Lifeskills teaching

McGRAW-HILL series for Teachers

Consulting Editor
Peter Taylor
School of Education, Bristol University

Henderson and Perry: Change and Development in Schools
Holt: Schools and Curriculum Change
Hopson and Scally: Lifeskills Teaching
Hutchcroft: Making Language Work
Saunders: Class Control and Behaviour Problems

Lifeskills teaching

Barrie Hopson and Mike Scally
University of Leeds

McGRAW-HILL Book Company (UK) Limited

London · New York · St Louis · San Francisco · Auckland
Bogotá · Guatemala · Hamburg · Johannesburg · Lisbon
Madrid · Mexico · Montreal · New Delhi · Panama · Paris
San Juan · São Paulo · Singapore · Sydney · Tokyo · Toronto

Published by
McGRAW-HILL Book Company (UK) Limited
MAIDENHEAD · BERKSHIRE · ENGLAND

British Library Cataloguing in Publication Data

Hopson, Barrie
    Lifeskills teaching.
    1. Lifeskills – Study and teaching (Secondary)
    I. Title   II. Scally, Mike
    373   LB1628   80–40797

    ISBN 0–07–084099–7

1 2 3 4 5   M & G   8 3 2 1 0

Printed and bound in Great Britain by
Morrison & Gibb Ltd, London and Edinburgh

To: Jen and Margaret

If men are unable to perceive critically the themes of their time, and thus to intervene actively in reality, they are carried along on the wake of change. They see that the times are changing, but they are submerged in that change and so cannot discern its dramatic significance. And a society beginning to move from one epoch to another requires the development of an especially flexible, critical spirit. Lacking such a spirit, men cannot perceive the marked contradictions which occur in society as emerging values in search of affirmation and fulfilment clash with earlier values seeking self-preservation. The time of epochal transition constitutes an historical-cultural 'tidal-wave'. Contradictions increase between the ways of being, understanding, behaving, and valuing which belong to yesterday and other ways of perceiving and valuing which announce the future. As the contradictions deepen, the 'tidal-wave' becomes stronger and its climate increasingly emotional. This shock between a *yesterday* which is losing relevance but still seeking to survive, and a *tomorrow* which is gaining substance, characterizes the phase of transition as a time of announcement and a time of decision.

[Freire, 1976]

Contents

Preface

This book has been in our diary, our days and our nights—too many nights—for more than a year. It has been within us much longer. Its origin was an endeavour to make contact with young people and adults in a variety of learning situations. It grew from the mistakes we made when working in systems that at times seemed reluctant to recognize, much less to liberate, the potential of the people who were part of them. It was possible sometimes to step outside of the institutionally etched roles of teachers and learners into the excitement and warmth of a true learning community; where facades were for buildings and not the people in them, where joy and pain and confusion and laughter were normal rather than embarrassing. Those were times when one glimpsed other possibilities—when one felt how things could be, given awareness, sensitivity and individuals skilled enough to create that climate.

We believe in education, because through learning we discover not only the world we live in, but ourselves. We can begin to see ourselves as instruments capable of being in tune with our environment or terribly discordant and at odds with it. The tuning comes not from outside of us but from within. We are each our own drummer and we must find our own beat. Sadly, we are only too aware that much of what passes for education falls short of this. Education should be *by* the people, but all too often it is merely *for* them; it should be expansive rather than restrictive; stimulating not boring, peaceful not aggressive; accenting strengths not highlighting weaknesses; fun not dour; uplifting not depressing; communal not solitary; about self-discipline not punishment; about ideas not rituals; creative not conformist; focused on achievement not intentions.

In this book we do not claim to be objective—that belongs in the history books with Victorian science. We are not free from bias: we are heavily biased. We are biased in favour of helping people to help themselves, to take greater charge of themselves and their lives. We are biased in favour of institutions that help people to do just that. We believe that schools and colleges *can* help to empower people in this way. We also discover that many do not—rarely because of maliciousness or establishment plotting, but more often because people have become enslaved to the dailiness of institutional habits; they lack awareness of alternatives, and of a sense of their own direction.

The book began with a concern that, with schools being made to feel accountable to their paymasters, and with criticism from employees and parents about the relevance of schooling to living, that there was a danger of defining schools either as a conservative by-product of an economy greedy for relevant occupational skills, or as simple purveyors of literacy and numeracy. Sociologists typically define schools as being in the vanguard of social change, propagandizing conveyors of the dominant culture. We believe that this need not be so. Schools have a role as agents of social change, not simply of social conformity, but only if they become aware of the nature of the societal changes now occurring. The post-industrial revolution is here.

Chapter 1 outlines the major factors that identify our present era as one significantly different from anything we have experienced before. We examine the possible consequences of post-industrial society from the perspective of education in general and our schools and colleges in particular. Chapter 2 examines the concept of education more carefully and looks at the relationship between schooling, education, and lifelong learning. Chapter 3 begins with the assumption that anyone involved with education has some picture, however hazy, of the type of person she wishes to develop, and the kinds of organization she wishes to promote. We outline our model of a self-empowered person and of systems that empower rather than depower the people working and living within them. Chapter 4 focuses on schools *per se* and examines ways in which teachers can attempt to introduce lifeskills teaching into their schools. Chapter 5 outlines the skills required to work with groups in the classroom necessitated by this approach to learning. The skills of contracting, designing, producing, managing, evaluating, and following up lifeskills teaching are described. Chapter 6 describes a wide range of resources available to help teachers to teach lifeskills as we have defined them in this book. Chapter 7 anticipates the misgivings and scepticism of teachers who find it difficult to see how lifeskills can be taught in our present-day schools.

Writing a book is part dedication, part ambition, part therapy, and part vanity. As such, authors deserve all they ask for. Our primary reason for writing this book and *Lifeskills Teaching Programmes No. 1* is because we believe that schools and colleges should play a positive role in preparing young people to survive and develop in post-industrial society. That to do this requires a skills-based curriculum taught within the context of a value system that promotes autonomous people and empowering systems. We hesitated before introducing yet another piece of jargon into an already over-jargoned area, but we do mean something very specific by 'self-empowerment', and we do see a discussion of power to be central to any discussion about the aims of education.

We also had a lot of fun writing this book. The joke about writing a book concerned with accelerating social change is that, each time you finish a draft, you discover new information that needs to be inserted. We have enjoyed the contact with the hundreds of teachers, headteachers, careers officers, youth workers, employers, and health workers with whom we have shared these ideas on courses and conferences over the past 12 months and whose arguments, support, and information have helped us to produce our lifeskills model.

This is usually the spot in the preface where the authors thank their partners for their support—assuming of course that it has been given. Some relationships have foundered on the rocks of book deadlines, unsocial hours, unsociable demeanour, and even anti-social behaviour. Not so here, though all factors were present. Support was freely and warmly given by Jen and Margaret. We would also like to thank our support group of three people who helped us to prepare the manuscript—Stefaney Bailey, Melanie Allen, and Eileen McCabe.

> We grow as human beings if we know how to explore where we are, understand where we want to be, and act upon how to get there. And to facilitate the exploration, understanding and action of others. Unable to do so, we are left only as life's observers and not as life's participants. [Carkhuff, 1976]

Barrie Hopson and Mike Scally
Counselling and Career Development Unit, Leeds University

Acknowledgements

We wish to thank the following for permission to quote extracts from their work:

Jack Chambers, *Young People in Transition: The education and training of 14–19 year olds*, National Union of Teachers.
Adam Curle, *Education for Liberation*, Tavistock Publications Ltd.
Fordham, Poulton and Randle, *Learning Networks in Adult Education*, Routledge and Kegan Paul Ltd.
Paulo Freire, *Education: The Practice of Freedom*, Writers' and Readers' Publishing Co-operative 1976.
Paulo Freire, Letter to the Co-ordinator of a Cultural Circle from *Conscientization*, World Council of Churches.
P. London, *Behaviour Control*, Harper and Row.
Rollo May, *Love and Will*, Souvenir Press.
Everett Reimer, *School is Dead*, © 1971 by Everett Reimer, Penguin Books Ltd.
John Rowan, *Ordinary Ecstasy*, Routledge and Kegan Paul Ltd.
Dr Kowit Vorapipatana, from an article in *World Education Reports*, No. 8., World Education Reports.
Bruce Tuckman, Developmental sequence in small groups, in *Psychological Bulletin*, Vol. 63, 1965, American Psychological Association.
Charles A. Reich, *The Greening of America: How the Youth Revolution is Trying to Make America Liveable*, © 1970 Random House Inc. and Allen Lane.

1. Personal competence in post-industrial society

There is increasing evidence to suggest that for the past 20 years Western society has been embarked on an historical quantum leap, the like of which happens but rarely. The last comparable event was the Industrial Revolution, which resulted in the majority of the population moving away from agricultural work to manufacturing work, with fewer and fewer agricultural workers supplying the food needs of the masses. Two hundred and fifty years ago 95 per cent of the labour force worked on farms to support the remaining 5 per cent; in the UK, less than 2 per cent of the working population now feed the remainder. Even in the United States, less than $3\frac{1}{2}$ per cent of the labour force work on farms, supporting not only the other 96 + per cent but much of the rest of humanity too.

Over the past 20 years a comparable process has happened in relation to the proportion of the labour force engaged in manufacturing products for the rest of the population. Increasing numbers are transferring to service occupations. By 1951 nearly half of all workers in the UK were employed in manufacturing; by the 1970s, for the first time in history, there were more people employed in service industries (58 per cent), and manufacturing's share was reduced to 40 per cent, the lowest since the mid-nineteenth century.

It has been estimated (Stonier, 1978b) that the next generation may find that it needs no more than 10 per cent of the labour force to provide it with all the material goods needed. We are so close to this new era it is difficult to know yet what to call it. Tom Stonier talks of the 'Electronic Revolution' leading to the 'Communicative Era', in which electronic devices permit the introduction of new modes of production and create an entirely new set of economic factors. Because of this fundamental change in processes of production, the new era has also been dubbed the 'Cybernetic Revolution', referring to self-monitored and -regulating production and control systems. We simply refer to it as the 'post-industrial society'.

> Industries which are labour intensive tend to move to the Third World where labour is cheaper. Alternatively, such industries become mechanised and automated, in which case they need by far

1

fewer employees . . . the really profitable manufacturing industries involve enterprises such as pharmaceuticals, chemicals, electronics, computers. These are characterised by three features: first, they are relatively labour non-intensive because the plants are all built in accordance with latest technological production techniques. Secondly, they are all capital-intensive and normally involve multi-national sources of capital. Thirdly, *they are all knowledge-based.* [Stonier, 1978b; our italics]

To become more productive, industry has to become more automated, and this means fewer jobs. ICI is one of the UK's most profitable firms and is engaged in expanding its activities over the next 10 years. Yet that very expansion can be achieved only if ICI loses nearly 3000 employees every year for the next 10 years, i.e., one-third of its employees. One wonders what is likely to be happening to our struggling industries like cars and shipbuilding if our most successful firms have to cut back in order to expand. The Manpower Services Commission (MSC) carried out a study of the investment plans of Britain's 90 largest manufacturing firms in 1977 and found that any new investment in capital equipment would result in up to 30 per cent reduction in their labour force (MSC, 1977).

For many years it was believed that automation would eventually provide more jobs than it eliminated. It is now clear that this is a myth. The US Department of Labour estimated in 1971 that over 4000 jobs a week were being eliminated through automation.

Even semi-automated machinery can have dramatic effects. The new semi-automated mining equipment now being introduced by the National Coal Board demands an 88.6 per cent reduction of labour. A typical seam requiring two shifts of 22 workers yielding 5000 tons per day now requires two shifts of 5 men, each yielding 10 000 tons per day (Stonier, 1978b).

For firms planning new factories it costs on average only an extra 6 per cent to make it fully automated, with all the consequent advantages—fewer labour relations problems, 24-hour use of plant, lower unit costs (Stonier, 1978b).

The trend is worldwide. Between 1972 and 1976 the big seven Japanese colour television manufacturers almost halved their labour force from 48 000 to 25 000, while production rose by 25 per cent from 8.4 million sets in 1972 to 10.5 million by 1976.

American Telephone and Telegraph (AT&T) have reduced labour force from 39 000 in 1970 to 18 500 by 1977, arguing that not only can telecommunications equipment be produced

2

more efficiently, but the new equipment is so much more reliable that there will be a 75 per cent reduction in the need for maintenance staff.

Fiat is using a new mobile multi-programmed Robogate line needing only 25 workers instead of 125.

Computerized type-setting is not only deskilling the job of type-setter but reducing labour costs by between 20 and 60 per cent (Jenkins and Sherman, 1979).

In Australia 24 people make nearly all the beer cans for the country while 12 part-timers produce enough for all of the South East Asia market! The machines they use are self-diagnostic and signal the contractor to service them if needed.

The single most important factor responsible for these changes—and, indeed, for our leap into a post-industrial society—is the development of silicon chip technology. The advent of microelectronic techniques is presently the object of much speculation on scenarios for the future. They are described variously as recipes for heaven or for hell. Whatever the outcome, the initial impact is already being felt in a number of contexts other than that of the manufacturing jobs previously described:

• Many semi-skilled clerical jobs will disappear with the introduction of word-processing equipment, desk-top computers costing no more than a colour television set, photocopiers, and pocket calculators.

• Some service jobs have already been replaced; for example, 100 000 jobs have been lost in the UK as a result of the introduction of self-service petrol stations.

• Centralized information services will lead to further reductions of jobs; for example, already in the United States and the MOA system in France there are experimental schemes in existence which link a variety of shopping facilities in an area to people's bank accounts. No money changes hands: one's account is automatically debited when purchasing goods until the account runs into the red, and then your buying ceases until you have negotiated with your bank manager! At a stroke a wide range of jobs have been eliminated. Most supermarket chains in the USA and in the UK now have check-out machines which feed data into the stock control system, thereby eliminating the job of shelf-checker and drastically reducing the amount of clerical work.

• The falling costs of microelectronics are reducing the costs of telecommunications and of storing, handling, and retrieving information. Some research indicates that at least 45 per cent of business meetings could be replaced by teleconferencing facilities (mainly desk-top audio systems) by 1990 (Central Policy Review Staff, 1978). This could mean more professional people spending more time working from home. It would also have an effect on transportation systems.

● Computers are being used increasingly to provide a wide variety of services; for example, most large firms have computerized billing, invoicing, and stock control systems. A London hospital is experimenting with MICKIE, a medical history-taking machine, which in some respects gets a more favourable response from patients than the conventional interview (they are more honest with the machine). The CAPITAL computer system in London is a jobseeker–vacancy matching and information machine operating in a number of job centres.

● Interactive computer systems are already operating widely in the USA and to a much lesser extent in the UK in careers guidance facilities in schools and colleges, and are even providing counselling services (Watts, 1978).

● The new television information systems TELETEXT and the Post Office system VIEWDATA could have wide social and educational implications. The Post Office system already has the capacity for over 100 000 pages of data that can be transmitted via telephone call and television receiver. Interactive systems are now being piloted, for example a careers information system for schools.

● Computerized banking, and cashpoint machines, eliminating the need for as many desk-based bank clerks, is already common.

● Home entertainment and home education possibilities are being radically changed and multiplied by cheap videocassette recorders and interactive systems (used almost solely for games at the present) that plug into a television aerial socket.

The *Harvard Business Review* in 1978 published a league table of the probable winners and losers when computer networks have spread to the home and reduced the need for offices.

This, they claimed, was a medium-term forecast. Today, one does not have to read books like this for evidence of the changes in our society. One has merely to look around at the new products, systems, and ideas that emerge daily.

An important point to remember in a discussion on the likely effects of microelectronics is that, although the number of jobs may be reduced, wealth should continue to accumulate. This could provide the economic underlining for a host of alternative ways of living and working, a variety of indices by which one's work is judged by others and, most importantly, by oneself.

Winners	Losers
Financial institutions: more fee-based consumer and business services.	*Airlines:* less need to travel for business.
Electronics, computing, and communications utilities.	*Petrol and car companies:* less commuting and shopping travel.
Educational institutions.	*Television networks:* competing networked entertainment and information.
Insurance: lower life, health and property claims.	*Paper industry:* fewer office letters and printed publications.
Large retailers: electronic promotional techniques.	*Postal services:* electronic mail.
Entertainment systems.	*Construction industry:* fewer offices, simpler peopleless factories.
Speciality retailers: wider reach at lower cost.	*General retailers:* in-home shopping; wholesalers bypassed.

1.1 What are the consequences of the post-industrial society ?

Social, economic, and political forecasting is a road paved with the bones of statisticians, economists, and social astrologers buried in the act of trend-gazing. Who would have predicted the Arab oil embargo in 1973 and its short- and long-term effects on Western economies? Who could have predicted the drop in the birth rate in Western countries since the Second World War, a process now beginning to find echoes in some Third World countries? But with greater understanding of human behaviour and more political acuity the data already available could have predicted these events, if not the actual date of their occurrence. And evidence is accruing rapidly to suggest the challenges and opportunities of our Electronic Revolution, although there is controversy as to what will be the socio-economic implications of these developments. There appear to be four major groups of crystal gazers.

1. *The optimists:* who predict the end of monotonous, routinized labour, freeing people to enjoy leisure, to find new meaning in their lives, to be more creative and caring.
2. *The pessimists:* who see conditions of great social turmoil resulting from the transition to a post-industrial society. Their scenario is one of revolution, urban guerrilla activities, global wars, famine, and stress-related illness.

2. *The sceptics:* who feel they have seen this all before. There will be changes but nothing so dramatic that people cannot handle it; there will be pockets of unemployment and social unrest but this will be temporary.

4. *The ecology critics:* alarmed by the prodigious use and misuse of the resources of this 'spaceship earth', they predict a time in the next 50–100 years which will see the drying up of many natural resources, an end to the exponential growth pattern of industrial society, and a return to earlier forms of smaller, co-operative work ventures, intermediate technology, self suf-ficiency, and a greater focus on a balance between human values and action, resources and needs.

Whichever scenario is the correct one, if any one of them is, the end result will be the same—namely, that we are living through a period of transition—and the demands on young people and adults will be similar. People will need to be adaptable, flexible, and more personally competent than at any other time in our history.

Our own predictions can be summed up by reference to the two Chinese symbols for denoting a crisis: one represents 'danger', the other 'opportunity'. We have least sympathy for the sceptical approach. We have a belief in the tremendous opportunities for the future, while fearing for individuals in the short term. We are concerned at the profligate misuse of dwindling resources and see this as an opportunity not simply to develop new energy sources, but to reassess our priorities and values.* We do believe that the future provides an opportunity for a greater variety of alternative life-styles, work patterns, leisure interests, creative pursuits, learning opportunities, and personal and social development than has been presented to us in any previous era.

This book, however, is primarily about education. Until now there has been scant reference to it. We would now like to make a list of predictions for the future, firmly rooted in the present. At the end of each section we will attempt to draw out the implications for those involved in education.

And by 'education' we do not simply mean 'schooling'. We see

---

* It is worth noting that very minor savings in our present profligate use of energy would produce dramatic changes. Widmer and Gyftopoulos (1977) estimate that a 1 per cent increase in energy efficiency every $2\frac{1}{4}$ years could allow an uninterrupted growth in the US gross national product of 3 per cent per annum without any increase in energy usage. The overall energy effectiveness of Western economies is about 8 per cent, with manu-facturing about 13 per cent. There is considerable scope for saving in all areas of usage, even after allowing for the high initial capital investment usually required.

education as a life-long process of learning, growing, developing, training; sometimes in schools and colleges, sometimes in places of work, in the community, at home, at leisure. The focus of this book will be on statutory secondary education, but the following section is directed to educators involved in formal and non-formal systems geared to people at all ages and stages of human development.

1.2 Features of a post-industrial society

Providing and receiving knowledge and skills is the most rapidly growing area of the economy

The development of automated and cybernated production methods, the movement from a cash-based economy to one based on credit transfers, the shift from a national to a trans-national economic system, the development of computers and interactive data-retrieval systems, and the fact that the growth of new products, technology, and ideas is now exponential, instead of linear, means one thing: that there is a greater dependence on information and innovation than ever before. The real wealth producer in post-industrial society is neither land nor manufacture, but knowledge. The ownership of land and natural resources all help to develop a nation's wealth, but, as Stonier says, *'the most important single resource is the skills and knowledge which its people possess'* (1978).

Jenkins and Sherman make the point that 'information is a vital resource; it is also non-depleting. When gathered or disseminated the sum total of information not only does not fall, like oil, gas or minerals, but generally increases, because of the feedback to the original information' (1979).

We are already witnessing the trend away from making a living by operating machines, to making a living by creating, transmitting, organizing, storing, and retrieving information. We are now experiencing an increase of scientists, managers, statisticians, educators, consultants of all kinds, planners, technology maintainers, systems analysts, trainers, leisure-based occupations, etc., on a formal career level. At the informal level the last decade has seen an explosion of self-help groups—between 500 and 600 known groups in 1978 in the UK (Humphreys, 1978). These groups, as well as providing mutual support, are keeping people with similar concerns in touch with latest developments.

If we also bear in mind the numbers of young people involved in full-time education, and the increasing numbers of adults involved in full- and part-time education and retraining (and getting paid for being involved), we can see that one can also make a living, for some period at least, as *receivers* of knowledge and skills.

The result of all this is that today the population as a whole spends less and less time making things, and more time inventing them, planning systems to produce them, training people to service the productive technology, training managers to run the production plants, training managers to manage the managers, retraining workers whose jobs become outmoded, negotiating with unions who represent those workers, providing career counselling for workers, providing social facilities and health facilities, producing house journals, advertising the products, maintaining good public relations, researching markets at home and abroad, training export staff to learn new languages and customs, keeping up with new legislation on quality control, work conditions, employment regulations, company law, tax changes, government and international regulations, services, and funding opportunities, selling the products, entertaining and influencing customers and potential customers, commissioning consultants to evaluate the production systems, management and decision-making systems, the financial operations, borrowing money, issuing shares, investing profits, researching new products, negotiating with competitors.

One begins to see how the production of one screw, pencil, transformer, or cupcake develops a superstructure as vast as any world balanced on the shoulders of Atlas. And we have not begun to discuss what all these people do when they leave work—spending their money in shops, at leisure, or on further education. Knowledge, skills, and services are the keys to our future.

QUESTION FOR EDUCATORS
How well are we preparing our young people with the knowledge, skills and attitudes necessary for living a fulfilled life productively in this new era?

There will be chronic unemployment judged by traditional norms and values
In the UK, at an average growth rate of 2 per cent (which has been the norm for the past 15 years) by the year 2000 there are likely to be 6 to 7 million unemployed (Lutz, Meriaux, Mukherjee, and Rehn, 1976), *if* we maintain our current concepts

of work and career patterns.* The key word in that last horrific sentence is '*if*'.

Whatever happens, people are going to have to live with the expectation that for some periods in their lives they may well not have a job in the traditional sense. The implications for education are clear: people will need to be trained in how to cope with unemployment psychologically; they will need job-hunting skills, self-marketing skills, knowledge of how to get information on retraining opportunities, government grants, and schemes, and further and higher education options. Even if we achieve a growth rate of $2\frac{1}{2}$–3 per cent, which was achieved for only a few years in the late 1950s and early 1960s, the turn-of-the-century figure would be between $2\frac{1}{2}$ to 5 million unemployed. To do this means a $2\frac{1}{2}$–3 per cent growth rate *each year* until the end of the century; economists believe there is little reason to suppose this country will suddenly improve its growth rate consistently even to that level.

The impact on young people is particularly distressing. In 1978, one-third of young school-leavers could not get jobs. One-third of these had not found employment within six months; one-quarter had been unemployed for a year. The average length of unemployment was 11 weeks, compared with 1970 when it was 3 weeks. Between 1970 and 1978 unemployment increased by 260 per cent for boys and 466 per cent for girls. One-third of all unemployed people are aged under 18. Those school-leavers with no qualifications are likely to find it most difficult. The Manpower Services Commission (1976) has expressed its concern that failing to get a job could permanently alienate school-leavers from the world of work and from society. This is particularly worrying as youth unemployment tends to be disproportionately concentrated among ethnic minorities in the inner cities.

Unemployment is often cumulative, and a recurrent pheno-menon for particular people. Mukherjee (1978) quotes studies that show that in Britain, once a person has lost his job through being made redundant, there is a greater than average chance that he will again find himself in a redundancy situation. People once made redundant cannot, in their next employment, claim special consideration for length of service; quite often there is occupa-tional downgrading, and this is frequently associated with moves

---

*There is some debate on these figures, but after reviewing the predictions of a number of forecasting groups, Jenkins and Sherman (1979) conclude that if we reject the new technologies and remain as we are, we face unemployment of up to 5.5 million by the turn of the century; if we embrace the new technologies we will end up with 5 million unemployed.

by persons concerned into marginal jobs which are always at greater risk in a tight labour market.

An American study (Stein, 1963) found that, if a person is out of work for 6 months or longer, 'the worker may begin to experience an erosion of his former skills'. An OECD study (Sinfield, 1968) showed that the longer unemployment had lasted the less chance there was for the person to escape from it. People out of work seem to pass through successive stages of shock, then optimism, followed by pessimism and finally fatalism (Martin and Fryer, 1974). The unemployed person's growing depression creates family strains which reinforce the vicious downward spiral.

One ironic point to bear in mind is that 'unemployment' as such is a relatively recent concept in the economic arena. It came into being only as a contrast to 'employment'. Employment as we have begun to understand it recently means working for someone else for a set number of hours, and has been the norm only for about 150 years. Professor Elliot Jaques has said that he cannot trace the word back before 1846. Prior to this, people were self-employed or worked by tradition and birth for families, estates, the aristocracy. It may well be that the kind of economic employment that was required by the Industrial Revolution has been brought to an abrupt siliconized end by the post-industrial revolution.

In addition to the personal costs of chronic unemployment, there would appear to be some social costs. A British study (Flynn, Flynn and Mellor, 1972) found high correlations between unemployment and assault (0.9), burglary (0.8), and theft (0.8). One cannot argue from correlations to causes, but it would not be surprising if the condition of unemployment were to stimulate people to anti-social acts.

Because of this we are likely to experience experimentation with a number of possibilities, most of which involve a radical rethinking by people of traditional concepts of work, leisure and careers:

● *Government funded schemes* like the Youth Opportunities Programmes (for young people) and STEPS (for older workers): people will be employed for short periods or for a particular project, at the end of which they get a traditional job, move to another scheme, retrain, or enroll for more education. Currently (1979) this initiative will provide alternatives to employment for 250 000 young people and 50 000 adults.

● *Reduction of the working week* to 25 hours or less while keeping the same wage rates: this could double the number of jobs available.

- *Job-sharing:* the Americans have developed a concept which calls for a two-person team to share a job that is done seven days a week. There are numerous possible variations of this.
- *Abolition of 'overtime'* as an institution: in the UK in 1978 this would immediately create 750,000 more jobs.
- *Recurrent education:* this centres on the concept that after leaving school or college one works for a period, then, either because of redundancy or a personal desire for a change, returns to full-time education, then to a further period of work, a period of retraining, more work, or any sequence of these (see the extended discussion of this concept in Chapter 2).
- *Self-employment:* we foresee the possibility of greater opportunities for self-employment, if the government uses its funds to provide non-repayable grants and repayable loans. If young people develop greater skills in decision-making, creative problem-solving, knowledge of how to use resources, and how to generate personal commitments, the opportunities are legion, given financial underwriting. Increasingly, large firms cannot produce items for a specialist market or where profit margins are low. There are great opportunities for small groups to set up businesses to satisfy these demands. It is significant that in the USA in 1979, two new jobs in three are created in firms employing less than 20 people (Birch, 1979). As society gets more complex there will be myriad opportunities for developing community projects. Young people need to be taught how to prepare and sell proposals, and to whom, *but* funds have first to be made available.
- *Sabbaticals:* there is growing interest in this option by which an employee is released on full pay for anything from a few weeks to a year, full- or part-time, for further education, to work for another organization, or for pure recreation (Goyder, 1977). Sabbaticals for workers were first introduced in the USA in the early 1960s, and have since spread to a variety of professions. Many of the people released are expected to use their skills on community projects. In the UK the Action Resource Centre was founded in 1973 to act as 'brokers' linking skilled people from contributing firms to smaller firms and community projects in need of those skills. Educational leave is another variation which is spreading slowly among a number of British firms. Paid educational leave is already an individual right in France, Belgium, Italy, Yugoslavia, Sweden, and the Netherlands. The British government has adopted the ILO recommendation for paid educational leave in 1974, but has lefts its development to negotiation by collective

bargaining and voluntary action. The TUC supports the concept. Research on these schemes suggests that there are a number of benefits to the employing organization: returning employees are often remotivated, career blockages have been bypassed, and new job opportunities are made available to the subordinates of the person on sabbatical (Goyder, 1977).

● *Early retirement:* many organizations, often with government aid, are introducing early retirement schemes. However, there is increasing social pressure to extend the age of retirement. In some countries, e.g., the USA, Sweden, and Japan, the argument is that to retire people on the grounds of age is pure discrimination. As from 1 January 1979, in the USA mandatory retirement before the age of 70 has been banned by law. Consequently this may not be the easy alternative to producing jobs that some governments had thought.

● *Part-time employment:* in the USA and Scandinavia it is already not unusual for professional people to begin to negotiate 50 per cent, 75 per cent or 80 per cent contracts with their employees. This is less common in Britain as yet, and there is often a distrust of the commitment level of part-time staff. Traditionally, part-time workers have been women doing semi-skilled jobs. This is likely to change, but to enable this to happen the same employment protection legislation is needed for part-time as for full-time jobs, and also an attitude change to the effect that anyone wishing to work part-time is creating another part-time job for someone else.

● *Income coming increasingly from more than one source,* for example from a part-time job, a community-funded job, possibly some freelance work, even some 'topping up' from social security: keeping a 'work diary' will not be a necessity simply for the professional groups. One suggestion is that of a minimum 'social wage' paid to everyone and covering basic needs only (housing, food, clothes) with paid employment an option beyond this. If this sounds unthinkable now remember how ridiculous the idea of universal old-age pensions first appeared—or child benefit; or unemployment benefit.

One thing is clear from all this. The right to work may continue to be a fundamental right given to all people, but no more can it be promised for a lifetime. The massive unemployment we are seeing now and are likely to see increase is partly a result of the move to a post-industrial society and the feeling that 'service jobs' are somehow inferior and not to be encouraged, but in a large part is due to a rapidly changing economy which will necessitate a bigger pool of people 'in transit' between jobs, retraining, and further education. This latter role is likely to increase as a normal part of a person's career pattern. But then the variety of roles one occupies in one's daily life is likely to become of greater importance: from the roles of employee and homemaker to a plethora of roles in which we work, play, and find significance.

Donald Super's new concept of career development recognizes the plurality of roles that a person occupies (Super and Bowlsbey, 1979): this rainbow of roles comprise: child, student, leisurite, citizen, worker, spouse, homemaker, parent. We have added to these the roles of consumer, friend, and person 'in transition' (Hopson and Scally, 1979).

QUESTION FOR EDUCATORS
With this concept of life roles, the task for education in helping to prepare young people for them looks very different to the equivalent task 20 years ago, when the notion was to ensure that people had a good general education, some help to get them into *the* job to which they were most suited (unless you were a girl, when it did not matter so much anyway! Boys took jobs—girls took husbands!) We now have both sexes needing the skills of adaptability, wedded to the notion that non-work roles will have to provide a major slice of their life satisfactions, knowing that education is a life-long process, excited by the options now available, aware that sometimes they will not have jobs, with a higher proportion of their time being 'discretionary' and a smaller part concerned with earning a living. What is the implication of this for the curriculum of our schools, and how is it to be taught?

There will be an increase of 'discretionary' time for everyone, but more for some than for others
The concept of 'time at one's discretion' as used by Jack Loughary (Loughary and Ripley, 1978) we find more useful than the traditional split between work and leisure. Loughary distinguishes between the time that we spend looking after ourselves—eating, cleaning, laundry, cooking, shopping, etc. (*maintenance* time), the hours we sell to other people for money—jobs—or for the promise of money—educational courses (*sold* time)—and whatever is left is our *discretionary* time. In one sense, all of one's time is at one's discretion, but we are referring to that time not taken up by commitments freely entered into like a job, raising children, or maintaining a home. Quite clearly, many people are going to be

13

faced with an ever-increasing amount of discretionary time, although this is not likely to be equally distributed. Some people will be as busy as ever with their jobs, while others are likely to have no jobs at all unless we see some dramatic changes in government policy. It is of interest to reflect that in 1973, when all industry was reduced to a three-day week, 80 per cent productivity was sustained. The government and society clearly have a variety of options.

There is sufficient evidence available to suggest that not everyone will welcome more discretionary time. In the past it was believed that a relatively jobless economy would introduce greater contentment than ever before, but only 23 per cent of Americans polled in 1977 in a national survey believed that union proposals for a four-day week and three-month annual vacation would result in happier homes. Industrial sociological studies confirm the apprehension. Many doctors have stopped prescribing holidays for tense and anxious people because they can often make the situation worse. Holmes and Masuda (1973), in their research into which life events are stressful to people, found that each holiday experienced in a year added points to your 'Life Changes Scale', which in turn was positively correlated with physical and mental illness. Suicides, depressions, and other self-disabling behaviours increase over holidays and weekends when hidden conflicts can no longer be repressed by the rigours of routine. In many cases leisure appears to generate domestic conflict or withdrawal. Studies of retired people confirm that some marriages are maintained during the career years simply because the people seldom see one another. Unless relationships are good, and people are skilled at handling them, increased discretionary time could be a nightmare.

QUESTIONS FOR EDUCATORS
Do we provide our young people with the skills to be able to make effective use of their discretionary time? If not, what are the skills and how can they be passed on? When is the most appropriate time to pass them on?

We are already living in an era of 'overchoice'
'We live in a transient society where the only constant phenomenon is change, where the only security is the knowledge that tomorrow is going to be very different from today, and that yesterday will be the subject matter for next year's history syllabus' (Hopson and Hough, 1973).

14

Alvin Toffler, in his apocalyptic book *Future Shock* (1970), claimed that a combination of transience, increasing diversity and novelty in our life-styles, organizations, and institutions produce the syndrome of 'future shock'—a pathological state which is increasingly afflicting people who cannot cope in an age of 'overchoice'. Jobs are changed more frequently, homes moved, fashions adopted and discarded, knowledge gained and outdated, ideas created and consumed faster and faster. Not only do possessions and information become increasingly temporary, but sub-cultures, life styles, and work patterns become increasingly diverse. Totally new concepts in science and technology can reduce us to the status of naive visitors watching a world riding an acceleration course towards advances far exceeding anything that up until now people have been psychologically or morally prepared to live with in comfort.

The symptoms of future shock are with us already—massive increase in stress-related diseases, depression, apathy, and an increase in interpersonal violence. Its victims often display erratic swings in interest and life-style, accompanied by feelings of harassment and stress and a need to escape from a large number of decisions they are ill-equipped to make. A study of admission rates to mental hospitals estimates that 7 per cent of men and 11 per cent of women can expect to enter a mental hospital at least once in their lifetime. The Institute of Psychiatry found that about 10 per cent of all people treated by GPs were treated for formal psychiatric illness and a further 5 per cent for other psychiatrically associated conditions. Toffler maintains that we are already living in an era of 'over-choice' and that there are limits to what information humans can store and the decisions they can make. Because of this people will choose how to deal with over-choice. Some ways will be ineffective, self-destructive or merely antithetical to personal growth; others will be proactive and growth-inducing, enabling people to ride the tiger of change.

QUESTIONS FOR EDUCATORS

Change cannot be prevented but it can be managed. How are educators going to teach people to cope effectively with accelerating change? How will they teach people to make decisions, to clarify their values and attitudes, to facilitate their decision-making, to cope with being overstressed (or sometimes even understressed, for example when unemployed) and to manage their time so as to maximize and minimize frustration?

Living in an era of increased interdependence puts a greater value on effective communication skills

The problems of modern society, economics, cultures, and governments rarely come down to a lack of ideas or resources but rather to difficulties in how we communicate with one another. If, indeed, we are moving into the 'Communicative Era', the skills of sending and receiving messages, of communicating clearly and appropriately, are going to be more important than ever. As the world's cultures perforce have more contact with one another as their economies become more interdependent, so communication channels have to be opened and cleared.

The likelihood in the future is that the opportunities for any individual working alone will diminish. The concept of work teams is developing, whereby a team is formed for a particular project, then disbanded, with the individuals forming into new project teams or joining other organizations. Consequently, it will be vital that people are equipped with the skills of working co-operatively in groups. The lonely craftsman is a thing of the past or a present leisure-time pursuit. In almost any job one can think of there is an increased role for communication. Take a car mechanic: increasingly a mechanic is a member of a team, with whom he will have to relate to get the job done. He has to keep abreast of massive new inputs of information, and know where to get it from. He often has to relate to customers and know how to get accurate information from them, and also must know how to give instructions clearly. In 1977, in the USA the National Automobile Dealers Association announced a unique two-year programme at community colleges for aspiring car mechanics. The dealers are convinced that simply learning how to repair a car is no longer enough: a mechanic must also have a greater knowledge of society and be able to communicate effectively.

QUESTIONS FOR EDUCATORS
What are effective communication skills? How do we teach them to people?

Personal relationships will be more temporary

In 1977, for the first time, young people in the UK were told that new marriages entered into under the age of 21 only had a 50 per cent chance of surviving for a lifetime. One out of every five people now stand to experience divorce before the age of 45.

For all the talk of alternatives to marriage, 97 per cent of women and 93 per cent of men still get married. The change is that people marry more often! Toffler first introduced the concept of 'serial relationships' which now looks to be the most common alternative.

However, it is not just in our most intimate relationships that a revolution is taking place. The average life of a mortgage in this country is less than eight years; there are 7 million job changes each year; 35 per cent of people moved house at least once during the last five years; in professional groups, over 50 per cent moved house at least once in five years, and 20 per cent moved twice or more. People are having to learn to create relationships quickly in the knowledge that many of them will be temporary and need also to learn how to end relationships. Creating, maintaining, and ending relationships involves skills that we are only just beginning to identify; skills that were simply not required by the majority who lived in the community they were born into, rarely left the neighbourhood, and relied on blood ties for their security and identity. Ending relationships causes great problems, with guilt left over from the expectations of a bygone era (much to the delight of Christmas card manufacturers, who know only too well how difficult we find it to say 'goodbye': instead, we send cards for two or even three years, then cross off the 'dead' relationships to bury them finally).

> The ideal life will not be marriage, children, and a house in the suburbs, but rather the experiencing of a series of deep and fulfilling relationships in a variety of environments. We cannot expect permanency in the relationships of men and women in a very impermanent world. Up to a point, a man and a woman may contribute to each other's growth, but at a certain juncture, they may grow apart, and it should occur with diminished guilt, trauma, and depression. [Walz, 1974]

QUESTIONS FOR EDUCATORS

What are we doing to prepare young people for the range of alternative life-styles that are now developing? Are we teaching them the skills of making, maintaining, and ending relationships, or are we reinforcing models of interpersonal relationships that may be less relevant to the new era.

We will have to move towards a new concept of work

'To the question "What are you going to be?" youngsters might now say "I already am—and you should recognize me as a person whether I'm employed or not, whether I'm through with school or not" ' (quoted by Robert Strom, 1975).

Until this point in this book we have used the term 'work' as most people use it—to refer to their jobs. This is the last time we will use it in this way. From here on we will use 'work' to refer to any 'conscious effort aimed at producing benefits for oneself and/or for oneself and others, other than that involved in activities whose primary purpose is either coping or relaxing' (Work in America report, 1973). A 'job' refers to a person's paid employment; 'leisure' is the amount of discretionary time.

We must help to eliminate the equation born of industrial society which links 'work' with a 'job'. A person will work in the act of planning and implementing any of his or her roles. The age has passed during which people could define their identities simply in terms of the jobs they do. Why is this?

1. There will be fewer jobs available for people to do.
2. People will change jobs more often. In the USA already skilled workers will have to be totally retrained at least four times in their lives; it has been found that the British male worker can expect to hold between two and three jobs per decade (Richardson, 1977).
3. It has been discovered (Abbot, 1977) that 45 per cent of employed Americans now work less than full-time for the whole year.

The implication of this is that fewer people are (1) going to have full-time jobs and (2) going to have them continuously throughout their lifetimes. In which case, what happens to the rest of us?

We believe that it remains the responsibility of a society to help people find meaningful work; but it may be through a job, a series of jobs, a leisure pursuit, education, or most likely a combination of these.

Traditionally the sphere of life satisfactions for a man and a woman looked like the representation in Fig. 1.1. The dangers for both of having all of one's eggs in one basket becomes obvious when the basket is taken away, as it always is: for men there is always retirement and, increasingly, redundancy; for women the children always leave home. Both sexes must now be concerned with maximum fulfilment from the variety of roles they will play. Yet the fiction continues. As parents, often supported by the media, we encourage boys to think of jobs as their 'work' and life's purpose, and girls to think of being homemaker as their life purpose. In doing so we are presenting them with a snapshot of society that already looks like a still from *All our Yesterdays*.

The remnant of the Protestant ethic, the belief that working at a

18

Fig. 1.1

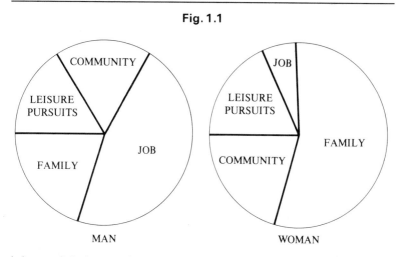

job, any job, is essential and a sign of one's moral integrity, must be eliminated. People must not feel guilty or be made to feel guilty because they do not have a job. This is difficult in a society that still sees holding a job as the first prerequisite for self-respect and respect from others. In large part, of course, this is because only by having a job can most people obtain a reasonable income. This belief is forcing the government to make huge payments (in 1977, £640 million was spent on schemes to combat unemployment) each year to people who do not have jobs. An alternative is to pay them for doing other things, like retraining, further education, community projects, grants to help people set up their own businesses, self-help groups, or community ventures. To a small extent this is beginning to happen, but it is seen only as a stopgap, second-best measure. We predict that this will be a pattern for the future, and not just from governments. In the USA over 6 million union members are being supported by union funds to attend colleges to get higher qualifications to further their career development.

QUESTIONS FOR EDUCATORS

What are we doing in our schools to help eliminate the Protestant ethic and to alert our young people to the new facts of economic life—that everyone has the right to work but not everyone will have jobs and certainly not continuously? Are we giving young people an opportunity to answer the question, 'Who am I?', not in terms of occupational role but in terms of the rainbow of roles available to them? What are we doing to help people ask new identity questions: not 'what is your job?' but 'what is your work?', meaning 'what are the activities from which you derive self-meaning and a sense of personal worth, and oh! yes, from where do you get your income?'

There will need to be a new concept of career

There is much confusion over the concept of 'career'. Some people use it only in relation to jobs, some even in relation to professional jobs only, while others use it to refer to a whole conglomerate of liferoles (as outlined earlier on page 13). To keep it simple we will use the more traditional concept of a career as the succession of jobs that constitute a person's role as an employee. In this sense there has always been a diversity of career patterns for men and often different patterns for women. Built into the consciousness of many people, however, was the belief that their career should progress 'upwards'. This concept of vertical career development is deep-rooted in all of our institutions. People evaluate themselves according to their position on the ladder of success or failure. Many people leaving schools today will have inherited this concept and will take it with them as a yardstick of their development. They could be in for a very nasty surprise.

All over the Western world organizations are reporting career 'bottlenecks', often at low- to middle-management level ('plateaued managers')—in factories, offices, schools, universities, hospitals, etc. The reason is that as jobs get fewer at all levels there is less mobility; this makes people more security-conscious, and this reinforces the tendency to stay put even more. Result: frustration, as people have been led to believe that progression is a vital criterion of success.

Vertical career development can no longer be taken for granted. People will need to find new ways of developing in their careers. Organizations are already having to produce alternative structures to produce new yardsticks for self-evaluation. One of these is the concept of horizontal career development.

The essence of horizontal career development is to provide opportunities for people to develop new skills, solve different problems, work with a variety of colleagues, but without necessarily obtaining promotions for doing so. The practice of cross-sectional work groups and task forces is one variation of this. Secondment to other parts of an organization or to a customer is not uncommon. Sabbaticals also contribute to the notion of horizontal career development. The key word in the concept is 'development'. This is different from simply moving a person around haphazardly from one job to another.

QUESTIONS FOR EDUCATORS

What are we doing in schools and our employing organizations to prepare people for the changes that have occurred relating to career development? Are we telling them that development does not necessarily mean upward progression?

There will need to be a changed concept of the 'welfare state'

It is no accident that in the UK today political capital is being made out of 'social security layabouts', 'spongers', 'shirkers', etc. There is increasing vocal criticism of people who seemingly exploit or cheat a system that was meant as a safety net to protect people from falling through the many holes in a capitalist economy. The most sophisticated welfare system in the world outside of communist-style countries is in Sweden. In that country increasing criticism of the massive taxation needed to keep the system flowing, together with concerns that individual initiative was not rewarded, leading to growing apathy among young people, resulted in a Conservative government being voted in recently for the first time in generations.

Illich (Illich *et al.*, 1978) has criticized the 'disabling professions'. It is difficult to know where to draw the line between helping and disabling. To give charity continuously is often disabling; to spend time and money helping people acquire new skills to help themselves is enabling. The way money is handed out by the present welfare state often reinforces lack of commitments and apathy. For example, people who are unemployed feel that they are being given handouts, and very inadequate ones at that, for being unsuccessful people, because that is the message conveyed from ministerial level downwards. One person unemployed by 1978 figures costs the government 75 per cent of his or her former salary, on average £3000 (Mukherjee, 1976). The question is how can that money be used to help that person find 'work', i.e., meaningful activity; to develop commitments and acquire new skills. Paying him or her for *not* having a job is negative. Paying the person for attending a course, setting up a new venture, being retrained, etc., is paying them for *doing* something.

We are suggesting that the present ideology, which equates work with jobs, leads to low self-esteem on the part of the people who do not have a job, self-doubt for people who have one but do not seem to be advancing in it, and a feeling of sinfulness for people who do not want a job (for example, who prefer the role of full-time homemaker whereas, on the contrary, the government should be delighted at people who voluntarily drop out of the job market). This will continue for as long as having a job is the only way of obtaining a reasonable income. *But*, you do not help people by giving them handouts as social destitutes: this is one of the many depowering dimensions in our society.

When economists and futurists predicted the long-term effects of automation and cybernation they were correct in their projections. However, in the 1950s when these projections were made the assumption was also made that the reduced amount of employ-ment would be equally distributed throughout the community. This has not happened. Instead, one group of the population is employed for as much if not more than ever, while an increasing minority has no employment at all. This is the new Rich and Poor dimension—between those with jobs and those without.

QUESTIONS FOR EDUCATORS
How can we combat the ideology that says that you must get a job, but if you do not the state will support you, as not everyone can succeed? Do we have a role as more active social change agents to pressure for a system that says that everyone has a right to share in the nation's affluence, and to contribute to it in a variety of ways—having a job, making things or providing a service, getting trained, becoming more educated, running a community project, raising children?

There will be a demand for a more adaptable labour force, and for people whom when unemployed can exercise initiative and generate commitment

At the rate at which knowledge is accumulating, by the time the child born today completes his education the amount of knowledge in the world will be four times greater than now. By the time he is 50, it will be 32 times greater, and 97 per cent of everything known in the world will have been acquired in his lifetime. [Robert Hilliard]

In the UK a working person can expect three or four major occupational changes in a working lifetime.

In the USA 25 per cent of present-day workers are in occupations that did not exist 25 years ago. It is estimated that by the year 2000,

75 per cent of the American population will be in jobs that do not yet exist. (Special Task Force, 1973)

These quotations sum up the pace of living today. Someone leaving school today in the UK can expect:

1. three or four different occupations in his or her lifetime;
2. six to ten changes of job;
3. to move away from the area of the country he or she was born in;
4. to have probably two marriages;
5. to be involved in education throughout his or her lifetime at different points;
6. to spend some time unemployed;
7. to have a variety of job patterns.

All economic projections indicate the need for a better educated if smaller labour force. For people without qualifications it is likely to be harder than ever to get the jobs that are going.

Retraining will be essential with the rate of technological change. The Electricians Union in the USA has 57 members solely rewriting textbooks because about 10 per cent of the technical knowledge in the industry becomes obsolete each year.

People will need to be able to cope intellectually and psychologically with changes of job definition, retraining and redundancy. With movements worldwide towards labour–management decision-making they will be expected to have skills to contribute to that process. With shorter working weeks, flexi-time, shift work, job sharing and autonomous job teams making their own production decisions, people will need a higher level of communication, decision-making, problem-solving, and coping skills than ever before.

QUESTIONS FOR EDUCATORS

Are we training young people to be adaptable, with the range of skills required to live in the Electronic Revolution? Are we giving them the learning structures that will help them to develop a range of commitments appropriate to the many roles they will play as citizens?

People will need a greater range of personal competencies than ever before in our history

Sociologists and historians have often pointed out that schools mirror the society they are part of; that is, they are in the vanguard, not the forefront, of social change. They have also shown how changes in education resulted from changed demands from the economic sector. Universal education resulted from a demand for a literate, numerate labour force. If this is true, then we are likely to witness some dramatic changes in our educational system.

We are writing this book from the belief that the more self-empowered a person is, the more the person will experience fulfilment, achieve his and her potential, and become more socially responsive, caring, and committed citizens. However, it is comforting to realize that what we are promoting primarily as 'a good thing' is likely to receive massive reinforcement because it coincides with what the Electronic Revolution requires.

To provide people with the range of competencies that they and society will need in the new era is going to involve far more than literacy and numeracy—the basic skills that we needed 50 years ago. Today a whole additional range of skills is required if a person is able to *survive*. However, we believe that living is more than simply surviving, it involves *growing* too. Consequently we are presenting our own ideas of elements for a core curriculum for education (not just schools). We call it a '*Lifeskills Teaching Programme*', and subtitle it '*Taking charge of yourself and your life*'.

The skills are grouped under four headings and are presented in outline form in Fig. 1.2.

QUESTIONS FOR EDUCATORS
How do we provide people with these skills? How many of them can we provide in schools? How many in further education? How many run through recurrent education opportunities? How many in non-formal learning environments?

We have identified some dangers and opportunities of the post-industrial society. Perhaps the greatest danger is that the vast incomprehensibility of the technology could engender an even greater degree of alienation for people than previous technological eras have done. The scale of remoteness for the individual could be massive; the potential for calculated manipulation and exploitation is so high that educational forces could be in combat with much more formidable counter-forces than they are now. If this is the case, the skills outlined here will be an essential antidote to dehumanizing, depowering large-scale technology, and administrative systems. Education *is* power—but it depends on who is using it, and for what.

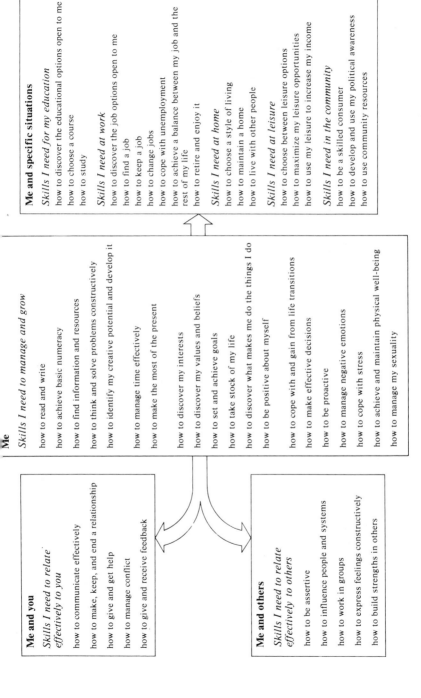

Me

Skills I need to manage and grow

how to read and write
how to achieve basic numeracy
how to find information and resources
how to think and solve problems constructively
how to identify my creative potential and develop it

how to manage time effectively
how to make the most of the present

how to discover my interests
how to discover my values and beliefs

how to set and achieve goals
how to take stock of my life
how to discover what makes me do the things I do
how to be positive about myself

how to cope with and gain from life transitions
how to make effective decisions
how to be proactive
how to manage negative emotions
how to cope with stress
how to achieve and maintain physical well-being
how to manage my sexuality

Me and you

Skills I need to relate effectively to you

how to communicate effectively
how to make, keep, and end a relationship
how to give and get help
how to manage conflict
how to give and receive feedback

Me and others

Skills I need to relate effectively to others

how to be assertive
how to influence people and systems
how to work in groups
how to express feelings constructively
how to build strengths in others

Me and specific situations

Skills I need for my education

how to discover the educational options open to me
how to choose a course
how to study

Skills I need at work

how to discover the job options open to me
how to find a job
how to keep a job
how to change jobs
how to cope with unemployment
how to achieve a balance between my job and the rest of my life
how to retire and enjoy it

Skills I need at home

how to choose a style of living
how to maintain a home
how to live with other people

Skills I need at leisure

how to choose between leisure options
how to maximize my leisure opportunities
how to use my leisure to increase my income

Skills I need in the community

how to be a skilled consumer
how to develop and use my political awareness
how to use community resources

Fig. 1.2. A lifeskills teaching programme

2. Education in the post-industrial society

In this chapter we will be examining the concept of education in general and looking at the popular equation of education with schooling. We will endeavour to equate education with learning, not schooling, and thereby establish it as a life-long process. We will then narrow our focus down once more to formal educational provision and to schools in particular.

For too many people 'education' is something that happens at school and consequently ends after one's final day at school. If one substitutes 'learning' for 'education' the ludicrousness of this assumption becomes more apparent; also the sadness—that so many people have unfruitful experiences at school that make them turn their backs on anything connected with school, like education. This view of education has been fostered by schools themselves. The 1944 Education Act has the assumption embodied in it that all the education that an individual needs should be crammed into this stage.

> In the jargon, this is often called the 'front end' (or 'front-loading') model in which as much education as possible is taken on board at the beginning of life. The student is thus issued with all the necessary educational supplies to cope with another 50 or more years of adulthood. [Advisory Council for Adult and Continuing Education, 1979]

If we view education as opportunities for learning, we see that automatically education must be viewed as a life-long process. We learn skills and concepts in a variety of contexts, from a range of people, from a plethora of experiences. Within this definition we can see that formal schooling, though vital—as it takes place in highly influential years—is only one among many media for learning. We find the following distinctions between formal, non-formal, and informal education useful. They are taken from P. H. Coombs *et al.*, *New Pathways To Learning*, prepared for UNICEF by the International Council for Educational Development in 1973:

> *Formal education:* the hierarchically structured, chronologically graded 'educational system', running from primary school through to university and including in addition to general academic studies,

a variety of specialised programmes and institutions for full-time technical and professional training.

Non-formal education: any organised educational activity outside the established formal system—whether operating separately or as an important feature of some broader activity—that is intended to serve identifiable learning clienteles and learning objectives.

Informal education: the truly lifelong process whereby every individual acquires attitudes, values, skills, and knowledge from daily experience and the educative influences and resources in his or her environ-ment—from family and neighbours, from work and play, from the market place, the library, and the mass media. [Coombs *et al.*, 1973]

All the indications are that we are about to witness a large growth of non-formal educational opportunities which, when combined with an increasing provision of formal education (see pages 32 and 33), will ensure that recurrent education will become the dominant model in all societies.

Much traditional adult education has tended to be non-formally based, while much child education in schools has been formally based. There is likely to be more of a blurring of these pictures in the future. The community school has been described as an example of the interface between traditional schooling and non-formal education (King, 1976).

Post-industrial society is likely to see recurrent education as one of the major arenas of everyday life, with the role of learner an increasingly important one to people of all ages and backgrounds. Indeed, already approximately 1 adult in 20 is involved in post-initial education at any one time, and a much higher proportion are involved at different periods of their lives. We have emphasized the broader context of education to be able to place schools, as we know them, within its context and to examine their purposes. In later chapters we will be stating the case for people becoming more 'self-empowered'; more in charge of themselves and their lives. Education is the most powerful way of their achieving this.

'Durch Bildung zur Macht' ('Through Education to Power') was the slogan adopted by German craftsmen at the turn of the century and we, with them, believe that education is concerned above all with power—the power to influence one's own life; the power to make an impact on one's community; the power to contribute to others and the community at large; the power to shape the conditions under which one is born and brought up; the power that can be gained only from access to essential information; the power to participate in decisions that determine the nature of one's environment; the power to survive, grow and develop; the power to learn and to teach.

Our beliefs about education have been influenced by (1) Third World developments, and by (2) the 'ecological' approach to education.

2.1 Third World developments in education

The Third World has seen the emergence of people like Friere and Nyerere who are both philosophers and activists: indeed, a key ingredient in their approaches is the relationship between reflection and action. Either is futile without the other. Both have concentrated on developing non-formal alternatives for education.

The work of Paulo Friere (1972a, b) in Brazil, as Secretary of Education and General Co-ordinator of the National Plan of Adult Literacy, has many lessons for all teachers. He was exiled from his country after the coup in 1964 and later became Visiting Professor at the Harvard Center for Studies in Education and Development. His methods for educators emerged from his attempts to tackle the appalling illiteracy that existed in many parts of his country. Trying the orthodox methods of teaching had little success. The people were apathetic, unmotivated, could see little point in learning to read, and hence achieved little. He had to start somewhere else. His policy of 'Conscientization'—awareness-building—was born. It was a group process, where the first task was to make the people believe in themselves.

Friere decided that his method would have to begin by creating and building self-confidence. The first principle of the method is that people learn as a group from one another without the usual formal 'teacher–pupil' relationship. It has to be a process through which members of the group develop a wider understanding of each other's views of the world. This process, in turn, causes people to question their own ideas and way of life and to start to realize that there are alternatives. Friere tried to create, through this kind of group experience, a situation in which the individual stops being a passive object crammed with information by his teacher. Instead, he begins to look critically at his environment and the influence it has on him, and to make his own decisions. In Brazil, Friere tested his ideas with groups that became known as 'cultural circles'. People gathered together in the presence of a co-ordinator who, for example, would show pictures of everyday scenes or

28

objects for discussion. Every new discussion helped those taking part to stand back from their own situation until finally they saw it more clearly and critically. For people who had always accepted that the factors affecting their lives were beyond their control this was an important step forward. Drought, hunger, hard labour, and debt to remote employers—all part of a way of life they had believed to be immutable—now became problems to be studied and thought about. The goal was to liberate the individual, not to stamp him into a mould by giving him a mass of facts and figures; to make the individual a subject rather than an object. Friere was developing in the group the idea that the 'locus of responsibility' for each of them lay within himself. Each of them was capable of being 'more' tomorrow than he was today. Friere wrote the following letter to the 'co-ordinators' of the Cultural Circles:

> For you to be a good co-ordinator of a Cultural Circle it is necessary, above all, that you have faith in man; a belief in his possibilities of creating, of changing things. You also need to love. You must be convinced that the fundamental spirit of human promotion as in education, is the liberation of man, never his domestication, and that this liberation commences in the measure in which this same man reflects on himself and on his condition in the world in which, and with which, he is. In the measure in which he is conscientising himself, he inserts himself in History as a subject.
>
> A cultural circle is not a school in the traditional sense in which a teacher, almost always convinced of his own knowledge, which he absolutises, gives classes to pupils, who are passive and docile and whose ignorance the teacher also absolutises.
>
> A cultural circle is a living and creative dialogue in which everyone knows something but is ignorant of something else, and all strive together to understand more.
>
> Therefore you, as co-ordinator, must be humble, in order that you might move with the group, instead of losing humility and pretending to move the group ahead, once it is judged 'advanced' enough.
>
> During the discussions, make it possible that the whole group participates. Take care to learn the names of the participants and avoid referring to them with impersonal expressions such as 'you' etc.
>
> When making questions, always direct them to the group, unless you are trying to motivate a less active member. Nevertheless, ask the question first and only later direct it to the person whom you wish to motivate.
>
> During the discussion make good use of the replies,

reformulating them as new questions for the group. Integrate yourself with the group. In so far as possible make yourself one of them. Never talk too much about your personal experiences unless you have something interesting for the discussions.

Although the real-life situation being discussed has a content that you know, don't enslave yourself to it, to the point of forcing the group to follow it. This means that we must respect the interpretation that the group has of the situation. It is almost certain that the group, faced with a situation, will begin to describe it in relation to their own existential experience which is not, nor can it be, the experience of the co-ordinator. His role is to search along with the group for a deepening of awareness and critical analysis.

The co-ordinator cannot anticipate how this will proceed. His task is not to do the analysis for the group but to co-ordinate the discussion.

In every group there are always those who talk a great deal and those who speak less often. Stimulate both in an appropriate manner so that an equilibrium will be reached.

It is important and indispensable that you are convinced that every meeting with your group will turn out to be enriching for both yourself and for the group. To achieve this you must strive for a critical posture. The more you and your group are inclined to the problematisation of the situation, the more you will become critical. This questioning, which must be exercised by you and your group, will overcome ingenuous consciousness which is characterised by losing itself on the periphery of problems, convinced that it has arrived at their essence. This questioning, rather than acceptance, of facts gives the participants an active role rather than a passive one, and implies that they can act for change, not simply accept their situation as it stands.

We would see the approach to teaching and learning of our Lifeskills Teaching Programmes requiring much of this approach.

The medium is the message. Friere was making people believe in themselves, in their potential, in the things they could do. He was saying: 'reflect on yourselves, on what it means to be you, on what you can be, and act to achieve it'. Acting, reflecting, and acting again, becoming more and encouraging all others to do the same, made people see literacy as part of their development, as something they could achieve themselves. They chose it and owned it and therefore cherished the process more. Literacy levels improved appreciably. The people wanted 'education' and made it happen. Friere said the first step was to believe in oneself, to be positive about oneself, to have a positive view of oneself as a starting point for so many possibilities. That is also where we start in our approach (see Chapter 3).

Other educators in other countries have discerned the real gains to be made in starting at the same point—avoiding our giver–receiver, teacher–learner, subject–object approach to education.

Even in remote Thailand the Ministry of Education has a programme to produce the personal competencies and self-management we would like to see at the centre of Western schooling:

> In the Thai nonformal education programme a process known as 'khit-pen' has been identified as the tool for harmony. Some people translate the word 'khit-pen' as critical thinking, others as rational thinking, still others as problem solving. It is, in fact, the combination of all these processes, *and more*. A man who has mastered the process of khit-pen will be able to approach problems in his daily life systematically. He will be able to examine the causes of his problems. He will be able to gather the widest range of information on alternative courses of action and weigh the merits of each alternative, based on his own values, his own capabilities, his personal situation, and the degree of feasibility of each solution.
>
> If, due to outside circumstances or lack of necessary knowledge or skills, the solution of his choice cannot be implemented right away, the khit-pen man will not become frustrated. Instead he will adopt a lesser solution while preparing ways to make the solution of his choice possible. This can range from acquiring certain specific skills or knowledge to creating necessary conditions in the environment. Educational programmes should, therefore, encourage people to use their khit-pen abilities. We would like to mention here that in general a man, and in particular the ordinary Thai, already possesses the process of khit-pen in himself.

> *Khit-pen people*
> 1. recognise their own potential in producing changes in their lives;
> 2. identify problems and relate them to their causes;
> 3. are capable of gathering information on alternatives;
> 4. select the most acceptable to their own values in relation to their political and social environment;
> 5. accept, at least temporarily, lesser solutions while making way for the solutions of their choice;
> 6. are able to justify their decisions, at least to themselves; and
> 7. accept the consequences of their actions.

In Tanzania and India non-formal education has brought about dramatic improvements in public hygiene (Institute of Adult Education, Dar-es-Salaam, 1974; Council for Social

Development, Delhi, 1976). The 'barefoot doctor' approach in China has enhanced health and longevity without using expensive and sophisticated medical services. Botswana has mounted a largescale exercise in public education using radio to explain and consult about a new grazing policy (Republic of Botswana, 1977).

Plunkett (1978) has argued that, 'with its settled bureaucracies and silent majorities', the West has now fallen behind the Third World in understanding social and economic change. As a result, he argues, 'coping with change may now be a skill that is better developed outside the West'.

Like Freire, we are concerned with promoting 'problem posing education':

> The point of departure lies in men themselves . . . in the 'here and now'. . . . Only by starting from this situation . . . can they begin to move. To do this authentically they must see their state not as fated and unalterable, but merely as limiting and therefore challenging. [Freire, 1972b]

2.2 The ecological approach to education

In their work on developing non-formal learning networks on a housing estate near Portsmouth, Fordham, Poulton, and Randle (1979) define their ecological approach to education. Ecology is about the changing relationships of living organisms to each other and to their environment:

> As a generative concept an ecological approach is capable of giving rise to new sets of educational questions and priorities. This is partly because it is concerned with the relationship between formal educational systems and other areas of life. It cannot consider the formal systems in isolation, for instance, but it must question the contribution made by formal education to a social ecosystem. [Fordham, Poulton, and Randle, 1977, p. 191]

They stress the importance of the geographical basis of most people's lives and the implications of these geographical limitations for the pattern and location of educational resources. They emphasize the essential nature of the teaching relationship— the medium is the message—and the degree of informal learning opportunities in people's lives.

The term 'ecology' implies a concern for the environment, and much of their work with adults involved people in a process of action and reflection upon themselves in relation to their social, political, economic, and psychological environment:

The object of education defined ecologically can be related to increasing the independence, freedom and autonomy of people with regard to both the objective and subjective features of their environment. This includes helping people to make full use of their own potential and of the learning resources that are locally there to hand. Defined thus, the goals of education relate much more to confidence, action and power than they do to generalized Knowledge. The natural resources themselves are, most often, people or networks of people. [Fordham, Poulton, and Randle, 1979, p. 193]

Their approach is summed up beautifully by their phrase, 'education by the people instead of education for the people'.

Like the Third World educationalists referred to earlier, they place great emphasis on the interdependence and interchangeability of teacher and learner. The surest way of learning something is, in the final stage, to teach it to somebody else. At all times everyone, including children, has something to learn and something to could teach. Everyone has skills. The problem with much formal education is that people are often in environments that constantly reinforce the skills of the teachers and the lack of skills of the learners. Take the teachers out of school and they become simply people, with a range of learner needs like everyone else. Take the students out of school and they will have an opportunity to show their skills in mending bikes, playing games, helping people, knowing the cheapest shop to buy records, knowing how to spot when the fish will be ready to bite, knowing how to manage their weekly budget or how to make a skirt.

2.3 More formal education for all

We would argue for a rapid increase in the provision of non-formal educational opportunities in the UK. However, we are shortly to see greater provision in the opportunities for formal education too. Almost half of our present school-leavers starting jobs at 16 or 17 receive little or no systematic education and training after entering work: the 'front-loading' model again. The government has been experimenting with a pilot scheme aimed at these 300,000 young people which eventually could provide vocational training opportunities for them at work and in colleges (Booth, 1978). This is called the Unified Vocational Preparation (UVP) scheme. The initial outline of the scheme, commenting on the absence of any systematic preparation for work for many young people, said:

At least part of the trouble is attributable to the separate development of education and training. For many young people entering the world of work, the only available supplement to minimal on-the-job training has been part-time further education of a kind which they are inclined to reject as being no longer appropriate for them. To encourage their interest and win the support of their employers, a new and unified approach is required. [Department of Education and Science, 1976]

The emphasis is to be equally on girls as boys, for even today boys under 18 on day-release schemes outnumber girls by four to one.

The education/training (and the distinctions will become progressively more difficult to spot as recurrent education becomes more established) takes place at the workplace as well as colleges, planned jointly by college staff and the training departments of the employing organizations. The stated objectives of the UVP are:

1. to assess young people's potential and help them to think realistically about jobs and careers;
2. to develop the basic skills that will be needed in adult life;
3. to understand their society and how it works;
4. to strengthen the foundation of skill and knowledge on which further training and education can be built.

As a result of this programme there will be few young people over 16 who will not be in either full-time or part-time higher education, occupational training courses, or a UVP scheme. Already the proportions of young people staying on into higher education are increasing: in 1960 6.9 per cent stayed on; in 1975 it was 13.4 per cent.

2.4 Schools in the post-industrial society

Where does this analysis leave schools and teachers?

As we have seen in recent years the schooling system is under attack from all sides. Besieged by 'deschoolers' on the left and 'Black Papers' on the right, schools now have government ministers, employers, higher educationalists, parents, and 'national debaters' of all persuasions knocking at their doors and demanding to see the 'household accounts'.

Inside most schools the luxury of debating the different philosophies and methods is rarely available. Like most sizeable systems, they have a life of their own, and a pace of existence, which makes 'time out' for such niceties a rarity. Timetables, exams, school functions, merely managing a building containing so many energetic differences, are an all-consuming task. To stop the process and re-evaluate—to ask the head, the staff, the governors 'Where are we going?'—is nigh impossible.

For many teachers confusion and uncertainty result in doing one's own thing 'to the best of one's ability' and leaving the grander questions to others. One remembers very well, from one's own time in school, reading Illich, Goodman, Holt, and others and sensing the 'ring of truth' that ran through all of them, but then having to return to classrooms, feeling commitment to the students there, and feeling that one had, in any case, a sizeable personal investment in teaching as a 'noble, caring' career. Did one 'throw it all in' or salvage what one could?

There were often incidents that helped one's decision-making. One remembers well the first year of 'ROSLA' (raising of the school-leaving age) in English schools—1974—a year of extra, compulsory schooling. Pupils who had been 'alienated' for many years already now had to forgo earnings and 'freedom' for a further 12 months. They were 'trapped'—their word—and they registered verbally and non-verbally, often violently and abusively, their wish to be elsewhere. A particularly 'disruptive' group from the fifth form of one northern school decided they had 'had enough' one day and disappeared (again!). An appreciative, if silent, but unofficial round of applause went round the staff room. How much more positive the whole school could be when that group was absent—energy could be spent on teaching and relating to other youngsters rather than on containing 'that group of zombies'. A week later they were back. John, the brightest and the 'hardest', and Brian, the 'fall guy' and the jester, who were the group leaders, came to their social studies class. They liked talking and would have been endlessly entertaining and informative if only the system had not expected other things. That morning they gave their views on education. They hated the school and felt they were wasting their own and everybody else's time. During their week 'off' they had gone to a 'free-school' which was running experimentally in the city at that time. 'Why didn't you stay?' the teacher thought, but said instead, in his best 'open style', 'What was that like, John?' John replied, in the serious tones that surfaced from time to time, 'It was terrible! It makes you think you're lucky to come to a place like this. That place was broken down, filthy cold and nothing like we've got here. [N.B. He had an appreciable record of vandalism!] The whole set-up was stupid. People just wandering about doing nothing. Nobody was teaching or learning anything.' 'So you don't want to go there, John?' the teacher's ray of hope was dimming fast. 'You must be joking! You wouldn't get an education in a place like that. I think any parents who let their kids go to a place like that just don't care and they are irresponsible!' Here were characters who, one felt, would have been to the left of Illich in the deschooling debate actually saying 'We can see some use and purpose in the school—maybe its not for us as it is—maybe it's too late in the day for us—but even we can see, if you get it right, some ways of "schooling" are better than others.' Across the pitted and blasted 'no man's land' of that ROSLA year waved a flag of truce—a sign of peace if the terms of the settlement could be negotiated! It is interesting to note here that John's and Brian's very personalized views were found to be well established nationally among their peers, by the Government Social Survey inquiry carried out by the Schools Council and published in 1968 as *Young School Leavers' Enquiry No. 1*. This report showed that three-quarters of those who wanted to leave school at the earliest opportunity thought being at work was preferable to being at school, and only one-tenth thought school was preferable to work. Work was better because:

1. it offered freedom and independence;
2. it was paid;
3. there was less discipline and more treatment as an adult;
4. it offered the chance to be free of teachers.

Teenagers at work, even more of whom preferred work to school, gave as their reasons:

1. a greater variety of tasks available at work;
2. they 'did things' rather than 'talked about them';
3. they met more and different kinds of people;
4. they were able to do things they could do rather than struggle, unsuccessfully, academically.

Bazalgette (1971) found that schools were regarded, by young workers, as being second-best to work in the areas of 'personal relationships with adults', as 'learning environments', and in offering 'opportunities for personal development'. Baxter (1972) found that young workers were more 'socially mature', 'satisfied', 'successful', and made an easier transition to adult life than did those who remained in education. Johnson and Bachman (1976) found that only 18 per cent of school pupils found that they were able to develop skills and utilize their talents at school—compared with some 80 per cent of employees in most occupations. Bill *et al.* (1974) found that only 7 per cent of pupils felt that they were very successful at school. It has also been found (Schools Council, 1968) that over half of school-leavers found more than half of their school subjects both 'boring' and 'useless', but that 80 per cent of 20-year-olds who had left school at 15 liked their jobs, liked their employers, and found their jobs interesting. Raven (1977) found that one-third of the pupils in their study sometimes or always hated school.

There are many pupils in our schools who are discontented, frustrated, and waiting to get out. There are many staff whose burden it is to 'contain' and 'deal with' those pupils. There is much non-productive energy dissipated on both sides of that relationship. A great deal of thought and effort has gone into alternative curriculum content, but it is difficult to be original and outgoing all the time. We will be saying in this book that there may be more productive ways of working with the less motivated using little more than the resources that are the pupils and teachers themselves.

2.5 How can we best use the time in school ?

The authors of a recent 'Black Paper' (Cox and Boyson, 1977) focused on many anxieties that exist inside and outside schools about how useful and productive current schooling is. It is indeed fascinating how schools and teachers are in a 'valley of death' predicament: 'Black Paperists' to the right of them, 'deschoolers' to the left. Those who support the Black Paper view say that salvation lies in getting back to the basics, in doing things we did well in the past, in the way we did them. It was G. K. Chesterton who defined heresy as being 'truths taken to extremes, half truths turned into whole truths'. To many teachers, members of a profession where there is much caring and commitment, it seems that is what the 'deschoolers' and 'Black Paper writers' have done. It is true that all is not well in schools, that things could be better; but salvation, it seems to us, does not depend on the 'heresies' of total abolition or 'reactionary dogmatism'. Reading 'Black Papers' and returning to classrooms did not seem helpful or hopeful. Schools are different now, society is different, the economy is different, values are different, knowledge is different, communication is different, roles are different, families are different, life-styles are different, and above all the future is different. One may lament or applaud the facts, but to deny them is futile or perilous. One has only to have taught a generation of pupils reared on television to realize that the impact of that single factor has been enormous. 'The written word is dead', one prophet

37

has written. It sounds like heresy for many teachers and parents, who found and still find the written word of enormous use and often of appreciable beauty. Maybe the heresy lies in the extreme presentation of the truth, that 'the old ways are no longer good enough'. The old ways would most definitely not have got the ROSLA group to the negotiating table. They will not end the process of attrition at work in many of our schools.

Even among the 'achievers' in our schools there is appreciable scepticism about the usefulness and relevance of much of what they are doing. Academic success once equalled security and prosperity. Many graduates in the dole queues today will tell you that this guarantee is no longer there. Many now do not enter university, or they drop out of a course, because acquiring a degree, they say, is not the most attractive way to spend one's time if a career is not there to justify the effort. Unemployment, recession, economic and political forces, and technological 'overdrive' are producing unpredictability in such enormous amounts that the present is being undermined. The 'deschoolers' would say that the 'Black Paperists' are merely 'rearranging the deck chairs on the Titanic'. A reaction from 'one of the crew' is that there may not be much purpose in playing around with the deck chairs, but that it might be very sensible and important to ensure that all the crew and passengers have lifebelts, lifeboats, and survival kits, so that whether the ship founders or sails there will be few casualties or (hopefully) none at all.

2.6 Towards relevance and usefulness—caught between yesterday and tomorrow

In the northern school already mentioned there had been many thoughts and much energy put into preparing for the 'ROSLA' (that horrid label) year. The Newsom Report insisted that the extra year of compulsory schooling should be a year that was 'different', not just 'more of the same'; but it bargained little for how few resources there were and how unwieldy and immovable many of our school systems were. In that school, however, attempts were made to provide more relevant courses for the 'early leavers', as staff called them, or the 'late stayers', as they saw themselves.

They were taken out of school as much as possible: community service, visits to places of work, to places of local interest; community surveys, youth hostelling trips, 'know your city' schemes, projects weeks, etc. The community was brought in: old folks' parties, play groups, visiting employers, beauticians, policemen (different from the one who called 'on business' from time to time); Buddhists, bankers, Hindus, Gingerbread groups, and so on. The 'consumers' responded well, though it was never easy. It was, they said, 'better than what we had been doing before'. As in most schools, the teachers who wanted to do this kind of work could have the 'non-exam kids' for as much time as they wanted them. With the 'exam groups' it was, and is, different—it was a fight to get them out on a careers visit, to see a film or visit a theatre. A youth hostelling trip was unthinkable— 'all that exam work missed'; 'their education disrupted'. 'Learning about life' is OK for 'non-exam kids' but is a luxury, in many schools, not afforded to the so-called achievers. In this particular school there were four groups in each year whose main diet was GCE or CSE work full-time. From that group of approximately 120 there came, one day a fascinating document headed 'A Petition'. It was neatly written and artistically presented and went on:

> We the undersigned think that a lot of the work being done by the 'leavers', on their 'Contemporary Studies' Course is very important, very educational and prepares them for life after school. We, in the exam group think the work is equally important for us and we ought to be doing the same.

It was signed by most of the exam group. For the team of teachers involved there were mixed feelings. The soundness of the argument was inescapable. It was nice to receive the stamp of approval, but it was very difficult to have to meet that group and justify to them the school's insistence that their priority had to be exam success in eight or nine subjects. The words of justification rang hollow. Much exam content and method is of the past rather than the present and the future, and is remote from the realities of many of the students' lives.

A perusal of many O-level and A-level syllabuses will show the prominence given to yesterday's knowledge and facts. The 'past' seems to be out of proportion, to many of the pupils on the receiving end. We would argue that the past has its place, let's not dismiss it, but we can move into it from today and go where the search for relevance might take us. The method of teaching for exams very much anchors us firmly in yesterday. We are, much of the time, dealing with second-hand ways. Whitehead warned in his *Aims of Education*: 'First-hand knowledge is the ultimate basis of intellectual life. What the learned world tends to offer is one second-hand scrap of information, illustrating ideas deriving from another second-hand scrap of information. The second-handedness of the learned world is the secret of its mediocrity'; and is the secret of why much exam work is dull, unexciting and seen as a painful necessity.

Eric Midwinter (1972) very humorously and effectively questions the usefulness of his many hours of his own education. Like many of us, he never meets the irregular foreign verbs to decline, or roots to square, or poetry to parse, or catechisms to recite, that took up many hours of our adolescence. The really essential skills for living are rarely taught directly in schools, with the exceptions of literacy and numeracy. It is hoped that in some mystical way these skills are passed on via the teaching of traditional school subjects. Raven (1977), echoing some of the findings of the Schools Council (1968) report, found that the goals that were given primary attention by students, parents, teachers, ex-students, and employers, such as the fostering of personal qualities like initiative, self-confidence, and the ability to deal with others, received scant attention in schools and, as a result, were poorly attained. Teachers and students worked not towards the goals they believed to be the most important from an educational viewpoint, but towards goals that could be assessed in a manner acceptable for the award of educational qualifications.

> If you wanted to find a youngster who had 'The ability to co-operate with others in the achievement of common objectives', or 'The capacity to face problems and work for the means to solve them', or 'The ability to adapt to changing situations both at home and at work' . . . or 'The appropriate levels and command of "lifeskills" which would include the ability to communicate with and listen to others', it's most unlikely . . . that one could identify any O-level GCEs that would relate to *any* of those characteristics. Yet those characteristics are the ones that have been identified over and over again by parents, employers, further education, even the DES—yes indeed, and by teachers too—as the most important requirements that should be embodied in the curricula of schools. [Chambers, 1978]

The DES in their contribution to the education debate (Department of Education and Science, 1977) have also emphasized the importance of developing in students a capacity for the acceptance of retraining, a better balance between factual knowledge, concepts, and skills, equipping all students with study

40

skills and problem-solving techniques. These should be part of the core curriculum for 11- to 16-year-olds.

It is interesting to browse through a school's careers library and ask: 'Are there many careers (or any) that require more than six O-levels or their equivalents?' Many schools still have pupils in large numbers pursuing success in nine or ten subjects. 'Are employers interested in exam success if the job applicant has less than four O-levels or their equivalent?' Many pupils return to schools dismayed (cheated?) that nobody has ever bothered about their grades 2, 3, 4, 5, in a whole range of CSE subjects. If you get less than four O-levels the employer is more likely to ask 'Are you honest, can you work without supervision, are you punctual, regular in attendance and will you be prepared to learn?' Much of what is achieved by way of motivation of pupils in school is based upon the myths that people outside are interested in your grades other than passes (largely they are not!), or that exam success unlocks the future (if it once may have done, it does not necessarily now). How many careers teachers can hand over a careers pamphlet today to a pupil, and say with confidence 'There's a job that will give you security and a future'? All the teacher can do is make sure that the individual pupil has the personal equipment to face the uncertainty and unpredictability and to survive whatever the future holds. Much work at the moment, especially with the brighter pupils, is not preparing them for that kind of future, and is much more about acquiring academic knowledge than about developing personal maturity and lifeskills. Many university counsellors will testify to the unpreparedness of some students for many of the personal demands of university life, and would say that much of the high drop-out rate is due more to the inability to cope personally than to academic shortcomings.

The Industrial Training Research Unit at Cambridge has carried out a very significant piece of research relevant to the debate on the nature of the school curriculum if preparation for work and adult life generally are high priorities. They were interested (in 1979) in what makes for differences in adjustment to jobs between 16-year-old school-leavers who leave with minimal or no qualifications. Some boys and girls who do poorly at school make a good start at work and improve as time goes on: what distinguishes them from those who fail to improve? The differences between the two groups as reported by their employers were as follows:

Improvers	Non-improvers
Versatility	Doesn't follow instructions
Takes initiative	Bad timekeeper
Pride in job	Dislikes supervisors
Good personal relations	Careless about quality
Listens to instructions	Can't concentrate
Wide viewpoint	Chats, gazes around
Seeks work when slack	Personal problems
Quality-conscious	Bad personal relations
Good timekeeper	Over-confident for ability
Asks questions	Doesn't pull weight
Methodical and neat	Doesn't like change
Reports faults	Doesn't report faults
Remedies the problems	No loyalty to company

The ability to do the jobs concerned did not merit consideration in the study, as employers did not think of this as a problem. The list of qualities required to succeed emphasizes the importance of the lifeskills outlined in Chapter 1. The other issue raised for us was about where the skills thought essential to job success were on the curricula of most schools: how to make and maintain relationships, how to communicate effectively, how to think and solve problems constructively, how to find *and keep* a job, how to manage conflict, how to work in groups, how to find information and resources, how to manage time effectively:

> What this survey does is to show where the main improvement areas lie for the young people in the bottom 40 per cent of the ability range. There is a reservoir of capacity among them from which to produce this improvement, judging by the good progress made by many who had unpromising school careers. Most of this improvement hinges on changed attitudes. . . . Invariably this touches on their own self-image which is usually a poor one. An unsatisfying school experience and the low status given to the jobs of the unskilled by schools and society alike have a depersonalising effect. The result may be the denial of establishment values, opting out of the 'system', personal lack of confidence, and a disgruntled and aggressive bearing. [Industrial Research Training Unit Report, 1979]

2.7 Towards more personal competence

So the teacher is in the middle, hearing and seeing that all is not well. The cry comes from all sides and from 'above' and 'below': 'Let schools be "useful", "productive", "efficient", "interesting".' The problem for the teacher is that those words have different meanings if you are a government minister, an employer, an economist, a parent, a headteacher, a governor or a student. Is there, in fact, a common call? Maybe there is! Isn't the demand that everybody is making one for individuals who are 'personally competent', responsible, caring, and committed? People who can learn and develop the skills they will need to survive, provide, cope, and prosper in a variety of different situations. Isn't all this the other side of the coin of inadequacy? It is difficult to govern, employ, work with, provide for, support or teach those who are not adequate to meet the challenges of life in the rest of this century. This is not to say that there are adequates and inadequates, or that these are permanent conditions of human beings! Some cope and prosper better than others, some cope better in some situations than others, and there are many reasons for this. We are saying it is possible for every one of us to be more effective and self-fulfilling than we are today, and to the degree that 'underdevelopment' exists, it is wasteful on individual, social, and economic grounds. Each individual, at school or post-school, is saying 'We want to survive and prosper, be adequate and competent. The more skills, competence, and confidence I have the less I need fear tomorrow.' As Winston Churchill once put it, despite his markedly lack-lustre school career, 'Give us the tools and we will finish the job'. It is a matter, we think, of identifying for ourselves today what actually are the 'tools' that would give us the adequacy and versatility to be more effective individuals tomorrow.

2.8 Putting the school in its context

We have already seen that schooling and education are not synonymous. Because, in the past, they have sometimes been regarded as such, we have produced such myths as:
— education happens only in schools;
— education lasts only until you leave school;
— some people are always teachers, some are always learners;
— being educated means knowing many facts;
— being clever means passing exams;
— 'experts' and those in authority always know best.
This belief, that schools are the one source of 'light and truth' and teachers the only mediators with 'omniscience', has not been the healthiest foundation on which to build. It can be a narrowing and depowering concept. It can negate and discount all the incredible learning that goes on in each one of us before we ever go near a school at the age of five. Goodman (1970) points out that the language learning done in infancy in the family, in the street, in

the playgroup, and in informal, unstructured contacts has lessons for all would-be language teachers. He contends that, were the language learning extracted from the home and given over to the schools, it would be timetabled, formalized, academically presented, written down repetitively and artificially, and of course examined, and thereby would cease to be the dynamic and effective process that it is. It is easy to see how much learning occurs in other ways and places other than schools: from television; at home; from magazines, comics, newspapers, radios; from conversation in pubs, clubs, restaurants; from holidays and travel; from colleagues and workmates; from church and community groups; in leisure activities with others; and from special interest groups like literary and music circles, canoe clubs, philatelist groups, pigeon fanciers, debating societies, Cubs, Scouts, and Guides, and so on. The narrowness of schooling against the breadth and width of life is sometimes depressingly apparent. Some say that compulsory schooling, with its containment of large numbers of people in one building to do predetermined subjects in artificial time-packets, in isolation from 'reality' and the community and with an emphasis on 'sitting down' and 'keeping quiet', is counter-educational. It stops much learning which would otherwise be going on in 'reality-based' situations. A withering thought, this, for us, as we see the amount of the rates and taxes the system devours. Does what we do achieve justify the outlay? Are the lessons learned ones with a life-long use? Is schooling a launching platform to the educational process that is the rest of one's life? Does it open opportunities or narrow visions? Does it achieve its objectives? Does it 'turn on' its recipients to the learning possibilities in the rest of their lives? Is what we intend teaching what is actually learnt? Adult educators will tell you of difficulties of getting across the concept of recurrent education to prospective consumers. A lesson learned by many in school seems to be that learning means schooling. Very large numbers of pupils leave schools having had negative experiences, lack of success, or large amounts of time-filling. Education has been tasted, has not excited the taste-buds, and has left a legacy of indigestion. When later they hear a call to 're-enter education', that it 'is a life-long process', they do not feel impelled towards more of the same. Some, of course, do well, and pursue education as a career. The 'treasures of everyman' are hoarded and guarded in castles of privilege we call colleges and universities. Many of the treasures become elitist and exclusive. 'Education' is for the few, and is not seen as a staple diet, something each of us needs to fulfil ourselves in the present and to move on to our next life-stage.

There is as much to know at the age of 5 as there is at birth, at 16 as at 6, at 26 as at 16. How much one's ideas, needs, and situations change within a decade! Leaving school and choosing a career, how many realized the effect upon that career of being married and having children? What expertise and skills relationships and parenthood require! Our career ideas change. We lose a job: how can we be most effective in that situation? Life produces its ongoing demands to which education can respond. We become ready to learn about renting or buying, banking, hire purchase, taxation laws, insurance, at a time when they become part of our lives. We would welcome some information on the possibility of re-routing motorways that threaten our neighbourhood, some skills in keeping the car running or building that extension. We would welcome some lessons in making some sense of our political system, or our welfare state, or our trade union; some chance to develop other leisure activities as we outgrow our previous ones. At 36, 46, 56 the list of things we need to know, or know about, or know how to do, will be different, but as long. Look at the recent interest in education for retirement. Retirement takes skills, and those retiring need information, and hence we can now take courses to prepare for that stage of life. Education is indeed from the 'cradle to the grave'; schooling is only a part of it. If this is the case, schools and teachers have a large responsibility. If schooling is an experience that 'switches off' rather than 'switches on', then people will carry from school to adult life a resistance to the idea of ongoing education. Schools, even with the best intentions and out of the highest motives, present to many a depowering, alienating experience, which some would say blocks off the notion and possibility of life-long education. We think it is possible to reverse this. We see that 'switching on' can be achieved by making schooling more 'person-centred'. A process that is about me—my interests, hopes, values, ideas, perceptions, ambitions, relationships, skills, and development—is one that can produce interest, energy, commitment, response, and responsibility.

2.9 Who is responsible for what is wrong ?

We are not introducing blame or guilt into this discussion—that would be inappropriate and unfair. As Reimer says in his introduction to *School is Dead*:

There are unjust men in this world and it is an unjust world, but it is not primarily the unjust men who make it so. It is an unjust world largely because it is composed of faulty institutions. These institutions, in turn, are merely the collective habits of individuals, but individuals can have 'bad' habits without being bad people. In general people are unconscious of their habits; particularly their institutional habits. The positive thesis of this book is that people can become aware of their bad institutional habits and can change them. The world would then be a better world made up of still imperfect people. [Reimer, 1971]

2.10 Changing our institutional habits

Information-giving or skill development?

Much of school is based upon information being passed from teacher A to student B, or from book C to book D. The content of much of the information, as we have already said, is out of date or 'second-hand', and cannot keep pace with the present rate of discovery and obsolescence. The *Sunday Times* recently quoted various attempts to up-date and make relevant some of what is happening in schools. At various times between November 1977 and March 1978 the paper reported the following developments: York University is producing a French language 'survival kit' to replace many irrelevant teaching programmes; at Cabinet level in the British government questions are being asked about 'political education' to combat the emergence of politically extremist groups; in New York they are working on an information 'survival kit' based on information needed to 'survive' in the 1980s in New York State. So much of the present information is barely worthy of preservation, and will in any case become obsolete quickly.

A question raised at a conference at York University in January 1976 by HMI Andrew Fuller seems to us an important one:

There are few crises in our society caused by lack of information; we have an abundance of knowledge. Most of our crises and our difficulties are caused by our inability to live with ourselves and each other—are our schools recognizing this and responding to it?

But the method as well as the content is questionable. The method has a message! However benevolent my intentions as a giver of information, some of what I am conveying as I stand in front of the class is likely to be:

'I know more than you, you know little.'

'What I am telling you is important whether you recognize it or not.'

'I am the only teacher in this room—learn by listening to me and not anybody else.'

'What I am saying is the most important thing happening here—whether you are sad, happy, bored, in love, dying to speak, ill, angry, bereaved, worried or whatever—giving facts is more important than recognizing where the receivers "are" or what they think or want.'

The depowering, alienating process is at work. Let us sit in the pupil's desk and feel what it might be like:

'If the teacher at the front keeps impressing us that she knows more, that we know little; that what we feel, think, need, and are interested in is of secondary importance; that passivity is better than initiative; that our peer groups are not worth contacting or listening to and can teach us nothing that is valuable; that knowing facts about other people and places remote from us is of prime importance; that we can learn only from teacher or books, then the switching-off begins. What we are hearing and what is being done to us (with the best of intentions!) feels like it discounts us and disqualifies our experience and our worth unless we are assertive enough (they call that disruptive) and challenge it.'

Information-giving as an educational process is likely to be fact-centred and not person-centred, and is likely to be a detached rather than involving, alive approach. The educated person of the future, we are told, is likely to be not the one who knows a lot of facts but the one who knows how to ask questions and find out a lot of facts. The Oxfam poster expresses the same idea: 'Give a man a fish and you feed him for a day—teach him how to fish and you feed him for a lifetime.' Development rather than aid. It is interesting in passing to note that many poorer countries now reject aid that is mere benevolent-giving. Receiving, as a replacement for doing for oneself, is not development and doesn't build for tomorrow. Skills and self-empowerment, learning by doing, are the investment in tomorrow. Develop information retrieval skills, information organization skills, study skills, thinking skills, problem-solving skills, and you have equipment to face whatever tomorrow requires by way of information. These are important skills, but they are only a tiny part of a whole skills-development possibility that schools could introduce.

2.11 Schools and teachers do make a difference

One of the major reasons why we have developed the Lifeskills Teaching Programmes and produced this book is because we believe that formal education in general and schools in particular

47

do have an important function. Research published in 1979 by Rutter and his colleagues demonstrates clearly that there are 'good' schools and 'poor' schools, and that the variables contributing to these differences can be identified. Their conclusion is that schools with a mix of ability, which set good standards, where the teachers provide good models of behaviour, where the students are praised and given responsibility, where the general conditions are good and where lessons are well conducted, are the most effective schools. Geographical location, class size, sex, teacher–pupil ratio, physical facilities, and methods of teaching were not related to the differences. This is firm evidence for what most teachers have always felt, namely that the quality of teaching and the personality of the teacher does make a difference.

Aspy and Roebuck (1977), in one of the most important pieces of educational research of the decade, showed how effective and less effective teachers could be differentiated according to behavioural skills. They found that teachers who were highest in their abilities to empathize with their students, who demonstrated respect (positive regard) in and out of the classroom, and whose behaviour and intentions were congruent (genuine) were the teachers whose students showed most cognitive growth, IQ gains, best attendance, and fewest examples of disruptive behaviour in the classroom. These three qualities have also been demonstrated to distinguish effective from less effective therapists, doctors, social workers, and managers. They also provided clear evidence to show that these skills can be taught relatively quickly (under 72 hours) and that the teachers can then teach these skills to other teachers. Sadly, one might ask the question, 'where are these interpersonal skills taught in initial teacher training in the UK?' and emerge with an answer that makes one wonder about just what *is* the value of many aspects of initial teacher training. Aspy and Roebuck's study was titled from a comment from one of the students they talked to and concisely sums up the research: 'Kids don't learn from people they don't like'.

These two pieces of research, we feel, more than justify the claim that schools can make a difference, and within schools there are effective and less effective teachers. The qualities identified by Aspy and Roebuck are qualities that within limits can be taught, and will be essential to teach the subject matter we will be referring to in the way that we have been describing.

48

2.12 Whose responsibility is education ?

It was interesting in school at one point to debate this with a class whose homework was not produced. The question arose as to who should be anxious about that. The teacher had been saved hours of marking and felt some relief, but as the official, 'professional' response was to come down hard on this, the hassle began. What was doing homework about? Many of the 'doers' did it because they were told to and would be punished if they didn't. Very few saw it as for their own benefit or as an investment in their future. Whose responsibility was their education and progress? Very definitely, most said, it was the teachers. The teacher himself felt that was how most people would see it; he even felt it was mostly his own view of things. Dependency and over-dependency are learned at a very early stage and take a great deal of unlearning, if indeed they ever can be. If, at an early stage, the 'system' says to each of us, in the way it operates, that responsibility for our progress, development, behaviour, and welfare lies with somebody other than ourselves we are on the road to dependency. In the way many schools operate this is the message. 'It is somebody else's responsibility that I learn' is the first step to 'it is somebody else's responsibility that I eat, am clothed, and housed, that my children are provided for', and so on. 'Overgiving' in the teaching sense, like overgiving in the helping sense, is likely to disable, to retard development, to delay maturing, and to require later a sizeable effort to unlearn dependency. Our content and method need re-evaluating. The skill development programme we are describing as a Lifeskills Programme has, as an important objective, the development of responsibility for oneself and equipping each individual with skills and an approach to life that will reduce the over-dependency that is often as much a burden for the 'supporter' as it is for the 'supported'.

The theme of empowering the individual in each of the above approaches, and thereby inviting development, commitment, responsibility, and initiative, is one of the bases for our proposed self-empowerment programme. We borrow something from each of them, but develop them further. They are a starting point. We offer the possibility of concentrating the educational effort on self and personal skill development; of schools pursuing this as a priority. We predict that the results of such an approach would be highly significant and gainful. Very little, if anything, needs to be sacrificed. There need be no falling-off in students' academic performance. Our experience suggests that building a positive self-concept and working with individuals on themselves has appreciable spin-off even in the form of higher academic achievement. Friere found it; so have many others. For example, Wattenberg and Clifford (1972) found that self-concept was a better predictor of reading success than IQ. Children with poor self-concepts attained considerably less in reading skills than did children with good self-concepts.

There is in a 'person-centred' approach to education, we would suggest, real gains for everybody. It is appropriate to all the ability range. It is even an antidote to those pupils who are not 'interested in anything'—our experience says that they are interested in themselves, and can move from there into other areas. We are registering here that, while the responsibility for education lies within the whole community, schools and teachers are in a unique position as agents of personal, and through that social change. Not everything is within their grasp, but through the influence and impact they can have on individuals they can effect significant results in personal development and thereby bring about eventual social change.

We all need to 'be somebody', and we become somebody either in personally and socially desirable ways or in deviant ways. Can't we invite individuals in our school programmes to feel they are valued, important, and full of potential which it is in themselves to develop? As one of Paulo Friere's illiterates said, 'I want to read and write so I can stop being a shadow of other people.' Basic literacy is only one of many lifeskills that would enable each of us to be more fulfilled and capable, givers rather than takers, more competent and self-directing, less dependent and controlled, more fully human. Individuals like that would contribute to a highly active, more democratic, less vulnerable, type of society, with a greatly reduced need for Illich's *Disabling Professions* (1977).

Schools, we are saying, are capable, in their contribution to education as a life-process, of making a sizeable impact on individuals and society, if their priority objective became the self-empowerment of all involved in their systems. This would involve re-appraisal of what they are doing at the moment in terms of content and process and some re-direction. For us that direction is towards providing each one with the basic lifeskills necessary for human survival and growth in the post-industrial society.

In later chapters we will become specific about the implementation of this programme and the methods and organizational adjustments that will be needed to accompany it, and the skills teachers might need to develop to use it.

Adam Curle sees as the outcome of his education for liberation that:

> We will become human beings who are aware, capable of objective love, courageous in the defence of truth, careless of our safety and possessions, autonomous. This is real liberation. Education for liberation is that which attempts to liberate us from the habit of thought, action, and feeling which makes us less than human, which enables us in turn to liberate others and which transforms the system into the counter system. [Curle, 1973]

We see 'liberation' being very much about autonomy and responsibility, but also about sensitivity to others and the promotion of their liberation. We think it is also about developing the skills of each of us which will allow us to acquire, preserve, and use that liberation in whatever situations life brings to us and others.

3. Education towards self-empowerment

> Here is Edward Bear, coming downstairs now bump, bump, on the back of his head behind Christopher Robin. It is, as far as he knows, the only way of coming downstairs, but sometimes he feels that there really is another way, if only he could stop bumping for a moment and think of it.
>
> A. A. Milne, *Winnie the Pooh*

Anyone defining educational objectives and designing educational systems is simultaneously describing his own model of the ideal person and the ideal society. Education cannot be discussed in a value-free vacuum any more than it can be discussed in a political vacuum. Education is about values and politics (see Chapter 5, page 122); and we believe that when people present their views on education they will be reflecting their own views on what people and society should be like, and therefore need to be clear themselves on the values that fuel their thinking and objectives.

In deciding the questions that education should be asking at the advent of post-industrial society we too are clearly implying that it would be best if people were 'like this' and society was 'like that'. As a result of our own analysis we have identified the values that we believe are desirable *per se* but are also necessary to help individuals survive and grow in the new era.

Martin Luther King had a dream, and that dream helped him to see the reality of how things really were more clearly. Without dreams and fantasies our imaginations can become stultified in the 'dailiness' of everyday living, merely reacting to the demands that others put upon us through a process we label 'pinball living'. Balls in a pinball machine have no life of their own; they are set in motion by someone else and then bounce from one place to another without any clear direction, sometimes even making big scores, but then sinking into oblivion until someone sets them off again.

The opposite to pinball living for us is self-empowered living. What follows is a discussion of what we mean by self-empowerment and why we believe that it should be a prime objective for schools.

3.1 The depowering dimension

For many years now, through working in different environment and with different people, much of our work has been fuelled by five basic beliefs.

1. Many people restrict their own growth and development far more than they realize; i.e., they 'depower' themselves.

2. Many people live and work in environments that, partly by accident and sometimes by design, operate to 'depower' them further.

3. It *is* possible for people to become more aware of their self-imposed constraints and of those imposed on them.

4. It *is* also possible for people to acquire appropriate skills and resources to 'empower' themselves, i.e. to develop more control over what happens to them and their reactions to what happens to them, greater self-direction, more flexibility, more commitments in living.

5. The more people take charge of themselves and their lives, the more likely they will work to empower others and to develop empowering environments in which all people can live, work and play.

'Man is free who believes he is free, and has the skills to support his freedom. Man is determined who believes he is so and lacks the skills to deny it' (Carkhuff, 1976).

By 'power', we mean the ability to influence intentionally what happens to us in relation to other people and the physical world. To 'empower' is to get in touch or help someone else get in touch with these abilities. When people are 'depowered' they feel powerless, helpless, apathetic, alienated:

> the central core of modern man's 'neurosis' . . . is the undermining of his experience of himself as responsible, the sapping of his will and ability to make decisions. The lack of will is much more than merely an ethical problem: the modern individual so often has the conviction that even if he *did* exert his 'will'—or whatever illusion passes for it—his actions wouldn't do any good anyway. It is this inner experience of impotence, this contradiction in will, which constitutes our critical problem. [May, 1970]

3.2 The process of becoming depowered

Some people are born 'depowered', others become depowered, yet others have depowerment thrust upon them! Our point is that from whatever source depowerment comes it is always possible to be more empowered than we are at the moment.

First and foremost we depower ourselves

We do this by:

- the *belief* that we can do nothing to change our situation or ourselves;
- not developing a wide range of skills, thereby rendering ourselves dependent upon others, whether it is not knowing how to sew a button on our trousers to not knowing how to buy a house;
- building our own constraints without analysing why and without looking for alternative objectives or action plans.

In southern India the local populace enjoy monkey-meat, and they have developed a novel way of trapping monkeys. A coconut is hollowed out through a small hole in the shell. Boiled rice, which monkeys apparently adore, is placed inside the hole which is just big enough for an average sized monkey-fist to squeeze through. The shell is tied to a tree. Now, when the greedy monkey discovers the shell and the rice, he also discovers that he can just get his hand inside the shell, but as soon as he takes a handful of rice, he cannot get his hand out again! The monkey, you might predict, would drop the rice to escape. But instead he cannot bring himself to let go and sits watching the hunters come closer and closer until they club him to death. Most of us have our own monkey traps: things, ideas, people that we cannot let go of even if it means our stultifying and perhaps dying, psychologically and even physically (e.g., with stress-related diseases). We must have material possessions, or security of job, or the permanence of a relationship at all costs, or a belief of how the world *should* be as opposed to how it is. Looked at this way, perhaps it is easier to understand just how a monkey can be so stupid!

We also depower ourselves by living out our 'life scripts'. This is a term from transactional analysis (Steiner, 1974), which refers to the way that as children we pick up messages like stage directions which compel us to follow them as part of our life drama. The directions may be positive and/or negative, verbal or non-verbal, consistent or inconsistent. We are given sex roles, work roles, cultural roles. We are given roles within the family group. This means that much of our behaviour and values are pre-determined by our early experiences. We are carrying out the directions given us by parents and social groups, but are unaware of these influences because they are so much a part of us. In addition to the directions given us by others we add some of our own that influence us, often unconsciously. For example, Linda aged eight realized that when she could not cope with a task and she cried and acted helpless her father would do it for her. At that age she may well have had genuine difficulties, but now she is 25 and married and she continues to act in the same way. Maslow (1968) refers to this as a 'frozen need'; i.e., it may have been appropriate at eight but is now unnecessary, yet the habit lives on, frozen into Linda's repertoire as if she were still eight years old, and dictating her responses to totally different situations. Part of the process of becoming self-empowered involves becoming aware of how one is 'scripted'. From that awareness comes the freedom to choose whether to stick with that script or to change it. You might decide, for example, that part of your script includes being helpful to others and trusting people, and you may decide to retain this. In this case what was a *script* has now become a *commitment*. *The Oxford Dictionary* defines commitment as 'an engagement that restricts freedom of action'. This is what empowerment is all about—not merely the acquisition of freedom, but the use of it to provide a sense of purpose to one's existence. True freedom comes with the determination freely to restrict one's alternatives.

Scripts give people directions. Some of the more depowering ones are directions like: 'You're OK, I'm not OK', 'I can't think for myself', 'Life is just one damned thing after another and the sooner it's over with the better', 'However hard you try someone will frustrate you in the end', 'Fate determines all so there's no point in trying', 'I must be perfect in all I do, and if I can't I'd better not try at all'.

We allow other people to depower us

We do this by:

1. assuming that there are many things we cannot do and therefore we have to rely on others to do things for us;
2. assuming some people have an automatic right to tell us what to do, e.g., doctors, lawyers, priests, politicians;
3. being reactive, and making no attempt to influence what happens to us;
4. not developing a wide range of skills that would make us less dependent on others;
5. not ensuring that we have access to important information and that we know how to find out information. Information is power, which is why so many people keep information hidden. We need to know about ourselves, about other people in our lives, about the community in which we live, and about what is going on in the world at large;

6. assuming that we can have no effect on the society in which we live. This is often true, but we can always have some effect on the segment of life with which we are involved.

> Man is distinguished by his capacity to know that he is determined, and to choose his relationship to what determines him. He can and must, unless he abdicates his consciousness, choose how he will relate to necessity, such as death, old age, limitations of intelligence and the conditioning inescapable in his own background. Will he accept this necessity, deny it, fight it, affirm it, consent to it? [May, 1970]

We are sometimes deliberately depowered

This happens to us:

1. as a consequence of early learning. Seligman (1975) has shown in a significant series of research studies how feelings of helplessness are learned by people in response to situations in which they feel that what happens to them is not connected in any way with their actions. The result is depression—a belief in one's own helplessness. This can happen just as much from 'good' things happening to a person as 'bad' things. If the individual feels that she had nothing to do with what happened to her (or in psychological terms, if reward or punishment bears no causal relationship to her actions), then depression can follow. Seligman's work on treating 'learned helplessness' demonstrates the difficulty of extricating a depressed person from the belief in her own powerlessness. His experiments suggest that the most effective way of doing this is to ensure that people find out and come to believe that it is their responses that produce the gratification they desire. We have to structure learning environments to ensure that people have success experiences;

2. as a consequence of the social group we are born into. For example, low socioeconomic groups and minorities often report greater feelings of powerlessness—understandably (Irelan, 1967; Leibow, 1967), resulting in hopelessness, fatalism and apathy

3. because political groups and governments typically hide information from people to maintain them in positions of dependency;

4. because professional groups develop initially to provide a service, but often then become self-protective, their priority being to maintain their privileged position, so ensuring their own continuity by making people dependent on them. This is

the movement attacked so strongly by Illich in his book on *The Disabling Professions* (Illich *et al.*, 1978), and by Dore in his analysis of *The Diploma Disease* (1976).

3.3 What is self-empowerment ?

Self-empowerment is a process by which one increasingly takes greater charge of oneself and one's life. By our definition it is not an end-state. One cannot become a 'self-empowered person'. It is a process of becoming in which one behaves in a more or less empowered way. In this way it differs from the concept of self-actualization as described by Maslow (1968), which is a state of being that *can* be achieved.

To operate in a self-empowered way entails being able to:

1. look at oneself from outside of oneself and to believe that one is open to change;

2. have the skills to change some aspects of oneself and the world in which one lives;

3. use one's feelings to recognize where there is a discrepancy between what is and what one would like it to be;

4. specify desired outcomes and the action steps required to achieve them;

5. *act*—to implement action plans;

6. live each day aware of one's power to assess, re-assess, influence and self-direct;

7. enable others to achieve the power to take charge of their lives and influence the different arenas of their lives.

Underlying the whole concept is the belief that, no matter what,

There is always an alternative and we can choose.

Self-empowerment means believing that, and having the abilities to identify the alternatives in any situation, to choose one on the basis of one's values, priorities, and commitments. None of the alternatives in some situations may be desirable, but it is the knowledge that there is *always* a choice that heralds the beginning of self-empowered thinking.

How does one recognize self-empowered behaviour?

These are some dimensions that will help to differentiate between more or less self-empowered behaviour.

More	*Less*
Open to change	Closed to change
Assertive	Non-assertive or aggressive
Proactive	Reactive
Self-accountable	Blames others
Self-directed	Other-directed
Uses feelings	Overwhelmed by or fails to recognize feelings
Learns from mistakes	Debilitated by mistakes
Confronts	Avoids
Lives more in the present	Past- or future-oriented
Realistic	Unrealistic
Thinks relatively	Thinks in absolutes
Sees alternatives	Tunnel vision
Develops commitments	Keeps obligations
Likes self	Dislikes self
Values others	Negates others
Alert to other's needs	Selfish
Interested in the world	Self-centred
Balanced life-style	One arena of life developed to the exclusion of others
Enhances other people's lives	Restricts the lives of others

How does one become more self-empowered?

We offer the following operational definition of self-empowerment: to become more self-empowered one needs: awareness; goals; values; lifeskills; and information (see Fig. 3.1).

Awareness

One needs to develop the ability to stand apart from oneself and to examine oneself (a) from the outside—as others see one—and (b) from the inside—as no one else can see one. This latter involves becoming aware of changes in body state and feelings. Both (a) and (b) involve becoming aware of one's strengths, limitations, inclinations, values, prejudices, potential.

This area of awareness is labelled *awareness of self*.

One also needs to be sensitive to other people—to their moods, values, prejudices, strengths, limitations, and potential.

This area of awareness is *awareness of others*.

Everyone lives in networks, groups, organizations, social

structures. One must be aware of the ways in which one is being influenced by systems and in turn is influencing them.

This area is *awareness of systems.*

Awareness, therefore, includes awareness of self, others, and systems.

Awareness at any level can come about only through praxis, not through intellectual effort alone. In Friere's terms, the difference between naive and critical consciousness is that the latter is achieved 'through the authentic union of action and reflection' (1972a).

Fig. 3.1 Criteria for self-empowered behaviour

Awareness
- Self
- Others
- Systems

Goals
- Commitments
- Outcomes

Values
- People
- Systems

Lifeskills
- Me
- Me and you
- Me and others
- Me and specific situations

Information
- Me
- You
- The world

Goals

Self-empowered behaviour can take place only if a person knows why she is behaving that way, i.e. she has a goal. Unfortunately some goals are so abstract or general as to offer little scope for directed action plans, for example, 'I want to be happy', or 'I want to be successful'. Instead goals need to be specified in terms of desired *outcomes*, for example, 'I wish to obtain my satisfaction out of the administrative side of my work', or 'I want to be two grades higher up the scale by the time I am 30'.

Goals, however, even with specified outcomes, are not themselves evidence of self-empowered behaviour. The goals may not be your own. You may be living out someone else's script for you which says, 'by the age of 30 you will be a head of department, and if you are not you will be failing'. Goals need to be one's own, arrived at freely from an examination of the alternatives within the context of one's personal value system. This kind of goal would also qualify as a commitment.

Goals, therefore, need to have specified outcomes and to be one's own commitments.

Values

Goals in themselves are likely to reflect the values that we hold. As part of our operational definition of self-empowerment we are saying that behaviour will be self-empowered only if it embodies certain values. Concern has been expressed that more self-empowered people are likely simply to be more selfish and more skilled in their abilities to manipulate others. By our definition this could not be so as a vital element in the concept of self-empowerment is the desire and the ability to enable others to achieve more power over their own lives.

Our definition of values follows the distinction made by Raths, Merrill and Simon (1966) between a belief and a value. A belief becomes a value only if all the following criteria are met: it must be chosen freely, chosen from among alternatives, chosen after due reflection, prized and cherished, publicly affirmed, acted upon, and be part of a pattern that is a repeated action.

Below is a list of values that if acted upon should serve to ensure more self-empowered people and more empowering systems.

Values for promoting more self-empowered people
● Each person is unique, valuable and worthy of respect.
● Self-empowerment derives from operating through growth needs rather than deficiency needs (Maslow, 1968). Rowan (1976) has taken Maslow's distinction and derived behavioural examples of each type of need under the headings of Maslow's hierarchy of needs (see Fig. 3.2).
● Self-empowerment involves sensitivity to and the liberation of others.
● People are primarily responsible for what happens to them.
● People are responsible for their feelings, whether good or bad.*

* Readers who have difficulties with this statement might like to consult the teaching programme, *How to Manage Negative Emotions*, in *Lifeskills Teaching Programmes No. 1* (Hopson and Scally, 1980).

Fig. 3.2 A selection of growth and deficiency needs in the context of Maslow's hierarchy of needs (based upon Rowan, 1976)

Growth needs	Stage	Deficiency needs
Enjoying heat, cold or rain, bodily experiences	**Physiological**	Eating and drinking from hunger and thirst; sex out of a pressing bodily need; sleeping when tired
Confronting danger; anticipating danger to enable one to deal with it; using pain for learning and development	**Safety**	Escaping danger; avoiding pain or harm; seeking protection in real threat situation; suppressing hurt; cutting down on stimulation; attempts to stop environment changing
Enjoying the development of loved ones; love that reaches out to others, and gives others the space to grow	**Love and belonging**	Need for approval; fear of group; wants to please others; strong desire to belong to a definite group; changing oneself to fit in with what others want
Liking to be appreciated; warming to response from others	**Esteem**	Need for recognition and applause; need for hierarchies and stability
Respecting the identities of self and others; confidence in self; flexibility in action; authentic; creative; inspired; and inspiring; non-punitive; humour; letting peak experiences come; empowering others.	**Self-actualization**	Need for consistency; strong conscience with many guilt feelings; high standards which must never be infringed; searching for peak experiences out of boredom; exploiting others for one's own development.

- Any new situation, however undesired, contains within it some opportunity for personal growth.
- Stress and anxiety can be managed.
- Failures are learning experiences. There is in fact no such thing as a failure, only ideas or behaviours that do not work. A person cannot be a 'failure', although he may fail to achieve one or more of his goals. That does not make his total self a failure—unless he chooses to evaluate the experience in that way.
- All behaviours have payoffs, but some will be healthy payoffs and will reward the developing parts of a person, while others will be unhealthy payoffs and will serve to keep the person anchored in states of fear, hostility, depression, and insecurity.
- Values, priorities, and interests will change over the years: that is normal.
- The more self-empowered a person becomes the more able he will be to help others do the same.*
- People will not be able to respect, value, and love others until they have first learned to respect, value, and love themselves.
- Tomorrow need not be the same as today.
- People need continuously to monitor their own welfare and development.
- People should be concerned about the world in which they live and should work to improve it.
- Development never ends; self-empowerment is not an end-state that can be achieved.
- There is always an alternative and we can choose.

Values for Promoting More Empowering Systems
- An empowering system exists to serve the development of individuals.
- An empowering system will value and reward behaviour that conveys respect, genuineness, and empathy.
- A system is empowering if it encourages members to work co-operatively towards shared, identifiable goals.
- A system should be always open to re-evaluation and to internal and external influences for change.
- An empowering system is never static.
- Its members will give support and be open to receiving it from one another.
- The system will help people to identify their strengths and build on them.

* For evidence of this see section on page 75.

• People use problem-solving strategies to deal with problems instead of scapegoating, blaming or focusing on faults.

• There is consistency between their goals and their methods of achieving them.

• An empowering system is sensitive to the needs of outsiders.

• It will encourage power-sharing and enable individuals to pursue their own directions within the context of the shared goals.

• It will monitor its own performance in a continuing cycle of reflection–action–reflection–action.

• It will allow people access to those whose decisions have a bearing on their lives.

• It will have effective and sensitive lines of communication.

• Differences will be explored openly and compromise, negotiation, and contracting will be used to gain a maximum of win–win situations for all.

• An empowering system is always open to alternatives.

A quotation from Carl Rogers (1978) sums up our approach: 'It is not that this approach gives power to the person; it never takes it away.'

Lifeskills

The greater the range of skills a person possesses, the greater the range of alternatives available to her. There has been much discussion recently about providing young people with 'life and social skills', and there appears to be considerable diversity of definition as to what these skills are. Theoretically, the addition of any skill to one's behavioural repertoire will make one potentially more self-empowered. In practice, however, certain skills will be more closely related to self-empowered living than others. Knowing how to service your car will not empower you as much generally as knowing how to make relationships quickly. Knowing how to throw a pot will not help you through life as much as knowing how to be assertive.

We have attempted to define the vital generalized skills that will help a person to become more self-empowered. No doubt everyone will have his or her own additions to make and we would encourage people to do that. The remainder of this book is concerned with how to introduce and teach these skills in schools and colleges. Teaching resources and materials relevant to these skills are reviewed in Chapter 6, and a number of teaching programmes specially designed to teach a selection of these skills are contained in *Lifeskills Teaching Programmes No. 1* (Hopson and Scally, 1980).

The skills are subdivided into four areas (see Fig. 1.2, page 25): the 'skills I need to survive and grow generally', the 'skills I need to relate effectively to you', the 'skills I need to relate effectively to others', and the 'skills I need in specific situations'. The latter is to some extent the odd one out as it could include every possible skill imaginable. Because of this we have identified the five key arenas of living—education, work, home, leisure, and the community—and within each of these have isolated some key skills which appear to us to be the most generalizable. Again, other people will have their own priorities, and what we hope to do is not to persuade people to accept our list as it stands but to use it as a stimulus to help crystallize for them the skills that they see as essential for a more self-empowered existence. A list of these resources for teaching these skills is given in Chapter 6.

My skills: skills I need to survive and grow generally

How to read and write; how to achieve basic numeracy. These skills are the ones talked of most frequently by employers and Black Paperites. They are of course essential, and quite clearly not all young people leave school with them, as witnessed by the success of the adult literacy campaign. One unfortunate consequence of the concentration on these skills is that other vital skills—not so easily measurable—are ignored.

How to find information and resources. With 97 per cent of everything known in the world having been acquired in the lifetime of today's secondary schoolchild, the futility of teaching masses of information is obvious. Information is better stored and recalled electronically. The essential skills then become the ones of categorizing and retrieving information, and at its simplest level knowing which organizations and people will give relevant information. The skills can range from knowing how to use the Yellow Pages to knowing how to find out about one's rights as a citizen through to an understanding of library classification systems or viewdata television services.

Knowing the questions to ask, and of whom, will matter more than trying to remember all the answers. Information is disposable; processing and retrieval techniques are not.

How to think and solve problems constructively. The ability to think clearly and logically is central to all areas of living, and yet until very recently has rarely been taught formally.

Hudson's work (1967) has popularized the distinction between convergent and divergent thinking and the vital interdependence of them both. De Bono (1970) has recently been designing teaching programmes to develop divergent, creative thinking and problem-solving techniques.

How to identify my creative potential and develop it. With an increase in discretionary time forecast, the opportunities to indulge one's creative abilities will multiply. All too often early specialization in school cuts off whole areas of interest for students. In particular, those pursuing academic interests have often been prevented from developing their artistic and practical selves, while those engaged in vocational or technical studies have often been separated from opportunities to develop their literary talents. Both groups have typically been diverted from music as a pursuit, and it is probably thanks largely to pop music that many a student's musical interest has not died altogether.

How to manage time effectively. From all people at some time or another, from all organizations, is heard the plaintive cry: 'I don't have enough time!' Time is an ever-diminishing resource for all of us; therefore it would seem to be a high priority to ensure that we get as much as we can out of the precious years we have. This involves developing commitments, priorities and time-saving skills.

How to make the most of the present. The danger of becoming obsessed with managing your time is that you can spend much of your energy planning for tomorrow and reviewing yesterday.

> It isn't the experience of today that drives men mad. It is the remorse for something that happened yesterday and the dread of what tomorrow may disclose.[Robert Jones Burdette, *Golden Day*]

There are skills to being at ease with oneself and enjoying the moment.

How to discover my interests; how to discover my values and beliefs. Many people stumble over their interests, values and beliefs accidentally. This leaves the development of vital areas of being to chance encounters with people and situations. As with so many other lifeskills, these are too important to be left to chance. There are systematic ways of discovering one's interests and values that can remain with one throughout life, even though one's actual interests and values will change.

How to set and achieve goals. There is a saying, 'If you don't know where you're going, you'll probably end up somewhere else.'

Many people achieve little because they lack goals. However, having a goal is simply the first step; developing an action plan to achieve that goal is the only way of making it happen: 'a journey of 1000 miles begins with a single step'. Having goals is the surest way of avoiding 'pinball living'; knowing how to set goals will be the key to this.

How to take stock of my life. To avoid pinball living it is necessary to take time out periodically and to ask the following questions: 'Who am I and where am I now?' 'How satisfied am I with who and where I am?' 'How would I like me or my life to be different?' 'What do I need to do to make it happen?' Many people take stock only at times of crisis when they have to re-evaluate under pressure. How much better to re-evaluate when not under pressure! You may end up by staying as you are and continuing to do what you are already doing, but there will be a difference: your commitment will have been renewed.

> Practically all goals tarnish with time if not renewed in some way. [Campbell, 1974]

How to discover what makes me do the things I do. The skills of discovering the life script that conditions one towards certain beliefs, ways of being, and behaviour patterns: knowing how to analyse and challenge one's life scripts is the key to developing one's own commitments.

How to be positive about myself. Low self-esteem has been traced as the culprit in explaining the majority of human failings— aggression, despair, jealousy, selfishness. Unfortunately, we are reared in a culture that traditionally encourages modesty and self-recrimination and spurns 'boasting' and self-aggrandizement. We are certainly not recommending the latter, but we are saying that it is essential for young people to develop the skills of recognizing their own strengths and the strengths of others. When you are aware of your own strengths you know the base from which you operate, and will be clearer about the areas of yourself you wish to improve.

How to cope with and gain from life transitions. Going to school, changing homes, parents separating, leaving school, changing jobs, getting married, becoming a parent, parents and spouse dying—all are examples of major life transitions. In between those are a myriad of micro-transitions, some voluntary, some involuntary; some looked forward to, some feared; some predictable, some unpredictable. However much we may not have chosen for something to have happened to us, there will always be some possibility for growth and development. There are skills to help us prepare for and manage macro- or micro-transitions, and to discover the potential gains contained in every single transition.

How to make effective decisions. We make scores of decisions each day, mostly unaware of them, thereby not realizing the power that we have at each choice point. Periodically we make major decisions, and manage these in a variety of ways. Some ways have been shown to offer a greater chance of success than others. Decision-making strategies, once learned, can be applied to any arena of life that one chooses.

How to be proactive. Proactive people make things happen for themselves, reactive people wait for things to happen to them. How can you ensure that you *are* in charge, that you are not a piece of life's flotsam and jetsam being tossed upon a sea of unpredictable, unknown forces? Thinking and behaving proactively can be developed as a way of life.

How to manage negative emotions. You will not be very proactive if you are constantly subject to fears, anxieties, depressions, anger, or jealousy. There are skills by which you can learn to recognize, manage, and use these emotions to your benefit rather than your detriment.

How to cope with stress. We are constantly being told of the dramatic effects of the increasing stresses and strains of con-temporary living. In 1973 approximately 40 million days were lost to British industry because of 'mental illness, stress and headaches' (Gillespie, 1974). This is three times the number of days lost by strikes and industrial action. This statistic, of course, fails to illustrate the degree of human suffering involved. Stress, however, has an undeserved bad reputation. A certain optimal level of stress is necessary to keep people challenged and alert. The problems come when there is too much, or—and less discussed—too little. There are ways of preventing too much or too little stress, and methods for managing excessive stress when preventative techniques have failed.

How to achieve and maintain physical well-being. An essential ingredient to managing transitions effectively and in coping with stress is one's physical health and fitness. For too many young people fitness programmes and exercise diminish with the years after leaving school. The central element of physical fitness in combating heart disease and high blood pressure is now well documented. We are beginning to discover more, if sometimes confusing, evidence of the relationship between diet and disease.

Information on these and on the effects of smoking, drugs, and alcohol, together with techniques to further fitness, improve relaxation, and change unhealthy eating patterns, is a core survival item for the school curriculum. First-aid skills are essential survival skills too.

How to manage my sexuality. Sexual development is as vital to a more self-empowered existence as any other aspect of oneself. What is needed here is information, raising of awareness, and the skills of dealing with sexual emotions.

Me-and-you skills: skills I need to relate effectively to you

How to communicate effectively. The skills of sending and receiving messages, of understanding non-verbal as well as verbal behaviour, of being capable of using a variety of media—face to face, by letter, by telephone—are the skills that perhaps above all will be central to working with other people, setting and achieving goals, helping others and being helped, getting jobs, making friends, getting married, staying married, being an effective parent, surviving, and growing.

How to make, keep and end a relationship. For most of us a final assessment of our lives would consist of the sum of the quality of our relationships and the extent of our achievements. Without good relationships we are more likely to get ill, depressed, even die sooner (Hopson and Scally, 1980). In post-industrial society we are more mobile, marrying more often, changing jobs more frequently. An essential survival skill is to be able to relate well and quickly with new people; not to linger morbidly to memories of relationships past, yet to have the skills to keep those relationships we value.

How to give and get help. If you believe you are valuable, with strengths, then you will be more likely to offer help to others (see page 75). However, knowing how to give support is one thing; knowing how to ask for it is another. Someone who only ever gives precludes the receiver from the feelings of worth and self-respect that accrue from the act of giving only to give. To only give is to depower; to ask for help can be empowering of others.

How to manage conflict. Wherever people live, work, or love together there will be conflicts of interest and inclination, style and habits. Conflict is an integral part of human existence, not to be shunned or avoided but to be managed. Conflicts become destructive only when bad feelings accumulate as irritations remain unexpressed and preferences hidden. The skills of managing conflict are the skills of stating preferences, communicating unambiguously, confronting differences, looking for solutions that make winners of both parties.

How to give and receive feedback. We grow and develop as a result of information fed back to us by others. By ourselves we can be aware of certain facets of ourselves, but we need to see ourselves as others see us to obtain a rounded picture. In turn, others need feedback from us. We are all free to accept or reject feedback, but unless it is given there is no choice. We can be hurtful, even destructive, when giving negative feedback, and need the skills of delivering it constructively. We need to be alert to the positive attributes of others and to train ourselves to convey our positive thoughts and feelings to others to help them grow and develop. It often takes two to see one.

Me and others: skills I need to relate effectively to others
How to be assertive. Many people fail to get what they want either by being afraid to ask for it or by setting about it aggressively. Being assertive means clearly stating a preference but not at the expense of trampling over the rights of others.

How to influence people and systems. There are some ways of trying to make changes that are more likely to pay dividends than others. This is not about manipulating others but about planning your approach so as to maximize your chances of success without violating the rights of others. You will need to know how systems work and then you can work through them.

How to work in a group. In modern living, at work and in the community, it is essential to be able to get along well with other people. There are fewer and fewer opportunities for working alone. A person who irritates others is unlikely to be successful.

How to express feelings constructively. The British typically sit on their feelings with the result that preferences remain unstated, conflicts fester, and ultimately we get psychologically and physically ill. What are the skills of first recognizing one's feelings, and then using them effectively as aids to achieving what one wants?

How to negotiate, compromise, and contract. However clearly we communicate, no matter how assertive we are, there will come times when it is not possible for two people to get exactly what they want. This calls for the skills of negotiation and compromise. This becomes easier when it is taking place within the context of a clear contract: where expectations are shared, boundaries clarified, conditions laid down. Contracts do not have to be legal; verbal contracts, sometimes written down, have a central role in the organization and clarification of human relationships.

How to build strengths in others. Self-empowerment by our definition involves the practice of helping to empower others whenever possible. Each of us has the gift of being able to appreciate and reinforce the positive in others. The skill comes in putting that gift into practice.

Me and specific situations

SKILLS I NEED FOR MY EDUCATION

How to discover the educational options open to me; how to choose a course. With recurrent education becoming the norm, it is going to be vitally important for people to know what educational opportunities are available and from where they get relevant information. They will also require strategies for choosing between educational options.

How to study. It is quite remarkable that even schools that have traditionally prided themselves on their academic success rates have provided their students with almost no formal instruction in the techniques of studying, preparing and writing essays, taking notes, organizing homework schedules, revising for examinations, taking examinations, and reducing examination stress. With the development of recurrent or continuing education, the acquisition of these essential skills as early as possible should be a key priority for the curriculum. They are too important to be left to chance, yet where are they to be found in the curriculum planning of most schools at any level?

SKILLS I NEED AT WORK

How to discover the job options open to me; how to find a job; how to keep a job; how to change jobs; how to cope with unemployment. These are essential skills for young people to have before leaving school. We have already seen in Chapters 1 and 2 that jobs will be harder to find and that many people will have periods of unemployment, so that finding and keeping a job are high priorities. However, no one wants to stay in an unsatisfactory job, so job changing skills are necessary too. We do not believe that it is too depressing to prepare young people for possible unemployment. To adopt an ostrich-like stance towards unemployment is a disservice to students who need to be fully prepared for the world that awaits them—warts and all.

How to achieve a balance between my job and the rest of my life. People who derive all their satisfactions from a job have an unbalanced lifestyle. The danger of this is that associated with having all of one's eggs in the proverbial basket. The greater the range of sources of satisfaction, the more alternatives are available and the more self-empowered one is likely to be. The choice is always the individual's own to make, but he and she should be made aware of the advantages and disadvantages.

How to retire and enjoy it. This is certainly a skill that for most people will have little relevance until late in their lives—although hopefully not too late. The more one has enjoyed one's job, the more difficult it is to give it up—the content of the job, the activity, the regularity, the status, the social contact, and, of course, the money. Domestic readjustment is often called for, and new life commitments are required.

SKILLS I NEED AT HOME

Some of these will be relevant to a school curriculum, but others will achieve relevance only as the person ages, and would be more appropriately acquired in later life as part of continuing educational provision.

How to choose a style of living; how to maintain a home. Most of us will not be aware of the variety of life-style options open to us. We are blinkered by the horizons of our own upbringing. How many people are aware, for example, that two-thirds of all British households are not of the nuclear family type (father–mother–children), that one in 12 people do not live in families, and that one in 10 families are single-parent households? Choice of accommodation ranges from rented house or flat to bought house or flat, semi-detached, detached, old, new-estate, bungalow, caravan, with parents, alone, sharing, communal living, in the country, inner-city, suburbs, tower block, maisonette—the list goes on. What do we need to know about ourselves and about what is available? What are the myths about the so-called 'normal' ways in which people live? What do we need to know about setting up a home—mortgages, estate agents, rent laws, rates, do-it-yourself skills, interior design skills, knowing where to go for bargains, pros and cons of different heating and cooking systems, how to cook, clean, do simple repairs, wash and iron, shop?

It will be vital to get young people to examine sex roles and the stereotyping common in our culture. Both sexes can benefit from being subject to traditional sex roles. Girls in particular will gain from being made aware of the facts of economic life for women: over 40 per cent of the workforce is female; nearly half of mothers with 5–10-year-old children have jobs; and nearly one-quarter of mothers with under-5s work.

More self-empowered men are not dependent on women to perform a variety of tasks for them, and more self-empowered women do not wait for men to fix things around the house and make the key decisions. A woman need not follow the man's career plan wherever it leads around the country; she need not be the one to give up her job to look after the children; she need not be the one who keeps her job but then acquires a second job of homemaker and mother. Self-empowerment is about increasing the alternatives for both sexes.

How to live with other people. From learning to live with siblings and sharing our adolescence with our parents' 'middlescence', to living with friends and living with a spouse or intimate, we need to acquire the skills of living with other people's differences, being sensitive to their needs, asserting ours, compromising, negotiating, contracting.

How to be an effective parent. Some parenting skills are taught to some extent in some schools—unfortunately, often only to girls. This is probably another skill area that is best learned after leaving school, although the National Child Development Study (Fogelman, 1976) discovered that 57 per cent of Britain's 16-year-olds wanted to know more about the practical problems of family life, 55 per cent wanted to know how to care for babies, and 38 per cent wished to learn more about how children develop.

SKILLS I NEED AT LEISURE

How to choose between leisure options; how to maximize my leisure opportunities; how to use my leisure to increase my income. Awareness of leisure alternatives and the central role of leisure as a provider of life satisfaction is a process that needs to begin in school when leisure patterns are beginning to develop. Choice of leisure-time activities should be as high a priority in the curriculum as choice of job.

SKILLS I NEED IN THE COMMUNITY

How to be a skilled consumer. With advertising so powerful and persuasive, so many new products emerging, old ones being revamped, new drugs, dietary fads, new 'evidence' on smoking,

alcoholism, drugs, contraceptive pills, how is one to evaluate it all?
How to develop and use my political awareness. Without an understanding of how our political system works, of what the different parties represent, or of their propaganda techniques, we are pawns in the hands of the powerful. More directly, we need to know how local government works, how we can influence decisions that may affect our lives. We need to know how to use the law to our advantage, what are our rights as citizens, how to set up local action groups. Most of all we need to know how to develop political consciousness in ourselves and others.

How to use community resources. It is essential to modern living to know not only how to use a telephone but to use it to one's own advantage. We need to know how to use banks, the Post Office, public libraries, social services, citizen's advice bureaux, marriage guidance agencies, doctors, dentists and hospitals, insurance companies, job centres, further and adult education opportunities, job retraining centres.

The lists of skills under this last grouping—'Me and special situations', is infinite. It is for each educator operating in a school setting to decide which are the most generalized skills to teach.

Information

A person without information is a person without power. Governments, professional elites, bosses, and subordinates often try to keep information from people as a way of maintaining or increasing their power over them. To become more self-empowered we need:

● *information about ourselves:* data on our own abilities, potential, interests, values, vulnerabilities. We also need to know what data you have on us—records, your views on our strengths and weaknesses;

● *information about others:* your abilities and values, your intentions towards us and others;

● *information about the world in which we live:* the facts about jobs, leisure opportunities, new products, political machinations—to list but a few items. An uninformed person is open to manipulation on a micro- or macro-level.

The key to access to information is the lifeskill we have labelled 'how to find information and resources'.

3.4 Is self-empowerment possible The evidence

Little research work has been carried out on the exact definition of self-empowerment as defined here in terms of awareness, goals, values, lifeskills, and information. However, there is a large body of research relevant to some of the key dimensions in the concept.

Locus of control

Rotter (1966) originated the concept of 'locus of control'. He and his colleagues discovered that they could distinguish between people who felt that they were very much masters of their fate and people who felt that they had very little control over what happened to them. They called the former 'internals' (i.e., their locus of control was within themselves) and the latter 'externals' (their locus of control was perceived as external to themselves). There has followed a truly remarkable explosion of research—by 1979 we had found at least 200 studies—into the differences between 'internals' and 'externals'. The Coleman Report into educational equality (Coleman *et al.*, 1966) added urgency to the research with its finding that student achievement was more deeply affected by the students' sense of powerlessness (Coleman called it 'fate control') than by any objective advantages like teacher qualifications, parental income, geographical location of school, access to counselling, character of the library, etc. In other words, students who were able to say 'I am in charge of my life. I can make choices and decisions to get what I want. I feel good about myself' are more likely to achieve academic success than students who say 'It doesn't make any difference what I do. There's no point in trying because you won't get anywhere unless you're very lucky. Anyway, I'm not very good at anything.'

Phares (1976), in an exhaustive review of research on locus of control, produces clear findings that demonstrate that internals

1. have greater self-control;
2. are better at retaining information;
3. ask more questions of people;
4. notice more of what is happening around them;
5. are less coercive when given power (they assume that people are responsible enough to do what they are supposed to do);
6. see other people as being more responsible for their own behaviour;
7. prefer activities involving skill to those involving chance;
8. have superior academic achievement;
9. are more likely to delay gratification;

10. accept more responsibility for their own behaviour;
11. have more realistic reactions to success and failure;
12. are less anxious;
13. exhibit less pathological behaviour.

There has been some particularly interesting research which demonstrates clearly that internally controlled people are more likely to help others, and, in addition, tend to be more competent as helpers. In other words, the more people take charge of their own lives, the less selfish they are likely to be. This is hardly surprising. People who are low in confidence, anxious, and feel powerless are likely to be too involved with their own problems to have time to help other people with theirs. Their attitude is more likely to be one of, 'you'll have to put up with it, there's nothing you can do'. This is confirmed by the further research findings (Phares, 1976) that internals are more committed to social and political action than externals. This is very important because of the concern sometimes expressed to us that with all this emphasis on personal development, what about other people and the community in general? The message from the research studies is clear—the more young people feel that they do have some power to influence what happens to them, the more they will use that power for the benefit of others and the community.

A number of studies (de Charms, 1972) have demonstrated how teachers can be taught to teach children to increase their self-perceptions of internal self-control. They are taught to set realistic goals and to take personal responsibility for their actions. They discuss things that have happened in their lives and learn to ask questions like, 'Did I *allow* that to happen to me?' 'What could *I* have done about it?' These programmes have been found to result in increased motivation for learning and in improved academic achievement.

What factors predispose a person towards internality or externality? The research findings suggests that family environments characterized by warmth, protection, and nurturance along with consistency of parental reinforcement seem to lead to a belief in an internal locus of control. Absence of these or too much nurturance and protection can lead to a belief in external control.

Learned helplessness
Seligman's research (1975) has already been discussed (page 56). One promising feature of this work is that programmes have been

designed for schools to reduce feelings of helplessness and have been clearly shown to do just that (Dweck, 1975). Failure, in itself, has been clearly shown not to cause helplessness if people learn that it is possible to avoid failure by trying harder and by learning new behaviours. In fact, experience of success with a small taste of failure seems to result in more persistence in future problem-solving tasks than experiences of success with no failure (Kleinke, 1978)

A series of experiments on institutionalized elderly people have shown the powerful negative effects of loss of control (Schultz, 1976) and the changes produced by giving some control. Some elderly people had a student visit them on random schedule while others actively participated in arranging the schedule of visits. Both groups of elderly people reduced their daily medication doses, rated themselves as happier, and got more involved in social activities than a control group who had no visitors. However, the group that had a hand in arranging their schedules improved significantly more than those who had random visits. Apparently part of the value of the visitors consisted in giving the elderly people a feeling of control over their own lives. 'It appears that being well cared for by others is not nearly as important as being able to care for oneself' (Kleinke, 1978).

Effects of feeling positive about oneself

The relationship between self-esteem and academic success is well documented (Wattenberg and Clifford, 1972), and high self-esteem has been correlated consistently highly with low anxiety and fewer neurotic behaviours (Fitts, 1972). People with low self-esteem perform less well under stress and failure (Schrauger and Rosenberg, 1970), and are less socially effective overall (Rosenberg, 1965). Most research has found that people with high self-esteem are more confident and ambitious (Rosenberg, 1965).

Research by Bernice and Albert Lott (1968) has shown that when people have a positive experience in the presence of others they increase their liking for those who witnessed their success. Children who received attention and rewards from their teacher increased their liking for their classmates significantly more than children who were ignored by their teachers. Adults also appear to like people more as a result of positive appearances with them. When an empowering system emphasizes the positives and seeks for personal strengths, the effects of this would appear to be 'catching'.

Self-control

A key assumption behind the concept of self-empowerment is that human beings can change, often dramatically, and that they can learn to exercise more and more control over themselves. There has been an accumulation of research in the past 20 years that has demonstrated that, just as we can learn to catch a ball, drive a car, make a cake, so also we can learn to control a wide variety of our thoughts, feelings, and behaviours. An impetus was the work of Neal Miller (1971) and the subsequent explorers of the new technology of biofeedback who demonstrated that we can learn to exercise control over so-called *involuntary* bodily processes like heartbeat, skin temperature, and pain thresholds. Since then a variety of techniques has been developed to enable us to exercise more control over our behaviours—smoking, eating habits, sexual dysfunctioning, study habits, work habits, marital interaction, etc. (Goldfield and Merbaum, 1973). More recently techniques have been established that can enable us to change our feelings by changing our thoughts (rational–emotive therapy—Ellis, 1973; cognitive restructuring—Meichenbaum, 1977), using fantasy and imaginary role-playing (cognitive rehearsal—Meichenbaum, 1977), changing our body state through systematic desensitization and a host of relaxation methods. Anxiety can now be attacked directly through a variety of bodily and cognitive devices (Thoreson and Mahoney, 1974).

In short, there appears to be far more plasticity to the human experience than was ever thought possible. To some that will appear exciting, to others frightening.

> In order to defend individual freedom, it is necessary to enhance the power of individuals. If behaviour technology endangers freedom by giving refined powers to controllers, then the antidote which promotes freedom is to give more refined power over their own behaviour to those who are endangered. Since everyone is endangered, this means facilitating self-control in everyone. [London, 1969, p. 213]

In this section we have seen that there is strong evidence to support the desirability of helping people to develop positive self-images; of teaching them to believe that they really do have some power to influence what happens to them and that they always have the power to control their own reactions to events. We have seen that there are techniques available to give people more self-control over their behaviours, thoughts and feelings, and that schools can have an impact in giving a greater sense of control, and the skills of control, thereby reducing the degree of debilitating helplessness and powerlessness that might otherwise predominate. We have begun to see the first evidence which suggests that environments and systems need to be designed to become more empowering of individuals, and that the more empowered people become the more socially responsible and responsive they become, and the more they will help other people to help themselves.

3.5 Self-empowerment or social action ?

Some political groups have criticized our approach for being individualist, politically unaware, and culturally and internationally isolated. To that criticism we would admit that we do begin with the individual, but we state that we are also concerned with creating empowering systems; we believe that everything one does in education is political, and that becoming aware of how political pressure groups often work to depower us is essential; as for our cultural and international isolationism, we have learned a great deal from Third World educators and philosophers and in particular we have learned from Paulo Friere that you begin to make changes within your own immediate sphere of influence—which happens for us to be in British schools and colleges.

The social revolutionaries argue that the only way for us to move towards a more just, peaceful, loving world is to change the social structures in which we are formed and conditioned, if necessary by violence. We have two responses to this assertion.

1. You will not bring about a society of peace and love by violent means. The goal and the methods of achieving it must be congruent. The agents for change need to be living models of what they are working towards.

2. We do indeed need massive social changes to create better conditions—but who does the changing? If one elite group replaces the other and makes decisions 'for the people', the fundamental power structure remains unchanged; only the characters and the ideology has changed.

It is of interest to hear the changes of direction of one of the most best-known social revolutionaries of America in the 1960s—Jerry Rubin:

Awareness of self is the first step to awareness of cultural oppression. In fact, true self-awareness leads to the realization that full self-growth is impossible in a corrupt, repressed and polluted society [Rubin, 1973]

78

Sidney Jourard, on a similar theme, commented that, if a person is coping effectively with his basic needs, his energy and thoughts are freed for other interests and other people:

> When a man ceases to be a problem to himself, because he has fulfilled his needs for security, love and status, he will begin to see the world in a manner which differs from the way 'deficiency-motivated' persons see it. [Jourard, 1974, p. 89]

'Power to the people' is a non-starter until one has first identified the power in oneself. Without this we remain subject to the depowering dimension in ourselves, in others, and in the institutions about us— many of which are claiming to act on our behalf.

Too many social changes have been motivated simply by good intentions and love or by violent struggle.

> If we just have the love, the old ways continue their disgusting course, only touched with a certain glow, like phosphorescence; if we just have the struggle, we soon become wooden soldiers fit for nothing but being pushed around by some leader. It is about love and struggle. [Rowan, 1976]

We would add that it is about skills too.

Self-empowerment begins with oneself and spreads to others, but self-empowered behaviour is most effectively developed in systems that are structured to encourage, reinforce, and teach it. 'Social action or self-empowerment' is a false dichotomy. People can become more self-empowered by learning lifeskills, by teachers modelling growth-oriented values, and helping students become more aware of their internal and external worths, by giving them information, by helping them develop goals and commitments, *but also* by working to change our schools and other institutions into empowering rather than depowering places to live and work.

We are too easily overwhelmed by the thought of trying to change an enormous system of which we are but one small cog. This happens because, for example, we think that we have to tackle the entire educational system. We cannot. Only frustration and madness lie on those horizons. Remember, change the part of the system you are involved with. As a teacher that may mean minimally changing one's teaching methods; it could progress to influencing peers or parents or, further, to persuading the hierarchy to make changes. There may be an alternative route via union politics, local or national working parties, extracurricular activities. Reich optimistically tells us that:

the individual who is free of the conventional goals can make an amazing amount of independence for himself without any organisation, simply because organisations are so cumbersome, inefficient, and unable to meet the demand upon them. They are confounded by anyone who takes initiatives. [Reich, 1971]

The remainder of this book examines the ways in which schools can be changed into more empowering environments, and examines the resources available to teach lifeskills directly to young people.

There is no antidote to power but power, nor has there ever been. But there are ethical uses of power. In order to exercise justice against lawlessness, it is necessary to array lawful power. . . . In order to defend individual freedom, it is necessary to enhance the power of individuals. [London, 1969, p. 213]

4. Lifeskills teaching in schools and colleges

If the future is to produce a variety of life-styles, all of which demand of individuals that they are competent to meet many new challenges, how can schools today equip their students for that future? Our opinion clearly is that it requires:

1. much greater awareness on the part of teachers in schools of where current economic and social trends are taking us;
2. the spreading of that awareness to students and their parents;
3. the introduction into schools and colleges of courses of specific personal-skill development aimed at making individuals competent to face change and challenge;
4. a re-assessment of how much of our current content and method of schooling actually promotes self-empowerment.

None of these may happen quickly enough, but that does not prevent individual schools or colleges, or individual teachers, actually making a start on increasing their own awareness and skills and those of their students. Reflection and action ought to be integrated in any process of change, and we would like to assist that process in this chapter by providing some basis for reflection and possible starting points for schools or individual teachers who wish to get started.

To do this we would like:

1. to indicate the kind of school systems in which lifeskills teaching might most naturally take place;
2. to indicate how, with small beginnings, individual teachers or groups might introduce lifeskills teaching in various areas of school life.

4.1 Systems that empower

There are some schools that, we think, would not take naturally to the philosophy and methodology implicit in teaching for self-empowerment. The traditional, rigid, heavily authoritarian type of system would be unlikely to accept the concepts and approach that will be required to work with students in the areas of personal skill development. The kind of school that would be most suited to working with such programmes is likely to have particular features which will closely resemble the individual model for self-empowerment.

We offer here a version of the kind of system that would be most conducive to the development of lifeskills teaching programmes, as a basis for reflection by teachers who might want to introduce such work.

A system that will take most naturally to the approach will:
1. be aware:
   — of the human models it reflects;
   — of schooling as being only one aspect of education;
   — of how it uses its power;
   — of its strengths and weaknesses;
   — of how effectively the school functions as a system;
   — of what the school is preparing students for;
2. have clear, identifiable, and specific goals;
3. have shared values which promote self-development and social commitments;
4. provide lifeskills teaching in order to achieve these values;
5. provide information that is relevant to the lives, work and futures of students and staff.

Such a system will be aware:
— of the human model its approach reflects
This will be the basis of the educational method that operates. It is common to have conflict between different groups on the same staff over different treatment of, or attitudes towards, students. 'Give them a good thrashing and all will be well' is an opinion that can sometimes be heard alongside claims that schools would benefit from more student participation and decision-making. That there are very different approaches at large is obvious, but more fundamentally perhaps it is clear that there are different versions of human models under consideration. How we answer the questions:
● What do I think a human being is?
● How do I see the purpose of my relationship with those I teach?
will form the basis of our approach to teaching.

For many the answers may be ill-formed or unarticulated, but they will shape much of our teaching philosophy, style and methods. For example, some would see students as empty receptacles with intelligence that is largely genetically determined and measurable, needing to be controlled, corrected, directed, and instructed (Hitt, 1972). This view has been the one that underpinned much of our traditional educational method (Esland, 1971).

Another view (Hitt, 1972) is that each individual is capable of controlling his own behaviour and way of life on the basis of an individually perceived reality and meaning, acquiring values that he owns and develops through experience. This person is capable of self-direction and autonomy and need not be dictated to by others. Teachers accepting this model are likely to use more informal methods, give more control to the student, use the students' own experiences to learn from, see learning as basically exploratory, and blur the distinction between teacher and learner (Esland, 1971).

Out of these alternatives is likely to emerge the school's approach to its task of education. Schools or teachers operating on the basis of 'empty receptacles' are unlikely to be comfortable with, or suited to, developing lifeskills as we define them. An important first stage will need therefore to be able to identify how staff,individually and collectively answer the questions:

- What is the human model on which I base my teaching?
- What do I see is my role as a teacher?

Such a system will be aware:
— of schooling as only one aspect of education
If we are entering a period when paid employment will not, for an increasing number of people, take up a major part of their time, when retraining and life-long education will be a feature of our lives, then schools will need to get away from the 'front-loading' version of education. It will become more important than ever to make schooling a stimulating and worthwhile experience, providing the motivation and basic equipment for individuals to undertake their own development.

This will involve *accepting* and *teaching* that:

1. education is life-long; school is only one place of learning;
2. each of us learns continually and will learn best whatever we are interested in or need for our own development;
3. education is primarily one's own responsibility. We use others as resources; school is there to assist individuals, but each of us is responsible for shaping our own development. The belief that teachers educate us is potentially depowering; for better or worse, the task of developing our potential, of learning whatever fits for us, is our own task.

If a school wishes to proclaim that message it will need to be able to identify specifically *where* and *how* it is conveying it to students and parents.

Such a system will be aware:

— of how it uses its power

Power is a concept that arouses an appreciable amount of unease and discomfort for many individuals and systems. Many fight shy of referring to it, of recognizing it and certainly of owning it. Power, even if we ignore it, is not likely to go away, and we think it is important for a school to become aware of:

1. what power it does have;
2. what it uses it to do.

Power has been defined as the ability to influence or change another's thoughts or behaviour. The bases of it have been identified as (French and Raven, 1959):

1. *Legitimate power:* the kind that those in authority or official positions possess to legislate or direct. They can delegate this power to others;
2. *Reward and punishment power:* the kind of power that is possessed by those who can give others good or pleasing experiences, or painful uncomfortable ones;
3. *Charismatic power:* the kind that those people have who have likeable personalities or who are admired for other reasons;
4. *Expert power:* the kind that those with particular knowledge or skills have by being afforded status and prestige by others.

It is interesting to note that teachers are likely to have power based on each of these categories, though any one teacher is likely to rely more on one pattern than another. Power therefore clearly exists in schools, and it is important to recognize it rather than deny it. However benevolent and caring an individual or a system is, they cannot opt out of the issue of power and what it is being used to do.

It is interesting to examine the likely effect of too much power residing with any individual or group. The result for others can be resistance; alienation; apathy; the feeling of helplessness, of being 'depowered'. Consistent with the development of self-empowerment in students will be an analysis of how balanced the sharing of power is in the school. Balanced, shared power is likely to invite development, feelings of involvement, participation and responsibility. The use of power and responsibility should be learned gradually and naturally, and the earlier the process can begin the better. Power used to dominate or manipulate others is likely to be destructive, and it probably thrives best in a vacuum, in settings where checks and balances do not exist. Education for self-empowerment, equipping each person to be responsible and take charge of himself, is a sizeable check on too much power residing in any one area.

Schools embarking on self-empowerment programmes might spend time on making the following analysis.

- What power do we as a school have?
- What are the constraints/limits to that power?
- How well distributed is power among the staff?
- What power do staff have in school, how do they exercise it and over whom?
- How balanced is staff–parent power?
- How balanced is staff–student power?
- What power do students and parents have and how is it exercised?
- Who are the most powerful/least powerful groups/individuals connected with the school?
- Does this analysis suggest the need for any changes? If so how might the changes occur?

Such a system will be aware:

— of strengths and weaknesses

Each individual may be seen in terms of qualities or strengths, which he uses for the good of himself and others, and weaknesses, areas or features of himself that block or impair his own development or that of others. Each school is also likely to be a mixture of things it does very well and other things on which it could improve. Recognizing the strengths is important, because once they are recognized they can be supported and reinforced and can give the confidence necessary to work on whatever might need to be changed. It is nonsense for any individual or any human institution to believe it is faultless. Within every person and every system there is potential for development, and the first stage is to recognize what that is.

Schools that are confident enough to wish to proceed with self-empowerment programmes would be presenting a valuable model for development if they were to examine their strengths and weaknesses in the following ways.

- Groups of staff could be asked to identify individually and collectively 'What we do well as a school' and 'Ways in which we could do better'.
- The same exercise could be undertaken with groups of students and groups of parents. Their perceptions would be a valuable form of feedback for the school.

● From the lists of 'Ways in which we could do better' could be chosen priorities to work on. The task of identifying how improvements might actually be achieved could be made the responsibility of different groups, who might be most interested in particular priorities and would be prepared to work to achieve them.

Such a system will be aware:

— of how effectively the school functions as a system

Large organizations develop patterns of operating and functioning which take on a pace and direction that can eventually influence, control and shape the lives of the people who are part of it. Rules, timetables, traditions, habits, schemes of work, standards, and the physical layout of the buildings are just some of the features that will have a sizeable impact on the behaviour, attitudes, and feelings of the people in any school. Living and working in large groups requires an awareness of how systems and structures need to be monitored, to detect the points at which they cease to be sensitive to the people that they are there to serve.

Staffs of schools should give attention to analysing, from time to time, the perceptions of the way their organization functions. Questions that could form the basis for such an examination might include the following.

● What are the signs in our organization that people are valued and respected? What are the ways in which that value may be being denied?

● What indications are there that relationships are based on genuineness, so that people operate openly rather than defensively? Are there any indications to the contrary?

● What evidence is there to show that attempts to see each other's points of view and listen to each other's opinions is a normal activity?

● Do individuals receive constructive feedback about their work? Is praise and positive reinforcement more common than criticism and negative feedback?

● Do people take part in decisions that will affect their personal or professional life?

● Is conflict used and dealt with constructively? What are the ways in which differences are opened up and solutions sought? Do groups or individuals attempt to work through negotiations rather than by 'winning' at others' expense?

● In what ways do we communicate effectively? In what ways is our communication not so effective?

● How are the personal and the career development of people in the system provided for?

● Is consensus worked for, rather than simply majority decisions —which can displease minorities—or compromise—which can sometimes please nobody?

● Are there any rules under which we operate that are no longer necessary or would be better revised? Are there any rules for which we cannot give a rationale that would be widely accepted by the people it affects? (For 'rules' substitute habits, ways of working, or traditions.)

● What are the ways in which anybody with a grievance can find redress? Are grievances harboured? Are mistakes perpetuated? Is blame more apparent than working through mistakes and learning from them?

● How do we evaluate our work, our own and each other's contribution?

● Are there any ways in which we label, stereotype, make subjective/negative judgements of each other? What kind of records do we keep? Do these allow for development and change? Are they open or hidden? How do we justify any judgement made by one of another? If judgements are recorded how might they affect the individual now and in the future?

● What provisions do we make for the personal and professional support of each other?

● Do we have shared, identifiable goals and do we work co-operatively towards them?

Again it could be very useful for individuals to record their own perceptions of the way they experience being part of a particular school system, and then to have the opportunity to exchange perceptions with each other. By hearing how different people see the system should come a realization of which areas might be causing difficulties and consequently will need attention.

Such a system will be aware:

— of what the school is preparing students for

Unless schools are aware of the variety of possible scenarios out of which the future will emerge, it is likely to have a methodology that is anchored in the past.

A staff ought therefore to ensure that it develops its own, the students' and the parents' awareness of what models of the future it feels are possibilities. Study groups, using available information or materials, inviting speakers with particular knowledge, and using recorded television programmes which discuss future alternatives, could organize seminars to alert staff, parents, and students to the scenarios of the future towards which we are moving. It is likely that many Humanities Departments or Science Departments would be happy to organize such 'future-studies', and the possibility of combined staff, parent, and student sessions could be very fruitful.

At the end of the information-gathering stage it may be possible to come to some understanding of and discussions about the following.

● What are likely to be the social and economic features of life in 5 years time? 10 years time? 20 years time? What are likely to be the patterns and types of employment at those stages?

● How can schools and individuals best prepare now for the likely changes?

The possibility of introducing lifeskills programmes could well provide the opportunity for a school to re-evaluate its current approach and effectiveness. Such an analysis would hopefully produce the awareness, which is a prerequisite to development.

As well as awareness, the system in which lifeskills programmes will most naturally fit will:

Have clear identifiable and specific goals

Most educational institutions are of a size and complexity that goals are often taken for granted or regarded as understood. The population in any system will have an incredible variety of expectations, aspirations, fears, and objections. Because it is difficult to surface and correlate all of these, it is often found easier to regard all those present as accepting certain goals which are often general, vague and unarticulated. Self-empowerment involves having clear goals (if you don't know where you're going you'll probably end up somewhere else), and will flourish best in systems that are themselves self-empowered. An important first step to introducing lifeskills teaching would be for a school, college or further education (FE) institute staff to undertake a clarification of its educational objectives. One headteacher we heard about recently had his school's objectives clearly posted on the wall of his office. While not evaluating his particular goals or enquiring about the school's effectiveness in achieving them, we do think it is vital for any organization to have very clear objectives to which those involved subscribe, both in shaping them and working for them. The whole system should be able to answer:

1. What are we working to achieve collectively?
2. What are our different individual objectives? Is each of us clear about our own and each other's?
3. What is each of us doing to pursue the objectives?
4. How will we know when we have achieved them?

Our experience would suggest that the skill of clarifying and being specific about objectives is not widely developed. Too generally defined objectives are unlikely ever to be achieved. For example, many schools would claim objectives such as:

1. to encourage the personal development of students;
2. to provide a good, general education;
3. to promote initiative, sensitivity and maturity.

In the generally understood sense of each of these, there would be little to which to object. It is probably true however that within any staff room there will be significant variance between individual understanding of what exactly is meant by terms like 'personal development' and 'good general education', and probably wide disagreement about how much student 'initiative' is desirable and what in fact constitutes 'maturity'. What we are not saying is that uniformity of objectives, or absolute agreement on terminology, are to be pursued relentlessly. We do think, however, that each educational system needs to give time and effort to becoming very specific about its organizational objectives; to requiring each department or faculty to identify the part it is playing in the pursuit of those; and to examine differences between individuals and departments in methods and objectives.

Educational contracts

The notion of educational contracts seems to us to be a very important one also. Any educational system should be able to set out clearly, to its consumers and sponsors, exactly what it hopes to achieve, how it will achieve it, what its criteria will be for evaluating its success, by when it hopes to have achieved its objectives, and what it requires very specifically from participants in the contract, be they students, parents, or teachers. This would register the partnership that education surely is, and would indicate the need for co-responsibility which ought to be a feature of open, balanced relationships.

Ideally, each department should be able to identify specifically for itself and others:

1. what information it will expect its students to have by the end of their course, and at different stages along it;
2. what proportion of its time will be spent in information-*giving*, what information it will give, and what information students will be expected to gather for themselves;
3. what *skills* it will develop in the students and what *methods* it will use to develop these;
4. how it will contribute to the overall organizational goals and link with the work of other departments;
5. what in-service programme it has for the development of its own staff;
6. how it will evaluate its own effectiveness and how frequently it will do this.

Having clear objectives that emerge from procedures that allow everybody to have a say in the shaping of them is important in developing commitment. Motivation is likely to be present where people 'own' and choose their own direction; where they are consulted and invited to participate in decision-making; where they are listened to; and where action is seen to follow from discussion and preparation. Those who are in leadership positions in schools may sincerely believe they know what is best for the organization and the people in it. However benevolent and experienced is that leadership, unless it invites and encourages participation, it risks eroding initiative and motivation in others. Doing things for others is often a way of expediting matters, and ensuring things are done the way one wants. This procedure has hidden costs, however, because over time the energy and potential one might tap in others is atrophied. Participatory methods take time and can be frustrating, but they are consistent with recognizing that everybody can be a resource, and systems that do not give recognition to this should not be surprised if they alienate those they fail to value.

From goals and objectives shaped by those who are part of the system, priorities can be chosen. Individuals and departments can then be aware of the overall intentions of the organization and be able to discuss how their own priorities will contribute to those. Systems can tolerate different interests and approaches as long as these are communicated and there is an awareness of who is providing what.

For us, schools in the post-industrial society will need to give priority to personal skill development, as a basis for the cognitive development that has traditionally been the primary objective of most schools. Equipping students for the future will involve also moving:

- from processing second-hand, outdated information to identifying knowledge that is about today and tomorrow; using the past and not living in it;
- from teaching memorizing, verbal repetition and copying skills to teaching students to question, challenge and research;
- from encouraging dependence, obedience and passivity to rewarding self-reliance, initiative and originality;
- from regarding literacy and numeracy as appreciably more significant than interpersonal and practical skills;
- from valuing and requiring student silence to welcoming people saying more about themselves, their interests, feelings experiences, etc.;
- from emphasizing correction to reinforcing the positive;
- from suggesting that there are few teachers and many learners to a realization that everybody teaches and learns continually;
- from negative feedback and 'putting down' to strength-building and confidence boosting;
- from lecturing and 'talking at' students to experiential learning;
- from valuing private learning and competition more highly than collaborative processes;
- from regarding education as handing over a set of answers worked out by others to working with problems related to the students' own experiences and daily lives;
- from being 'win–lose' systems to being the kind of organization that works at negotiation and for consensus. Unfortunately, in some schools staff feel they are 'winning' when students are 'losing' (privileges, face, power, etc.), or students 'win' by making staff 'lose' (in confrontation, in challenges to authority, in defying rules, etc.). Indeed, in some school systems inter-departmental or personal rivalry is so marked that staff operate on the basis of win–lose with each other, competing for status, resources, the adoption of policies based on self-interest, etc. In such a process those who 'lose' are likely to work with little good will or motivation and can even work to 'sabotage' any worthwhile schemes. Systems in which an individual or groups are made to feel like 'losers' are storing up trouble for themselves. Outcomes and procedures in which everybody seems to have gained

91

something of what he wanted take time and effort but are likely to be very worth while.

If one were to represent each of the above in terms of a continuum, then it ought to be possible for each school, each department, each teacher to decide where they would place themselves ideally, and in fact, on that continuum. These placings could be the basis for exchanging perceptions of how they evaluate their work.

Any system preparing students for the future will need a clear appreciation of its:

Values
Schools that embark on self-empowerment are obviously putting their values squarely on the line. Some of the beliefs inherent in this approach to education are presented briefly here to invite the reactions of those who may wish to use lifeskills programmes. Teachers intending to use them should be clear about which they accept and wish to put into effect, which they do not accept, and which additional beliefs and values they themselves have. Our beliefs which we would like to see put into effect are as follows.

We are all learners and teachers
There is no individual who knows everything; there is no individual who cannot offer others learning from his own experience; teacher and learner are not permanent roles, and unless they are interchanged frequently then it is good for neither teacher nor learner: arrogance for one and depowering for the other could result. Teaching gives status and esteem, and the possibility of teaching should be available to every individual at various stages. Students should have frequent opportunities to see teachers as learners and to teach other students, and teachers.

We can do too much for people
Teaching is a noble, caring profession, but teachers should be clear about the line that is drawn between caring and doing too much for people. We can help to such an extent that we remove initiative, induce dependency and reduce the other person's capacity for self-reliance. That kind of help is disabling (Illich *et al.*, 1978) rather than enabling. Support others, give them confidence, help them to see alternatives; but do not decide for them or act for them if that can be at all avoided. It could be more

developmental for each of us to make our own mistakes and learn from them, rather than do what everybody else tells us is best for us. Teaching can sometimes give opportunities to appear almost God-like in advising, controlling, 'saving' others. The temptation is best resisted.

It is better for each of us to be responsible for ourselves

There is very clear evidence that people who generally feel that they control themselves and are responsible for themselves function more effectively (see page 75), find out more, retain information better, use information in a more organized way, are more aware, and generally learn better. They have higher academic achievement.

- They feel less need to dominate, control and manipulate others.
- They are generally more skilled and competent.
- They are more committed to social action and helping others in difficulty, even when it means discomfort for themselves.
- They are more persistent, consistent and responsible (Phares, 1976).

Teachers and schools that promote an approach that encourages their students to be independent, to decide, to be responsible, and to act for themselves are making sizeable contributions to individual and social well-being.

Positive self-esteem is a basis for growth and development

There is abundant evidence to establish that those who have a positive self-image learn more (see page 76), make better relationships, are less defensive and suspicious, do not indulge in bragging and boasting so much, are more responsible (Rosenberg, 1965), and even have a better chance of making a more successful marriage. If we can produce school environments that register positively the value and importance of every individual, where praise and positive recognition exclude blame and negative criticism, and where we find many and various ways of letting individuals achieve success, we will create learning climates in which people will want to spend their time. Each of us needs to be somebody, to feel significant. The trouble is that in some schools, for some students, that is a possibility only via notoriety. If we cannot make our mark in socially acceptable ways we will find anti-social ways of making it.

Questions may be more important than answers

It can be interesting to decide what exactly one's role is as a teacher. Is it to provide answers? Teachers sometimes appear to know so much, it can seem they have all the answers. Second-hand answers are likely to be less exciting than finding one's own. If teachers can be 'problem-posers' rather than 'answer-givers', then they could encourage an approach to education and life that induces less apathy and invites more energy. 'Critical awareness' as a way of learning will be a basis for life-long learning. Teaching students to challenge, to ask how or why things are as they are, never to take for granted, always to look for alternatives and better ways of doing things, is equipping them to learn from any situation. Owning their own opinions, ideas and experience is likely to be more significant than reciting other people's answers.

Thinking and talking should be inseparable from action

Reflection is a good preparation for action but real development requires both. Acting to change ourselves or our situations is a way of learning more and taking charge of the direction of our life. Our schools should teach the reflection/action process as a way of life and allow opportunities for students actually to experience changes that they themselves have thought through and prepared for. Experiencing control and responsibility, seeing the consequence of one's own action, is more important than mere intellectual exercises.

Tomorrow can be different from today

Developing a recognition that neither individuals nor the world is static, but that development and change are part of life, is an important stage of awareness. To invite individuals to become directors of their own changes and shapers of tomorrow's situations will make them 'subjects' rather than 'objects', people who make things happen, rather than adopting the fatalistic view that individuals can make little difference. Teachers need to develop the belief in their students that they can make tomorrow more like they would want it to be, given that they have awareness and skills.

Good intentions are never enough

'The road to hell is paved with good intentions' expresses the eventual uselessness of simply thinking 'good' thoughts or wanting 'good' things to happen. It is never a substitute for *doing* good. People cannot read our intentions, but they can observe our behaviours and make assumptions on the basis of those. Sometimes our intentions are one thing and our behaviours another. A teacher who says he is very interested in his students but constantly criticizes them, rarely listens to them, fails to prepare lessons or mark their work, takes part in no extracurricular activities, and is rigid and formal in his behaviour will have difficulty convincing them of his interest.

The battle, then, is to get our behaviours in line with our intentions. In teaching it is not enough to *believe* in the importance of the individual, in his self-reliance and individual sovereignty; we must *behave* and operate in ways that are consistent with that belief. Actions *do* speak louder than words.

We can't change the world but we can change our part of it

If we concentrate too much on how big are the problems we face, if we wait for the 'big change' that will make everything perfect, we will spend our time between hopelessness and inertia. We are not going to create Utopia, but that is not an excuse for not starting to do so. Macro-change is not a possibility for most of us; what is definitely possible is to influence and improve the bit of the world we are in touch with. We can start by changing and developing ourselves; we can influence those we meet, work, and live with; we can improve our work situation, our local community; we can, in our democracy, even influence larger groups. However, if only each of us worked to make our own immediate environment healthier, for ourselves and others, that would be an enormous step forward.

Schools with the future in mind must give a high priority to:

Teaching lifeskills

If schools are to be the places of real skill development they will need to be staffed by people who themselves are highly skilled. Historically there has perhaps been the tradition that the best teachers were in fact scholars. It was naturally assumed that somebody who knew a great deal about a subject was the best person to pass that knowledge on to others. This assumption has proved, in many cases, to be not entirely well founded. The model is weak because:

● knowing a great deal about a subject does not mean necessarily that one can teach it well; indeed, one can know so much that one cannot see the difficulties of somebody who knows little. *Scholars know about subjects; teachers need to know about people, and how to create climates favourable to learning;*

• since one has studied and enjoyed a subject, the temptation can be to assume that others can and should do the same. What one has learned oneself one can own and prize. To present that, second-hand, to a different individual and expect enthusiasm and energy can be unrealistic.

Unfortunately, much teacher-training is still designed more towards the development of scholars than towards that of teachers. The priority that is given to personal academic development, rather than to interpersonal and group skills, does little to equip many teachers for effectiveness in the classroom. Recent research has indicated how vital interpersonal skills are in teaching (Aspy and Roebuck, 1977; Rutter *et al.*, 1979). Where teachers are skilled in building relationships, academic results are better, student attendance is better, and many other positive results can be found.

In schools also there is generally a lack of awareness of the importance of other skills. Traditional methods of working up the promotion 'ladder' mean generally that teachers gain experience in the classroom and then gradually desert that role to take up more managerial positions, many to be heads of departments, some to be headteachers or deputies. Classroom effectiveness and systems management require very different skills, yet there are few courses that prepare staff for senior management positions. Those that exist probably focus on information-giving rather than skill development, and there are two likely reasons for this:

1. a lack of awareness of what management skills actually are;
2. a lack of people who are able to teach those skills.

Lack of particular skills at senior level in schools does have a pass-down effect on the whole system. The standards, norms, and skill levels of senior personnel will decide the level at which the whole system functions. Similarly, teachers who lack skills are not likely to be able to increase the skill level of students beyond their own (Aspy and Roebuck, 1977).

Schools interested in developing lifeskills programmes therefore should not simply regard skills development as being something that is good only for students. A great deal of learning in schools occurs through 'modelling'. Students learn through observation of adult behaviour and style of operating. Teaching lifeskills therefore is not restricted to the preparation of particular lessons, but should also involve teachers undertaking their own personal development and skill acquisition, modelling the competencies they wish to teach.

It is sometimes salutary to realize how much learning occurs by imitation. Staff 'models' are crucial as sources of learning for students. Hence it is useless for teachers to stress *verbally* the importance of, for example, tolerance, respect for each other, co-operation, forgiveness, kindness, honesty, generosity, non-aggression, etc., unless those qualities are clearly *visible* in staff relationships with each other and in staff–student contacts. Members of a school staff could well spend time assessing just what lessons they are offering to students in the form of their interpersonal dealings with each other. How they relate, communicate, and function collectively ought to involve the practice of any values and skills they would wish to develop in their students. Any gap between what we practice and what we preach is likely to produce a credibility problem which will undermine anything we would wish to teach.

A very useful preliminary to introducing lifeskills could be for the staff involved to undertake an appraisal of their current skill levels and areas they may wish to develop.

The process could involve three stages:

1. stocktaking of skills and getting feedback;
2. identifying skills each wishes to develop;
3. organizing training to acquire them.

4.2 For teachers

The following questions can be a useful basis for individual teachers to address to themselves.

● How much thought and preparation do I give to the subject content of my lesson?

● How much thought and consideration do I give to the needs, feelings and interests of the students in my classes? Is the balance right?

● Effective teachers are said to have and convey respect for their students. How many ways can I list in which I *show* that I value the students I work with?

● Effective teachers *show* that they can see things from others' (students') points of view. What are the ways in which I do this?

● Effective teachers convey that they are genuine, real people and do not preserve a remoteness, or distance themselves, from their students. In what ways do I indicate to my students that I am a person and an individual, not simply a teacher?

● What are the ways in which I give encouragement and confidence to those I teach?

- In what ways do I create a relaxed, positive learning climate for those I teach?
- How do I develop motivation in, give responsibility to, develop skills in, and give support to, the students in my classes?
- Do I have clear objectives for the courses I run and the students I teach? Are they aware of them and in agreement with them?
- Can I, and do I, justify to my students the content and methods of my lessons?
- What are my five main strengths as a teacher, and my three main weaknesses? What am I doing about these weaknesses?
- How do I measure my effectiveness as a teacher? Do I know how my students, their parents, my colleagues, and the head rate my effectiveness?
- How do I ensure that I provide for the differing interests, talents, learning styles, and abilities in my classes?
- How do I show I am interested in my students, other than in their progress in my subject?
- What is my idea of a *good* student? Do my ideas allow for individuality, independence, creativity, divergent thinking, antipathy towards my subject, and initiative on the part of my students?
- What would make me a better teacher? Can it be achieved?

4.3 For headteachers

As a basis for their development, heads can ask themselves:

- How much of my job is taken up with administration and paperwork? Am I happy with how I manage that? Would I like to make any changes?
- What do I do to show:
  1. that I value the efforts made by staff and students?
  2. that I recognize the skills of different individuals?
- How well and often do I give feedback to members of staff on their work? How much of that is positive feedback?
- What are the expectations of my staff? How are these communicated to them?
- What are my goals and objectives in my job? How, and how often, do I evaluate my effectiveness? What are my sources of feedback?
- How do I contribute to supporting staff under stress?
- Are there any indications that might suggest I favour some staff or some departments more than others? If so, what are the consequences of that?

- What are the signs that communication is clear and effective with my staff? In which areas could it be improved? Have I checked out staff perceptions of these?
- What decision-making procedures do I use? How do I encourage participation? Whom do I use as consultants/advisers?
- Are my responsibilities and those of others clearly defined?
- What provisions do I make for the personal and professional development of my staff?
- What are my five main strengths and three main weaknesses as a headteacher?
- Which of these skills would I like to develop:
  - making meetings work effectively?
  - team-building?
  - managing conflict constructively?
  - counselling?
  - developing support systems?
  - preventing and managing stress?
  - communicating effectively?
  - giving constructive feedback?
  - effective decision-making?
  - making and maintaining relationships?
- How do I delegate responsibility, share power and offer leadership to my staff?
- How could I become more effective in my job? What can I do to achieve that?

Having worked their way through the lists, it would be very informative and useful, for those who are willing to do so, to share some of their thoughts with a trusted colleague. Feedback from others is essential if we are really to know ourselves. Our own version of ourselves will not tally exactly with the way others experience us, and getting information about how they see us is essential to any assessment of what we need to work on. We need somebody who will be honest enough not simply to say the friendly, positive things but also to indicate just where our shortcomings may be.

It is important that each person takes responsibility for his own personal and professional development. It has not traditionally been easy in the professional field for teachers, especially heads, to admit there are things they do not know or skills they lack. Facades of omniscience or omnipotence are a disaster not only for their owners, but also for their owners' neighbours. Nobody is perfect; nobody is all-competent. Each of us has areas of ourselves that can be developed, potential that can be realized, and to recognize and admit that can be the beginning of growth. Having once recognized what skills they would wish to improve, teachers and heads should take steps to request appropriate training from advisory services, the DES or other competent sources. The recent INSET proposals indicate real possibilities of relevant developments in increased commitment to in-service training (Department of Education and Sciences, 1978). The only anxiety one has is the shortage of sufficiently skilled individuals to carry out the amount of training needs that could surface if schools look at current limitations.

4.4 Skills for other groups

Skill development for teachers and senior staff, parallel to the lifeskills programmes for students, does not complete the picture. To increase the awareness and skills of other groups with which a school has contact could be a sizeable investment.

Schools and LEAs could:

Increase parents' skills

More competent, self-reliant students, learning new skills at school, will have an impact on their homes and families. That could give schools an opportunity to make a contact with parents that is more constructive than simply the routine parents' evening or parent–teachers' dance. All the lifeskills identified in our teaching programmes have applications and usefulness in adult life. An enterprising school could offer evening sessions on such skills as 'How to Make Effective Decisions', or 'How to Communicate Effectively', giving parents a chance to experience some of the same work their children may be undertaking. The skills they work on however could have real application in their own lives. Moreover, the contacts made could introduce the possibility of setting up skills programmes on 'How to Be an Effective Parent'. This opportunity could be greatly appreciated by parents who may be experiencing the difficulties of coping with adolescent children. Local marriage guidance groups and other parents and teachers could be useful resources on such a course. Useful source books on parenting skills are listed in Chapter 6.

Increase employers' awareness

A recent piece of research into why some young people have

difficulties on starting work (Industrial Training Research Unit, 1979) indicates that they are likely to fail if:
1. they can't follow instructions;
2. they are bad timekeepers;
3. they don't relate well;
4. they have personal problems;
5. they don't like change.

A group with similar school performance, but who did actually thrive and prosper at work, were said by their supervisors to:
1. be versatile,
2. be capable of initiative,
3. relate well to others,
4. listen to instructions,
5. ask questions,
6. remedy problems,
7. keep good time.

Any school undertaking lifeskills programmes is obviously intending to develop more personally competent young people who are likely to be at the same time more employable. It could pay dividends for the school to take time and care to present their schemes to prospective employers. Anything that is likely to reduce the number of school-leavers who manifest the faults outlined in the Industrial Training Research Unit (IRTU) report is likely to be richly appealing to employers. The contact could begin a dialogue that might result in employers understanding better the aims and methods of the school, and possibly reducing their demand for more traditional academic qualifications, which apparently force schools to continue to teach outmoded syllabi, the content of which rarely has application in any job. Unless schools educate employers, they may be failing their students.

Increase the awareness of governors and school-managers

School governors and managers should not be left out in the cold. Traditionally they have token power and operate through contact with the head. There are moves afoot to set up training courses to provide them with the expertise that should go with their role. Updating their awareness of what different educational approaches the future might require will be an important service, and staff who develop lifeskills programmes should have an opportunity of explaining their rationale and methods to governors and managers. Besides being educational for all concerned, it could be a way for governors and managers to broaden their contact with the school other than simply through meetings with the head.

4.5 Information

That knowledge will be the wealth-creator of the future is one of the predictions of current economic and social analysts (Stonier, 1978a). As the microprocessor reduces the need for human muscle, people will become more preoccupied with creating, processing and applying new knowledge. Working with information in some form or other will occupy much of the time of most people. Schools today, preparing students for that kind of future, obviously have to recognize the significance of up-to-date information and the skills of working with it.

New knowledge is accruing so quickly that it will be difficult for anybody to keep abreast of all new developments, though it would seem vital that schools attempt to do so. This would suggest to us that schools:

1. re-appraise the information they are at present working with: textbooks that are out of date, syllabuses that are archaic and based on subject areas or methods that cannot be shown to be relevant to those who will live in the post-industrial society, will need to be replaced quickly;

2. appoint somebody who has the task of importing to the school and disseminating among the staff new information as it becomes available. Such a person would have the task of absorbing news items, research findings, the content of television documentaries, radio programmes, magazine articles, etc., and summarizing relevant facts and comment and making these available to staff as background to their work. This would largely be information of general relevance— commenting on politics, society, the economy, psychology, scientific advance, etc.—rather than information for teachers of specialist subjects, who would keep up to date in their own subject as a matter of course. The information specialist could also advise on latest educational technology, helping schools make the transition from book-centred learning to the age of video-recorders, television, interactive systems, and personal computers;

3. encourage students to build up their own information exchange system. It could be helpful in each class to have a time each week when individuals tell each other of the most interesting new facts they have learned that week, from television, radio, newspapers, other people, etc. Staff could also have a short time

each week where they exchange interesting information or background they have discovered from various sources;

4. arrange ways of keeping parents informed of the thinking and findings that are influencing their children's education. Students taking home 'fact sheets' to discuss with parents as part of homework, or staff arranging parent/student quiz evenings when new information could be the subject of questions, might be ways of making the link.

If knowledge is the wealth-maker of the future, then skills concerned with its creation and use will be an important element in any lifeskills scheme. Rather than merely feeding information from teacher to student, the emphasis should be on teaching students to:

1. carry out research;
2. analyse and evaluate information;
3. process and organize it;
4. disseminate relevant facts to others in the group;
5. communicate clearly;
6. absorb what is relevant to them and act on the basis of it.

Stonier (1978a) has pointed out that already many people are 'information operatives'; that is, they earn their living by:

1. creating new information (e.g. scientists, researchers, etc.);
2. applying it (e.g. engineers, architects, inventors, managers, entrepreneurs, etc.);
3. transmitting it (e.g. teachers, reporters, TV personnel, technical salesmen, secretaries, etc.);
4. storing and retrieving it (e.g. librarians, filing clerks, computer operators);
5. organizing it (e.g. statisticians, computer operators, etc.);
6. studying it (students).

Those who have skills based on creating and applying new knowledge will have an important foothold in tomorrow's world. If they also have the interpersonal skills to ensure they can work effectively with other people, they will indeed be well equipped. Jobs involving information or people will be one of the few vocational growth areas, and careers and guidance courses particularly ought to ensure that students' skills are fully developed to equip them for such occupations.

4.6 Where to start ?

We have said that the ideal step forward would be for a whole school to become convinced of the importance of a new approach and to embark on a thoughtful and well-prepared move to establish lifeskills teaching. Failing that the whole system adopt the development, is there anything an individual teacher or a small group can do to begin to implement change? We think there is, and suggest that the first stage might be an assessment of how change might occur and where it might start.

If as an individual teacher I wish to work for the introduction of a lifeskills teaching course I will need:

1. *to be clear about what I want to achieve:* I will need to have a rationale and some specific objectives that I can present to others;
2. *to be clear about whether I need support or not:* it can sometimes work to do one's own thing, but it is very often better to have support, which means persuading others to join you;
3. *to be clear about who has the 'power' in the school:* heads and heads of department need to be consulted, brought in to make decisions or just to give backing. There can be unfortunate consequences for ideas and schemes that do not take the traditional route. However, not all power lies in high office. It can be significant to enlist the backing of those 'personalities' who influnece the staffroom, i.e. powerful 'back-benchers';
4. *to recognize the norms and 'language' of the system:* it can be the death of good ideas if they are presented in flowery language or jargon. Explaining what one hopes to do in terms that can be understood and do not jar, irritate or threaten is likely to be worth the effort;
5. *to recognize where opposition may come from:* spending time with and giving attention to those who may block the introduction of one's ideas can be a sound investment. Opposition can help to sharpen ideas, and building working relationships with those who differ with us can avoid their sabotaging our efforts;
6. *to look for opportunities to inform the 'silent' majority:* identifying the lines of communication that give one access to the wider audience, and deciding the most productive 'arenas' for exchanging information (staff meetings, one-to-one sessions, social gatherings, etc.), can provide outlets for spreading one's ideas;
7. *to have available all relevant information and be aware of resources:* having background facts and information, and knowing where to find resources relevant to the ideas one is promoting, could make the difference to impressing others; viz. Chapter 1 and the resources section in Chapter 6.

8. *to operate in a way that does not betray the valuable ideas one wishes to promote:* interpersonal skills are highly important for those who wish to influence others. Even very good ideas will meet resistance if they are pushed down people's throats, preached at people, or proclaimed with arrogance or triumph. Therefore the change agent who does not treat others with respect, who is not genuine and open, who does not listen to others and attempt to see their point of view, will probably betray the cause he wishes to promote. The medium is the message.

As well as that, it will be important to be aware of the politics and dynamics that are at work in the system that we would like to influence. It can again be fatal for good ideas to be used merely for personal 'empire-building'. An individual operating in a way that comes across to others more as personal aggrandizement, than as genuine educational concern will build up resentment to herself as well as the ideas that are her vehicle. That is why it can be very important to any innovatory schemes or methods to work for a broadly based acceptance of them before they are launched.

4.7 When the time seems right

When a teacher feels it is time to start on a course of lifeskills programmes it can help to do the following.

Think through the implications of such work for herself, her colleagues, the students, their parents

The way one operates in one's own classroom will affect other settings. To encourage individual thought and speaking openly; to teach the skills of being assertive; to support students in decision-making, etc., can produce behaviour change that others may not be prepared for; therefore it will be important to alert students, colleagues and parents to what one is doing and why, and to the possible ramifications of that.

Decide where one starts

Is the work more appropriate to some groups than others, should it be compulsory, can it fit in with other work? Some teachers for example have found that, rather than planning a separate lifeskills course, it has been possible to fit in skill development at particular points in a student's school career; for example,

1. teaching decision-making skills to groups that are about to choose their subject options;
2. teaching the skills of preventing and managing stress to those who are facing examination pressures;

3. teaching study skills to all groups in a school;
4. teaching job-seeking skills to all 15- and 16-year-olds;
5. teaching the skills of being positive about oneself to those in remedial groups who have little confidence;
6. teaching communication skills to groups taking English lessons, or to those who have to face interviews;
7. teaching decision-making skills to students in schools that encourage individual choice in what to wear; what to eat from choice of menu; what to study; whether to do community service or PE; whom to sit next to in class; how to spend an activity/project week, etc.

Subjects that are approached in some schools largely through the giving of information might be open to introducing skill development as a component; for example, health education on a timetable, as well as giving students facts about smoking, disease, diet, etc., could also incorporate the teaching and use of some stress prevention and management techniques, or permit students to undertake their own individual fitness programmes, etc. Without lifeskills ever being a word that appeared on a timetable, much valuable work can be done by those with energy and enthusiasm.

It might be possible for a teacher wishing to make a start to offer to make a skill contribution to other subject teachers, e.g. to exchange classes for six periods with a teacher who has an A-level history group and to teach a unit on Study Skills or Time-management Skills to his students. Some of these more practical skill programmes can be shown to make a contribution to work being done in subject areas, and, because they support and enhance working being done rather than replace it, they can be used to develop acceptance of the whole lifeskills concept.

Think about climate-building in the classroom

Lifeskills programmes are likely to require work situations in which there is a great deal of trust and support. Trust will develop when:
1. the teacher is not asking students to do things she is not doing herself;
2. whatever individuals say is listened to respectfully, and not ridiculed or put down;
3. there is a clear understanding about confidentiality;
4. the understanding is that nobody will need to do or say anything that she does not wish to;
5. students learn, through time, that they can be open and the teacher will not take advantage of that.

Creating the right climate will require preparation in working out what will be:

1. the most effective way for the teacher to operate during the session;
2. the most conducive physical setting (rearranging desks—chairs in circles? etc.). (See Chapter 5.)

Give particular attention to students who might have most difficulty

Not every student will take easily to the work. It can help to think beforehand who might have difficulty, how that might manifest itself, and how one might manage the situation.

Link the programmes to the pastoral system

Too often teachers with pastoral responsibility find themselves filling a negative, corrective role rather than working positively. Lifeskills teaching can be, and ought to be, an important developmental element in the pastoral system. The emphasis is on the preventative approach rather than on crisis intervention. Teachers working in these areas do need the skills of working with small groups in the area of personal development, and this could be an important in-service priority for staff involved with lifeskills-type materials.

Look for other staff and subject areas to work alongside

Lifeskills teaching is obviously a possibility for teachers in most subjects, though it probably lends itself more easily to subjects on the timetable like careers, personal and social education, social studies, religious education, general studies, guidance, English or drama. Any teacher who gives priority to the skill development of his students rather than merely feeding them information is obviously equipping them to do more for themselves, and may find it useful to build in specific skill work based on materials indicated in the resource section.

Offers lifeskills teaching programmes as a subject option or extracurricular activity

It is often possible to pioneer a new curricular approach by offering to teach it as an optional subject, or as an element of a general studies course. Most schools and colleges have areas of the curriculum that allow students to opt for one or two study areas from a range. In that option area there is often a willingness to experiment, which allows an enthusiast or a pioneer to make an

107

impact by establishing what might initially be regarded by others a 'pet idea' or fringe activity. In such a way might an individual teacher, unable to get broad-based acceptance of a lifeskills approach, be able to demonstrate what contribution such a programme might make. Offerings made in this way, if they are well received by students and can be seen to be effective, have a way of gaining respectability and recognition and eventually becoming a more central feature of the curriculum.

If the possibility is not there of providing one of the options, and there is no other entry route to the timetable, it could be possible to offer lifeskills learning as an extracurricular activity. This could be in the form of inviting some students to join a lifeskills group, in the way they might join other school societies or clubs, to do some lifeskills work in their non-timetable time. Given a group of enthusiastic volunteers, it can be possible to undertake very practical useful sessions on 'Improving your Decision-Making', 'Finding Out What Is Really Important To You', 'Developing Study-skills', etc. Sessions such as these, involving a relaxed atmosphere, some fun, and some learning, could provide a foundation and a reputation that could establish the credibility of the lifeskills approach in the system.

Working alone to get lifeskills teaching started any teacher could feel the lack of support and encouragement, which is often the lot of the pioneer. Patience and determination will be needed by the teacher who has to 'go solo' to initiate the work. We feel strongly that teaching lifeskills will have ramifications that are much wider than the teaching of most subjects, and for that reason it will be important for the teacher working alone to explain the work to colleagues and heads before it starts. If the rationale is clearly presented and discussion undertaken about materials, methodology and possible outcomes, then the teacher could be inoculating himself against subsequent difficulties. Even so, working alone is never easy, and contact with individuals outside the school who will provide support and encouragement is likely to be important.

A teacher wishing to start could:

1. decide which skills from the lifeskills model (page 25) would be the most appropriate ones to start with for her students;
2. decide whether it will most naturally fit into work she is already doing or whether it will require a series of separate lessons;
3. give thought to how she can introduce the idea of skill development to the students;

4. study the resources section of this book, become familiar with the teaching materials one may wish to use, identify where they might fit in, and begin developing student commitment to the approach.

Experience would suggest that the concept of 'lifeskills' may not immediately be recognizable to students, who are most likely to attribute personal effectiveness either to chance or to innate personality features, rather than to acquired skills.

To overcome this difficulty some teachers have juxtaposed video-recordings of individuals operating at different skill levels and asked students to identify what are the differences as a way of establishing that some people are more skilled than others, e.g. somebody who presents well at an interview alongside somebody who does not; somebody relating well to other people against somebody who is abrasive or a loner; somebody showing qualities of leadership, compared with another who has little influence on a group he is part of.

The stages of lifeskills teaching may well need to include:

1. *developing awareness* in the teacher and the student of what skills each has already and what other skills each would like to develop. At this stage it is often easier to recognize skills that other people have rather than one's own, and it could be useful for a group to have a session in which they tell each other what they see each individual doing well;

2. *identification* of which skills individuals or groups wish to work on first. The learning will be more effective if the learners have expressed a desire to develop a skill, have considered the consequences and recognized the advantages of doing so;

3. *assessment of materials* or resources that will help in developing the skill on which people wish to work;

4. *analysis and understanding* of the components of each skill—each skill will be more easily learned if it can be understood and practised in identifiable simple stages;

5. practice of the component parts, getting feedback on performance, and reviewing progress;

6. *further practice* with reinforcement, recognition and support given for progress and effort;

7. *the use of the skill* in real-life situations;

8. *the achievement of a skill level* that is such that one can teach that skill to somebody else.

In the end the effectiveness or otherwise of lifeskills teaching will depend upon the skills of individual teachers. No other element will be more significant than how the teacher functions. For very few students is the subject as important as the teacher; for most students the teacher *is* the subject. The qualities of the good teacher have been clearly identified in recent research (Aspy and Roebuck, 1977), similarly the qualities of effective schools (Rutter *et al.*, 1979). It would take another book to explore fully those qualities, but some of the essence for us is in the invitation to a teacher to approach her class with something like the following:

> We are going together on a journey of exploration. I know parts of the country and you know others; just because you are alive and use your senses and have experienced things which I do not know. You may not realise that you know them but it is my job as a teacher to help you to become aware of what you know and to recognise its significance. We shall all learn from each other by sharing what we know. In this way we shall explore together much more of the country than we could have done alone. My responsibility is to make sharing easier and to contribute my own knowledge and experience to the common pool. [Curle, 1973]

5. Lifeskills teaching methods—working with groups in the classroom

We believe that the social and economic changes that lie ahead require new teaching approaches in schools and colleges. These new approaches are not limited only to the *content* of what is taught, but will involve also a reappraisal of *how* we structure learning experiences at the points of contact between teachers and students. In developing lifeskills, the most effective teachers are likely to be those who are themselves highly skilled, and are able to model the kind of competence they are promoting in those they teach. However, it is not simply in personal and interpersonal areas that there will be a call for a wider range of skills in teachers; there will be a need for those who are able to promote learning in ways other than simply imparting knowledge from teacher to student. It was Galileo who stated that 'You cannot teach a man anything, you can only help him to discover it in himself.' Like all generalizations, this would appear to us an oversimplification; however, while we would not totally accept that view, we do advocate a shift of approach from formal teaching to experiential learning, with emphasis being placed on learning rather than teaching, and with each student being given more responsibility for his own direction and development. This will call for teaching techniques that develop the role of the teacher more as a *facilitator of others' learning, than as an expert passing on knowledge of a subject* that has been acquired by specialist study. The skill required most by such a facilitator, to work effectively with our own lifeskills programmes or with most of the resources listed in Chapter 6, will be the key one of working with small groups, in classroom situations, on areas of personal growth and development.

5.1 Working with small groups

This method of teaching and learning is an essential feature of all the programmes, and our experience suggests that it is not widely employed at present in many schools and colleges. For that reason we would like to outline in this chapter the approach to such group work in classrooms, which will allow our own teaching materials, and those reviewed in Chapter 6, to be used to best effect.

5.2 Defining group work

'Group work' is a term that frequently promotes strong reaction, mostly unfavourable, in schools and colleges. It is sometimes seen either as a relic of the personal growth movements that originated in America in the early 1960s, or as the province of social case workers and psychiatrists. Its disfavour is possibly a consequence of some of the more extreme forms of group experimentation that occurred in the fashionable sensitivity training group experiences (T-groups) that abounded at that time. We agree that some of the criticism and suspicion of what occurred in some of those group events is justified. What we wish to avoid is that, in throwing out the bathwater of fringe, freakish group experiment, we do not also lose the baby, who represents the reality that people can learn so much from membership of a group which is not easily learned in other ways. So we do favour situations in which learning occurs from talking and listening to others *in small groups*, from working together and joining in group activities and exercises in the classroom. This kind of highly structured group work is very different from the ambiguous T-group type experiences, and we believe there is a great deal of personal learning available through its use.

The group work that we would like to see develop requires careful design and planning. It invites the teacher to see his whole student group as a collection of subgroups of various sizes and composition in which lies great learning potential. It is carefully structured and will call for skilled sensitive management by the teacher or person taking responsibility for the learning event. We believe that well prepared and well managed small group sessions have great potential for participants to learn about themselves and others, whether or not that is the primary objective of the group. Whatever the task or purpose of a group, there will be a bonus of learning simply from having to act and interact with one another, and we would like to make that bonus available to students as they develop specific lifeskills. Perhaps if one were to identify the one skill most crucial for individuals to develop, for many it would be how to be effective in the groups in which we live, play and work. That skill is likely to be best learned by operating regularly as a member of actual groups, as a part of the education process.

There are other advantages, and some disadvantages, of small group work both for students and teachers, which we indicate in the following section. We remain convinced that lifeskills learning will best be accomplished by individuals participating in learning alongside their peers and teachers, and suggest that *this learning mode is central to the most effective use of the lifeskills programmes.*

5.3 Differences between formal teaching and small group work

Here, we will set out some of the differences we see between more traditional subject teaching methods and teaching personal and interpersonal skills by means of individual and small group work in classrooms (see also Fig. 5.1). There will be some overlap as some teachers will teach their subjects sometimes using group work methods in classroom settings.

Fig. 5.1 A comparison of formal and group work methods in the classroom

Subject teaching by formal classroom methods	*Personal and interpersonal skill learning in small groups in a classroom*
Emphasis more on presenting information than on experiencing events—often passive learners.	Emphasis on experiencing and learning from sharing one's own experience and hearing that of others—learners are active.
Information given is largely about the experience of others.	The focus is on the ideas and experience of the participants. The teacher is helping to structure the learning for them.
Emphasis is on the subject or topic being dealt with.	The subject *is* the participants—they are learning about themselves and each other in different contexts.
Success is often measured by the student's ability to represent information previously presented by the teacher or collected from books.	Individuals are encouraged to see success in terms of self-awareness and skill development, bringing increased self-assessment, self-confidence, and more effective performance in a variety of arenas of life.

Fig.5.1 (continued)

Subject teaching by formal classroom methods	*Personal and interpersonal skill learning in small groups in a classroom*
The teacher is the 'expert'—learning flows from him. Teachers teach—students learn.	Each individual is unique and, as such, has something to offer others. Each person, including the teacher, has something to teach and something to learn.
The teacher's 'expertise' rests on academic record in a particular subject.	The teacher's whole personality, opinions, experiences, skills, values, weaknesses, etc., are used in presenting the whole person as a member of the group.
Questions are focused on testing listener's understanding of subject.	Questions are focused on assisting listeners to understand themselves and each other more.
Teacher is regarded as of secondary importance to subject being studied. Teacher sets work which students do.	Teacher uses self as a model—using appropriate self-disclosure and own experience as a model. Often does the same work as the students.
Feedback given only by teacher. Emphasis in feedback is on correctness of information.	Feedback from a variety of sources. Emphasis in feedback is on variety of reactions of other people.
Teacher as instructor—giving the lesson.	Teacher as facilitator—offering a format/structure to assist student learning.

Fig. 5.1 (continued)

Subject teaching by formal classroom methods	*Personal and interpersonal skill learning in small groups in a classroom*
Teacher decides content and method of learning.	Teacher attempts to build contract regarding what will be learnt and how it will be learnt. Ground rules are agreed and established for the way the groups will operate.
Confidentiality regarding what is said in classroom is not seen as a significant concern.	Confidentiality regarding classroom statements needs to be accepted by students and teacher.
Possibly little relevance for whole school or college system of what is taught or learnt.	Probably significant implications for the rest of the system of what is learnt and *how* it is learnt.
Little peer learning.	Possibly a great deal of peer learning.
Probably little need for parents and other staff to be informed.	Likely to be important that parents and other staff are kept informed of work planned.
Teacher is usually teaching the whole class as one group.	Teacher uses a variety of subgroups to increase participation.

Advantages of teaching/learning in small groups

● It can develop social skills through social interaction. Many of the skills that are applicable in a variety of life situations are relevant in the small group, e.g. communicating, listening, resolving differences, giving/receiving support, compromising, etc.

● It can increase self-awareness as individuals are encouraged to express opinions and relate their own ideas, preferences and experiences and receive feedback or get reactions from others.

● It can be very supportive and encouraging for individuals to feel accepted by other group members.

● It can increase self-confidence to hear other people have similar concerns and anxieties. Seeing that someone is prepared to discuss matters that are important to him can encourage others to do the same. More openness is likely to mean more trust and mutual help.

● It can 'harness' peer learning. Some would suggest that students learn more from their peer group than from teachers or other adults. Using groups in the classroom means that the peer dynamic can be channelled and used rather than being left to chance in playground or cloakroom. This can be more exciting and less boring than the routine reception of information from teacher or textbook which is sometimes so uninspiring for some students.

● It can give individuals a chance to experiment with a range of behaviours. In a group, which in many ways can be a microcosm of the wider community, we can learn the effect of our adapting to, deviating from, challenging or rejecting the other's point of view. We can experience the effect of our participating in or withdrawing from the group activities. The small group can be an ideal place to test the consequences of our many and varied behavioural options.

● It can produce increased trust levels which can improve staff–student and also student–student relationships.

● It can identify students who may need particular, individual help with specific issues.

● It can introduce a range of teaching resources, because each group member is potentially a source of information and perception, and consequently the focus of learning is not simply the person labelled 'the teacher'. It can give everyone a share of the status and esteem that is afforded to those who teach others.

● It can convey significant messages about the 'locus of responsibility' in classrooms. Usually, the techniques employed suggest that it is the teacher's task and duty to educate all those present. The use of small groups with their emphasis on the value of everybody's contribution can convey that each of us has something to teach, and also that each of us can direct our own learning by formulating our own ideas and by analysing, accepting, or rejecting the views we hear expressed. Central to the concept of lifeskills learning is the belief that each of us will benefit from 'owning' our own development, and small group work offers that opportunity much more than formal classroom teaching.

116

Disadvantages of small group teaching/learning

- It can require adjustment to new methods of learning by the participants. Introducing new norms can produce a challenge to the rest of the system and initial resistance and tensions will need patience and sensitivity to work through.
- It can encourage experimentation with the new mode, which can be upsetting to those who do not see this as a necessary stage towards growth and development.
- It can produce more overt interpersonal dynamics, which have to be recognized and managed, than would be apparent in many formal classroom sessions.
- It can mean less apparent control by the teacher and more need for student responsibility, which can be difficult for traditional systems and some teachers to accept.
- It can require more preparatory work than more formal lessons.
- It can be more difficult to evaluate the learning than in those lessons in which students can be given a written test and their answers marked right or wrong.
- It does require the students to develop the skills of group participation. It does require the teacher to have increased awareness, to be prepared to work with more challenging methods and to develop skills other than those of imparting her own knowledge.

5.4 What is a group ?

Some confusion may have been caused by the lack of a specific definition so far in what we mean by the 'group' in group work. After all, schools and colleges actually function very much already by dealing with students and staff in a series of groups. These can range from the huge assemblies of hundreds of students that take place on many mornings in many schools down to quite small special reading groups in remedial classes or equally small specialist subject sets in some sixth-form examination groups. Many teachers do in fact manage a variety of groups already as part of their general school work. Management of such groups requires skills, and different skills are obviously necessary if one is faced with an assembly of 1000, if one is teaching a mixed-ability group in a classroom, or if one is taking a whole year group on an out-of-school activity. Similarly, we believe there are specific skills that are particularly relevant to setting up personal learning experiences for small groups in classroom settings in schools and colleges. Not many teachers will ever have the luxury of working with small groups of chosen pupils in relaxed settings, with unlimited time available. The reality for most is to be timetabled for various groupings of 30+ students, in formally equipped classrooms, for rigidly allocated time slots. All our teaching programmes have been designed to be used by teachers and students in such settings. They are not written for small select groups but are intended for use with the 30+ student groups which are the norm in most educational institutions at present. What they do call for is a recognition that one need not always teach a whole student group at once. With skill and imagination, a teacher can refuse to be constrained by the fact that he is timetabled for a 30+ student group in a given classroom at a specific time. Within those constraints there will be opportunities to:

1. work with the students in a group of 30+, but using a whole variety of subgroups (pairs, trios, fours, sixes, eights) as the education medium;
2. vary the physical layout of the classroom so that it is not the formal place of chairs and desks in rows but a flexible, variable learning arena around which groups move and change as they learn;
3. use the time available for a range of activities and learning formats.

In thinking in these terms the teacher can begin to employ the methodology of small group work which offers more variety, involvement, and participation for students and teacher. Education entered into in this way requires more individual responsibility and skill from teacher and student. The student will be invited by the method to become more actively a part of the educational process. The teacher will be required to become a skilled creator of learning environments and events and will employ more skills than are necessary if the task is simply to pass information from teacher to student.

5.5 The skills of setting up group sessions

To work effectively, using a small group approach to creating educational events, the teacher will require skills in contracting, designing, preparing, managing, following up, and evaluating small group work in classroom settings. These skills are set out more specifically in Fig. 5.2.

Fig. 5.2 The skills involved in small group work

CONTRACTING

the skills of beginning to set up the teaching/learning event; being clear about objectives, outcomes and various options and consequences; approaches to contract building with parties involved

↓

DESIGNING

the skills of putting together a group learning experience; considerations before the event of the factors that will help or hinder the development of the required climate; awareness of the effects of timing, programme sequence and the physical setting on the learning

↓

PREPARING

the skills of selecting and producing teaching aids and materials required for the session; communicating correct information prior to the event to other staff, parents, and students; getting the best out of the physical environment

↓

MANAGING

the skills involved in working with small groups, face to face; awareness of options in, and effects of, different classroom strategies and techniques; the skills of beginning and ending sessions; ways of coping with group members whose behaviour produces difficulty; the skills of building trust; choosing the most appropriate teaching style; awareness and use of the dynamics of groups at work; producing and maintaining the most conducive learning climate; having options to deal with a range of possible eventualities

↓

FOLLOWING UP

the skills of attending to issues or items needing attention after group sessions; following up action plans, or group decisions;

recognizing work done; contacting individuals where necessary; giving feedback to those outside the group who may be affected by the work of the group

---

↓

EVALUATING

the skills of establishing in a range of ways how effective one is being in achieving one's teaching objectives, how much students are learning or how they perceive the value or otherwise of the work; assessing the effects on other staff or the system as a whole

---

They will enable teachers to make the most effective use of the lifeskills teaching materials and will introduce a methodology into the classroom that:
1. displays a belief in the concept of each individual as a teacher and a learner;
2. distributes the responsibility for learning and teaching more evenly between teacher and student;
3. gives much more opportunity for student participation and interaction and invites active rather than passive learning;
4. is consistent with the philosophy implicit in the lifeskills approach of affording to each person the opportunity to take more charge of herself and her life.

Defining the skills
A teacher's first task is to see in the class of thirty students a virtually limitless series of potential groups. From a whole group of thirty, one can decide to operate with five groups of six, ten of three, or three of ten, or have fifteen pairs working together for a session. Once it is accepted that the teacher does not have to be physically present in each small group for learning to take place, then tremendous freedom becomes possible in designing different educational events. The success or otherwise of such events will be decided largely by the skills of the teacher *before*, *during*, and *after* them. We would like to present our version of what might be involved at each stage.

Contracting skills
So many attempts to introduce new or different elements into the curriculum founder because initial contracts are unclear. Perhaps it sounds strange to talk of 'contracts' with the legal overtones

120

implied; we believe, however, that psychological contracts exist between people, whether they are written down or not. As with any form of contract, the clearer it is, the more likely that all parties to it are communicating clearly.

Contracting is a stage of planning for classroom work that begins prior to the design stage and continues through the design process into the preparing stage, and also to the management stage.

The first part of any contract is to be clear about what you want to achieve, what is negotiable and what non-negotiable, what happens if the contract is broken, who the parties to it are, and whether it is renegotiable. In schools, this means being clear on your own objectives, finding out what the students expect, and ensuring that consensus is achieved with them, checking out with colleagues, superiors and parents when appropriate.

Skilled contracting will necessitate:

Being clear about teaching objectives

We are convinced of the need for teachers to have a clear, presentable rationale for what they are teaching. Knowing *why* we wish to teach something should mean that we avoid the kind of teaching that is simply routine, or repeating syllabuses and style that have been established so long that they are no longer challenged as to worth or relevance. Having clear, specific, well defined teaching objectives will also help avoid the vagueness of purpose typical of many of the syllabuses on which departments in many schools and colleges base their work. Teachers of lifeskills, using small group methods in classrooms, should be able to:

1. state clearly which skills they wish to develop in their students and the time they think it will take to achieve particular levels;
2. identify what they see as the areas of application of those skills;
3. adjust overall objectives for individuals within the group. Not everybody learns at the same pace or is starting from the same point, and some students can be victimized if standards set for a group are unrealistically high or unchallengingly low.

(N.B. It is likely to be very important to share teaching objectives with the group. It may or may not be appropriate however to discuss objectives one is setting for individual students with the student in question. These can sometimes be useful as an incentive for the person, but they can also be discouraging if they indicate a huge gap between that individual's attainment and general standards within the group. In this latter case, a teacher may decide simply to be conscious of what he hopes for in the case

121

of that individual and use that to monitor his progress.)

The more specific one can be about the desired outcomes of a teaching programme, the more likely it is that they will be achieved. It is important to remember that one's teaching objectives represent only one's purpose, and need to be translated into specific outcomes for the learners. Unless the students *learn*, the session has not achieved its purpose. Therefore, there should be clear ideas of what the learners will take away from the event. Outcomes defined should refer to things, people or behaviours that you can observe or at least infer. They can be categorized as:

- *information:* what facts or concepts will students be expected to have a grasp of by the end of a session? For example,

  — I would like the group to know the range of helping agencies available in the community;

  — I would like them to know how the pastoral system works in this school;

  — I would like them to have sufficient information to be able to answer questions on consumer rights, etc.;

- *behaviours:* acquiring skills should result in observable changes in students' behaviour. What different behaviours would you expect to see students using at the end of a learning stage? For example,

  — I would like the students to be able to carry out an independent piece of research in another part of the city and present a report to another group;

  — I would like a group, when given a problem-solving task, to be able to collect important data, organize them, assess them, examine various options, reach a group decision about a preferred course of action, and decide an action plan that would solve the problem;

- *attitudes:* some teaching is directed to developing particular values or beliefs in the learners. Attitudes cannot be observed but their existence can be inferred from observing behaviour. What attitudes do you wish to see being developed and how will you recognize them? For instance,

  — By the end of the course I would like students to be more autonomous and yet more prepared to help others. I will look for less reliance on me in the classroom and fewer requests for me to tell them what to do, and at the same time I will hope that most of them will volunteer to help with the Old Folks' party in the school at Christmas.

Being clear that students have expectations and objectives also

Our expectations are a powerful influence on the way we react to what happens to us. Expectations arise from past experience as well as from information we may have about the events in which we are involved. We tend to react negatively to happenings that do not match our expectations. Teachers therefore, in planning any new approach, are likely to need to ask themselves:

● How will what I would want to achieve match what the students want or feel they need?

● Will the content and style of the work challenge established norms in the group?

Innovation, unless very well justified and sensitively presented to all involved, can be experienced as gimmicky, freakish, or just change for the sake of change, and consequently resisted. Agreement between teacher and students on common, agreed objectives will not guarantee the success of group learning, but it will remove many difficulties that might otherwise sabotage the work.

Being sure you are starting from 'where the students are'

Sometimes, in our enthusiasm for new ideas we can present concepts and use language and methods that sound remote and strange to the groups with whom we wish to share them. Therefore, it will be important to ask:

● Am I able to link new possibilities to the current experience and interests of the students in the group?

● Can I present my ideas and aspirations in language and terms that will be able to be grasped by the group?

Being clear about the implications of the content and style of your teaching for others

Lifeskills teaching using small group work will not be carried out in a vacuum. It will have an effect, in varying degrees, on more than just those teachers and groups involved. The teacher initiating the introduction of the programmes might see herself as having an effect eventually on students, parents, colleagues, and the system (see Fig. 5.3). More skilled students, becoming used to sessions in which they are encouraged to discuss and express opinions, will carry their new behaviours into other situations and will produce new dynamics there. Therefore, the teacher introducing the work will need to consider:

Fig. 5.3

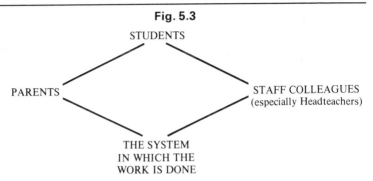

1. how to prepare parents, colleagues, and the students themselves for new possibilities;
2. how to prepare the school or college system for any likely impact of the new ideas and methods;
3. how to reduce the effect of any negative dynamics in the system on the work she, and the students, are undertaking.

The contracts with parents and one's own staff colleagues could require:

1. explaining *what* you hope to achieve in co-operation with them and *how* you hope to achieve it;
2. listening to any reactions they might have or providing further clarification they might need;
3. helping to examine any possible effects of the work for them and offering suggestions and help to reduce any negative ones;
4. offering continued contact to deal with subsequent difficulties if any arise.

Having set out, and checked out, what one's plans are, having consulted with each group of people involved, and having begun to shape a contract with them, one is set to move from primary planning into *designing* the educational experience, translating *what* one hopes to achieve into *how* one will achieve that.

5.6 Designing a group learning session

Beginning to turn one's initial planning into a teaching event that will be effective is likely to involve work in the following areas:

- clarifying objectives;
- building the contract;
- making the most of the learning environment;
- selecting appropriate procedures, structures, and materials;
- considering the learning sequence;
- identifying what needs to be done before the event.

We would like to become more specific about some of the considerations we see as being important in each of those areas.

Clarifying objectives

Only if we are clear what we want to achieve will we, at some stage, be able to evaluate how effective our work has been. The more specific we are about our objectives, the more likely it is that they will be achieved. We would hope that at the outset of any lifeskills teaching development, the teacher initiating the work would be able to complete the form in Fig. 5.4.

Fig. 5.4 Teaching objectives

I would like to teach the following:

information

skills

attitudes

to _____ (identify groups or individuals)

by _____ (identify when you hope to teach this by)

I will recognize that learning has occurred by

information (indicate how you will assess what information students have learned)

skills (indicate what new behaviours you will expect to observe students using which would suggest they had begun to develop new skills)

attitudes (specify what student behaviours you will look for that would indicate the acquisition of the desired attitudes)

Being able to be specific about what one hopes to achieve will help in preliminary discussions with parents and colleagues. Our guess is that both groups would be intrigued that any teacher would be prepared to:

1. take the trouble to consult them prior to any new development; and
2. risk being specific about how the effectiveness of one's teaching might be evaluated.

We hope that the modelling that will be offered by skilled teachers using the lifeskills approach will have the effect of producing more specificity in other subject teaching in schools and colleges, and will lead to parents expecting more accurate indications of what schools hope they are teaching.

Colleagues and parents are important people to give thought to in the preliminary stages, but whether they should be consulted before or after the group of learners themselves can be accurately assessed only in each new situation. At some point however the contracting has to be undertaken with the students with whom one hopes to work.

Building the contract

We place great emphasis on the value of teacher–student, teaching–learning contracts because:

1. they convey vital messages about shared responsibility for what happens in learning situations;
2. they invite individuals to participate actively in their own development;
3. they are likely to produce more student commitment to learning on the basis that each of us is likely to be more committed to something we choose than to something that is imposed upon us;
4. it indicates *interdependence*, which is consistent with the hope in the lifeskills approach of reducing dependency and by increasing personal skill and responsibility.

There may be opportunities *before* one actually embarks on a new teaching programme with a group to do some basic contracting. If a contract is understood to be an agreement between the teacher and her teaching group, then it will obviously have to consider:

- *what* will be taught/learnt;
- *how* the learning will take place.

One may need to gain access to groups one will be working with *before* one hopes to start, or to use the first actual session to work on the contract. At such a session the teacher can:

1. outline her own proposals for the content of the course she hopes to conduct;
2. explain her rationale for the proposals she is making;
3. make a statement about her reasons for wishing to offer a teaching/learning contract to the group;
4. ask for reactions to what she has said and respond to those;
5. ask whether anybody has any additional suggestions for the content of the course and include these if at all feasible;
6. ask about preferences and priorities in the group about the order in which the course content could be dealt with;
7. plan the course content and priority order in conjunction with the learners.

Having worked on the *content*, the teacher and students can now consider the *method* of teaching/learning. To help these issues be explored the teacher can:

1. explain her view of her own role in the learning experience. In the case of lifeskills teaching this will mean becoming less of an instructor and more of a conductor/facilitator of groups and individuals who are doing their own learning;
2. describe ways in which this role may seem different from the way she works in other subjects;
3. outline her expectations of the students in terms of how they work and contribute to their own and each other's learning;
4. ask for any reactions to this and respond to these;
5. suggest that any group that is going to work together as they are can benefit from identifying what each party can do that would help or hinder their work together. The group may then discuss:

    — what the teacher can do that would help or hinder the work of the students and vice versa;
    — what individual students might do that would help or

    hinder the learning for others;
    — distill from the above lists, in conjunction with the students, the *ground rules* that it will be mutually advantageous to observe in working together;
    — accept the ground rules as an agreed basis for work undertaken in the group.

We feel there are significant gains to be made in lifeskills work from agreement about ground rules between teacher and student. We think learning will occur best in learning climates in which people feel safe and are able to trust those with whom they are working. In work involving amounts of self-disclosure, for example, there will need to be agreement about confidentiality, so that all involved know exactly what the situation is in which they are involved. A teacher may wish to include ground rules which state, for example, that:

1. nobody needs to do exercises they definitely object to—anybody who wishes to opt out of a particular activity can ask to be excused and could be given other work;
2. personal abuse and ridicule of what somebody else says is not allowed;
3. criticism of people not present but identifiable is not allowed, as they have no chance to speak for themselves.

In general terms, the more control individuals have over their immediate environment, the more comfortable they are and the more open to learning they are likely to be, and ground rules collectively arrived at can contribute to that feeling of control.

The notion of teacher–student contracting may be so new in many systems that the idea generates disbelief or ridicule. Therefore, teachers introducing the concept may have to ask themselves whether it is worth delaying its introduction until students and colleagues are sufficiently aware of the philosophy of lifeskills work and the methods involved to see contracting in its fuller context. Hopefully, at that stage they will see that it is consistent with the content and style of the approach.

Some colleagues, and students, may fear contracting because it seems to overturn teacher control. We do not accept that it does this because a vital feature of any agreed contract will be for the teacher and students to be clear about *what is negotiable and what is not*. Those features need to be identified very clearly. So, for example, students' attendance at classes is required by the whole school or college system and therefore remains compulsory; school uniform requirements will probably still have to be observed; smoking will remain forbidden; etc. Contracts involve realities! They can give greater freedom and options *within existing boundaries*.

Contracting is also likely to be more suited to some groups of students than to others. Sixth-formers, for example, are possibly more likely to use the possibility more constructively than a 'remedial' group in the third year might. So it will require skill in the teacher to decide when and for whom contracting will be appropriate and the nature of the contract that will best fit that group, and their work, at that time.

Finally, it should be clear to all parties involved in contracting that agreements need to be reviewed at intervals, since situations will change, as will individuals' understanding, and therefore re-negotiation will be required from time to time.

Having given sufficient time at this design stage to building the contract, or deciding how one will eventually do so, one next has to consider the context in which teaching–learning will take place.

Making the most of the learning environment

Once one has become clear about what one wishes to teach, one has to begin to consider the factors that will create, or mitigate against the creation of, the most conducive learning environment. Even the best intentions and aspirations will not be enough in themselves to permit learning to take place. *What* one teaches will be heavily influenced by *when*, *where*, and *to whom* one attempts to teach it, and in designing a learning package, one needs to consider some questions relating to each of those factors.

Questions to ask

Time

Designers should ask:

- Is the time available appropriate to what I hope to achieve?
- Will the time of day, week, or year influence what I hope to achieve?

It is obvious that attempting to pack too much into any session can be very counterproductive. Sometimes in our enthusiasm we attempt to put across too many teaching points, and the result for the students is overload and confusion. One or two points per session, well made, with time for their assimilation, should be the aim. Having too much time for what one wishes to teach can be as much of a handicap as having too little. Time to fill, with little sense of purpose, can undermine student interest and produce boredom. Real skills exist therefore in making the most of the time one has, and real gains can be made by leaving students with a feeling of a task well done and a sense of achievement in what they have got through in any session.

In work that is personally involving for the participants, one needs to be particularly sensitive in one's management of time. To end a session abruptly, when someone is in the middle of discussing something that is particularly important to them, could produce negative reactions which could impair participation in subsequent sessions. In work in which members of a group have equal time to give their ideas on a topic, it is obviously very unsatisfactory to have a session when only some of them have had a chance to do that. As far as possible, then, be sure that what you hope to teach will fit the time you have to do it.

The period on a timetable that is allocated for the work one wishes to do will obviously have a significant impact. One can teach some things on a Monday morning, when students are renewed by a weekend's rest, which it would not be sensible to teach last period on a Friday afternoon, when students (and teachers!) may be overloaded and find that energy is low and concentration difficult.

A session that involves groups sitting down, listening to longish lectures after a heavy lunch, is likely also to mean a sleepy audience. Sometimes the rough guide that is given to what is the best time to do specific work is:

- *morning*—the best time for work that emphasizes *thinking*;
- *afternoon*—the best time for work that involves *doing*;
- *evening*—said to be the time when most people are most ready to undertake work that involves their *feelings*.

For schools whose students go home at the end of the afternoon there are obviously fewer options, but the time of day does influence what we can hope to teach and learn!

Similarly, there are some times of the school or college year that may make it more difficult or more easy to teach particular courses.

- The start of a new school year can be a time of fresh enthusiasm and receptivity to new learning.
- The pre-Christmas festivities often mean that serious work at that time is difficult.
- Dark winter days with wet break-times can reduce enthusiasm and make sustained concentration difficult.
- Post-examination times sometimes mean that students think that all hard work is over for the year. It can also mean they are ready to be involved in work that is a little different from the academic fare that has been theirs for most of the year.

Place

Feelings of physical comfort and well-being can help students relax and be more open to learning. In designing a learning event, therefore, it is important to give attention to making the most of the physical setting in which any teaching is to take place. Questions to ask oneself at this stage are identified in the checklist in Fig. 5.5. Factors in the physical setting that can help or hinder the development of the most conducive learning climate are here looked at in greater detail.

130

Fig. 5.5 Physical facilities checklist

(a) Is the room available suitable to house the group comfortably and give options for work in subgroups?

(b) Is there any additional space available if that is needed for subgroups?

(c) Will the decor in the room help or hinder the learning? Can I improve it if necessary?

(d) Will the furniture in the room give comfort, and what options does it offer for re-arrangement?

(e) Will the room be too hot, too cold, or too stuffy, and if so how can I remedy any of those difficulties?

(f) Is there freedom from distractions and interruptions? If not, what can I do to reduce the problem?

(g) Is the room so placed that any activity in it will intrude upon other groups, or are any neighbouring groups likely to provide factors that will inhibit my work?

(h) Will my work require any special features in the room (e.g. large amount of wall space for display of flip-charts, screen for overhead projector)?

(i) How will other uses that the room has affect the work I wish to do?

(a), (b) The use of space. Too little space or space that is badly used can produce feelings for those involved of being cramped or crowded and will make concentration, listening, or movement difficult. Exercises requiring movement in such circumstances can increase the confusion, frustration and loss of patience. Too much space can be equally off-putting. A small group sitting in the middle of a large, echoey assembly hall is likely to feel 'lost' or 'adrift', and could find it difficult to concentrate on issues requiring more personal disclosures. Teachers, therefore, who are timetabled for traditional-type classrooms or for areas not immediately sympathetic to more sensitive work may have to be imaginative in managing the space they are given. Removing desks or tables or stacking them, or screening off areas of rooms can help to produce feelings of greater group comfort, intimacy, and cohesion which will greatly help the learning. It is sometimes possible also to utilize adjoining cloakroom, stockroom, library, or study area space as overspill areas for subgroups to move into for discussion sessions.

(c) The room decor. The general appearance of a room can

131

influence the feelings and hence the work of groups that work in it. Scruffy, dirty rooms with tatty, out-of-date wall displays, rubbish lying around, and a generally ill-kempt appearance can encourage students to feel that this is an uncaring, unwelcoming setting; and it may be difficult to persuade them to relax there and do work that is about their own and each other's personal worth. If one has to teach in rooms that are not one's own base, then it is obviously more difficult to achieve the standards one would wish to set in terms of brightness, cleanliness, well displayed work, having plants or flowers around, etc. Well cared for rooms can indicate welcome to those entering them, as long as the decor is not treated as more important than the people. Some teachers having to use rooms other than their own have found it valuable to carry around with them a collection of posters to help cheer up surroundings, and to make the first group activity one of making the room as comfortable as possible.

(d) Use of furniture. If one is seeking to put students at ease and encourage them to work closely with each other, then furniture could help that process by being comfortable and giving flexibility. Sitting on hard seats can mean that one feels less prepared to be involved. Furniture that is heavy or noisy to move around can disrupt the flow of a session if movement is called for. Tables can become physical (and therefore psychological) barriers between groups and between group members. Space and comfortable, easily movable furniture can put participants at ease and give a whole series of options that can be useful at various stages. For example:

1. seating the whole group in one large circle, which makes it easy for anybody to talk to anybody else;
2. seating the group in a series of small circles for subgroup sessions;
3. seating the group in a horseshoe shape around the blackboard or the teacher, giving him easy eye contact with each member of the group and making him the focal point for the group;
4. having subgroups seated in a series of small horseshoe shapes around flip-charts on the wall on which their comments are recorded;
5. dispensing with seating altogether and letting students sit around on the floor or on cushions to increase informality;
6. allowing students to stand and walk around forming different subgroups in a session calling for a series of exchanges.

In some cases teachers have to run sessions in workshop-type rooms, science labs, or rooms in which the furniture is fixed to the floor. In an attempt to get over the restrictions enforced by such an allocation, it may be necessary to allow students to sit on the bench-type tables or worktops rather than be grouped around and separated by the fixtures. Inviting students to operate new norms like this can be a way of indicating that this work is different from other work and is, somehow, new and special.

(e) Room temperature and ventilation. It is obviously less easy to be involved in work or concentrate on it if one is in physical discomfort. Therefore, temperature control which can make sure that working groups are neither too hot nor too cold, and supplies of fresh air from open windows as that becomes necessary, are seemingly peripheral arrangements but ones that can make such a difference to a group performance.

(f) Freedom from interruption and distraction. Rooms with large windows overlooking playing fields or playgrounds, rooms with frequent visitors or passers-through, rooms in which telephones ring continually, and rooms with tannoy-type relay systems carrying announcements are all likely to make it difficult for a teacher to keep a group intent on work requiring concentration and important personal exchanges. If one has no choice about the room then one may have to resort to:

1. screening off windows or facing groups away from them so that distracting outside activities are not so obvious;
2. having a large notice which reads 'Please do not disturb! A very important work session is in progress until ———', which one can place outside the door;
3. taking the phone off the hook or, if it is an extension, insisting there are no calls put through until a certain time;
4. negotiating with users of tannoy systems to restrict announcements to a regular specified time, unless it really is an emergency. (One teacher, who made several vain attempts to get such an agreement, actually became so irate at frequent interruptions that he unplugged the wiring in his room! We are not recommending this action but offer the information to users of tannoy systems in the hope that they can be sensitive to the work of others!)

If a headteacher develops an admiration for the work of a particular teacher it can be a 'good news–bad news situation'. The good news is that the quality of the work is recognized; the bad news is that every visitor to the school is brought in to witness it! Part of one's contract-building with colleagues and heads can be to

133

indicate that spectators can seem like intruders to groups working on personal issues and for that reason are not welcome.

(g) Getting along with neighbours. As in buying a house, one can be lucky or unlucky in the neighbours one acquires, one can be similarly blessed or afflicted by classroom allocation, and neighbours can affect the work one wishes to do. Classes next door who are noisy can be very intrusive and distracting and, therefore, teachers working next door to disruptive groups, or music rooms, with choir and musical instrument practice to contend with, could find quiet, sensitive sessions difficult to sustain. Similarly, one can, oneself, be a difficult neighbour to others. If one wants sessions in which movement and energy are much in evidence, that could interfere with quiet study sessions next door. In short then, the message is:

— check what is going on around concurrently with your own teaching session, and if necessary
— negotiate an appropriate contract with your neighbours, or
— negotiate a change of room, if that is possible.

(h), (i) Equipment within the room and norms established by its other uses. It is apparent that the design options in any teaching session could be restricted by limited facilities in the rooms available. Lack of overhead projectors (OHPs), screens, blackout possibilities, video systems, even blackboards and chalk can limit one's possibilities. Perhaps, however, for most lifeskills programmes the most severe restriction might be a lack of wall space on which to mount the flip-charts that groups produce about their ideas. An awareness of what one may require therefore for any session, with enough preparation time to adapt to whatever is lacking or to acquire it, can ensure that the setting will be able to cope with one's design needs.

Some teachers will recognize that some rooms have 'atmospheres', based on the perceptions of the norms for that room. For example, a room that has a tradition of heavily formal teaching will continue to provide students familiar with it with expectations that they must behave in an appropriately serious manner while there. Similarly, in a room with a reputation for noisy, boisterous behaviour, where 'anything goes' has been the norm, it will be difficult to establish a new norm of quiet, thoughtful work. Consequently, it will be a consideration at the design stage of how the work that one hopes to do will differ from what usually happens in that location. If there are differences, then one will need to assess how one can quickly register the new norms one wishes to establish.

People

For most teachers there will be little opportunity to choose the groups they would like to teach. Were it possible to work with students who came voluntarily to lifeskills sessions, as could happen were they an option against other subjects, then the teacher would obviously be in a better position to expect commitment and application from them. Some teachers may be so keen to give the work voluntary status that they prefer to offer a range of options, even to groups they have no choice about taking. They can do this by offering a range of five or six activities which can be done in small groups, one of which is a lifeskills option, and allowing individuals to join in work they choose from the six possibilities.

If groups are not present with a teacher out of choice, then effective contract-building and skills of persuading them of the value of the work will obviously be called for. At the design stage, however, there are other factors relating to the student group to be considered (Fig. 5.6).

Fig. 5.6 Factors regarding the learning group

(a) Will their presence be voluntary or required? What will that mean for how we start?

(b) Do I have any previous contact with the group? If not, what are the design implications? If so, what will be their expectations of me, based on that experience?

(c) Are group members of about equal ability or mixed ability? What will that decide about how they divide up?

(d) Is the group a single sex or mixed? Are they used to working together in mixed groups or are they likely to be reluctant to mix for the work I have in mind?

(e) If the group is known to me, who are:
— the natural leaders?
— the most articulate individuals?
— the most withdrawn?
— members of close friendship groups?
— likely to be reluctant to work with each other?
— those who will require any special attention?

(f) What kind of learning methods is this group most familiar with? What is the general reading and vocabulary levels of the group? What bearing will these have on the type of work I am proposing?

(g) Is there anything I know about experience or interests within

135

that group, which I can incorporate and build on as a link with what I hope to introduce?

(h) In the light of some of the above considerations, if I wish to use subgroups would it be appropriate to permit them to self-select or will I want to decide the composition of groups myself?

There are obvious reasons for some of the considerations in that checklist; some others will need clarification.

Groups of similar general ability usually give fewer problems at the design stage. Mixed-ability groups tend to be regarded as more complex to work with, though the options provided by subgroups can reduce some of the difficulties. Subgroups can be used to cater for the different ability levels, or the more able may be given the task of teaming up with the less able, as long as there is an emphasis on the need for mutual support. Sometimes it can confirm damaging categorization continually to put the very able in leadership positions over the less able. Finding ways of giving everybody some experience of leadership would be more consistent with the general aims of the lifeskills approach.

If one is working with subgroups one can, of course, as the facilitator, make oneself more available to the group most needing help and encouragement than to those groups well able to manage their own work.

Even in coeducational settings there is sometimes a reluctance for male and female students to work together. Given the option, groups will tend to stick to single-sex patterns. There can be instances where this arrangement is appropriate for the work being undertaken. Whenever possible, however, we would urge that sexually mixed groups are used to begin to challenge some of the lack of male–female understanding that is common in our culture, and some of the sex-stereotyping that this promotes.

There are other techniques of group composition that can be relevant to what one wishes to achieve. For example:

1. placing the most vociferous individuals together in one group so that they are not able to dominate sessions as they sometimes do;
2. placing those who are not so forward or confident together, so that they do not have to compete, for once, with the more dominant;
3. recognizing friendship groups and using these as factors that will give group members greater feelings of trust and confidence which comes from working with people they like;

4. separating those who find it difficult to work together so that their interpersonal difficulties do not impede the work of others;

5. placing individuals who are in need of special sensitivity at particular times (e.g. the student experiencing difficulties at home, suffering a family bereavement, currently lacking confidence, etc.) with others who are naturally more supportive.

It is important to recognize that what one is doing is not simply hoping to teach the skills that are the subject of the teaching programmes. One does not teach only in the *content* of one's lessons: there are lessons for the student in the *style* of one's teaching. One is not teaching only new skills: one is teaching also a *new methodology of learning and working together*. The learning cannot be rushed. Students will take time to learn the new norms, and ways of working, and patience and support will be required as they adjust to these.

The more we are aware of students' expectations, which they will have formed through their previous learning experiences, the easier we will be able to aid the transition from old methods to new. The more we know of strengths, weaknesses, fears, hopes, interests, and experiences within our teaching groups, the more we can start from where the students are. We can use what they are familiar with as a launching pad to move them towards new awareness and new possibilities, but we must move at their pace and not our own, or we will risk losing them!

Through all this of course one is also having to consider the size of the groups one will work with. If one is timetabled for a class of 30, one has a great many options. Working with the whole group at once is likely to be appropriate for short inputs or to give instructions, but for any lengthier session will drastically reduce participation and require amounts of passive concentration from the students that they may not be able to give. The structure that will give the highest amount of student participation would be to have a task that could be carried out in pairs, and thus the teacher is working with 15 busy subgroups. For many activities, however, pairs do not give the range of experience, opinions, and responses that a larger group can offer. It is probable that to get the best balance between participation and representative range, the optimum group size is 6–8 members. Within a group of 8, one is likely to find a real cross-section of personality types, strengths, experiences, prejudices, values, skills, etc., against which to test any individual opinion. Below that number, one increases the potential for participation but reduces the representative range; above it, one gets a wider range but risks losing out on participation.

'Befores and afters'
The design stage also requires some focus on the fact that an educational event occurs in the midst of other realities. Students will not arrive at the door of the classroom untrammelled by other experiences, nor will they leave at the end to pass out of existence until you next meet. The designer therefore has to ask:
- What will my group have been involved in before they arrive at my session?
- What will the group be leaving to do at the end of it?

We have emphasized already the importance of teachers starting from 'where the learners are at' and not from where we might want them to be. Prior information, therefore—about norms, standards and dynamics in the group—can help us design appropriately. An important determinant of group climate will be the group's activities immediately before its arrival. To ask ourselves what activities members of a group will have been engaged in just before they arrive will help us to look at optional starting points. Unless one considers these, and chooses the correct option, then the main content of any lesson planned may suffer accordingly.

A group can arrive at the classroom door in a variety of states. For example, it can be:
1. very subdued after a difficult, tense lesson in the previous period;
2. very exuberant after a lesson involving high jinks and a good deal of stimulating activity;
3. very fragmented because some dispute is going on between group members;
4. very full of energy and pent-up because it is a wet day and they have been allowed no breaks outdoors;
5. seething with injustice after an incident for which they have been blamed;
6. tired and lethargic because it is late in the day and they have 'had enough'.

In any of the above cases, just to go straight on with what one has planned may mean that it fails to have the impact one had hoped for. One may have to be prepared to:
1. insert a short energetic interlude to liven up a low-energy group;

2. introduce a more relaxing, slowing-down type of interlude to allow the group to 'settle-in';
3. put aside what one had planned and allow the group to talk through the issues that are dividing it;
4. build in break-times to one's lesson so that people may have a chat or stroll about as a change from sitting working;
5. allow a group to talk about the feelings that are so evident in its members at that time, as a way of 'discharging' them. When we have strong feelings that are 'bottled-up', they are likely to prevent us from working as we would like to. We carry the feelings around like 'baggage'. A group leader is likely to have to allow people arriving at her session time to 'dump the baggage' by talking it through as a preliminary to starting work. An awareness that we may need a range of options to use as 'starters' to a session, related to what a group has been doing immediately prior to joining us, should therefore be part of our design consideration.

Also relevant will be the matter of sensitivity to what might be the next activity for students as they leave our session. It is obviously important in work involving personal issues or feelings to manage session time in such a way that people are not left in the 'middle of things', or that recognition cannot be given to efforts that people have made. The skills of ending a session include, however, more than just that. They include a realization that on leaving you students will be entering new situations where there will be different expectations of them and other requirements made of them. It could be important to assist that transition in a variety of ways; for example,

1. by allowing a group a few minutes to relax at the end of a session so they experience the feeling of a break between one activity and another;
2. by building in a gentle, calming exercise at the end of a particularly brisk, high-energy, stimulating session;
3. by giving a few minutes for students to think about what they are moving on to next and helping them to be aware of the differences they might meet by way of content, style, and expected norms of behaviour. Those minutes can also be used to check that there is no 'unfinished business' or need for clarification, reaction, or comment, so that individuals do not have 'baggage' to take along to wherever *they* are going.

All this is simply part of caring for those we are working with. Unless we are helping students to become more aware of choosing

139

behaviour that is appropriate in each context, then we may be inviting difficulties for them and others. It is interesting to hear a skilled disc-jockey talk about the art of running a disco evening. The sequence apparently is from a gentle start, using different tempo and volume of music, to build up to a crescendo of movement and excitement before ending with a final period of quieter music to 'bring down' his audience before releasing them on to the streets. Apparently, the disc-jockeys maintain that to end the disco abruptly, when the excitement is at its peak, could produce a whole amount of trouble afterwards in the form of aggression to people and property. While the results may not be so drastic following lifeskills sessions, we do make a plea for sensitive completion of exercises and helping students to move smoothly from what they have been doing to what they have to do next.

Questions of myself

A final crucial factor in considering the learning environment in which lifeskills teaching will take place will be to give some thought to oneself. It is easy perhaps, in the enthusiasm to teach a new course or try out new ideas, to ignore what is possibly the most important component of all—the teacher organizing and running the sessions! Teacher skill and performance level could well be the key to the success or otherwise of the event one is designing, and one should, therefore, consider the following.

● How do my plans for this event fit in with other demands on my time and energy from other teaching I am doing, from extracurricular activities I am responsible for, from my non-work areas of my life?

● What else will I be involved in, before and after the lifeskills session, that could affect my work or be affected by it?

● Are there any indications that I may be taking on too much work at this time? If so, what steps will I take to cope with the overload?

The lifeskills approach is likely to stand or fall on the effectiveness, or lack of it, of the teachers using the materials. There is a significant correlation (Aspey and Roebuck, 1977) between teacher effectiveness and physical fitness! We are not advocating (or maybe we are!) that every teacher owns and uses a track suit, but we are saying that a teacher's physical well-being will influence how much she can expect to achieve. Hence, each teacher needs to consider seriously the question of overload. For each of us there is an optimum level of stress at which we will work most effectively. If we can avoid exceeding that stress level then our work and student learning is likely to benefit. It is common that the most enthusiastic and dedicated teachers do drive themselves beyond normal levels of commitment and contribution. In the end, such energy and drive can be counterproductive, simply because they give so much that they burn themselves out, to the detriment of themselves and many good causes. Awareness then in general terms of the likely impact upon oneself of any new undertaking will be beneficial on many counts.

To particularize that awareness, one would do well to look at the whole day around the event that one is designing. What will one be moving from before the event and moving onto after it? Switching from physical education sessions to classroom sessions, or from careers visits out of school back into a classroom, may produce transition difficulties that one may need to consider. To know that one will have to complete a lesson promptly because one is on playground duty or in charge of the school bus duty that evening will mean there is no time to chat to students who may want to stay on after a session, so one may need to offer other time. Design considerations therefore include placing the event one is working on in a wider setting both for oneself and the students involved.

Selecting appropriate teaching procedures, structures, and materials

In the teaching programmes we have designed we have outlined procedures for conducting the exercises in the classrooms. We have stated clearly, however, that it will be necessary for each teacher to adapt the materials to suit her own preferences and teaching styles and the group she will be taking. With the other resources also indicated in Chapter 6, there will be need to shape the materials to fit one's own teaching situation. In designing any educational session, we think it is important to give attention to the question of which teaching procedures, group structures and types of materials will best achieve one's teaching objectives and match one's preferred approach. We think the questions at the design stage are as follows.

● What are the options I have in teaching methods, group organization and materials?

● Which of the options do I think best suit my personal teaching style?

● Which of the options best suit the ability and norms of the student group?

- Which of the options are most consistent with my teaching objectives?
- Which of the options offer most by way of variety and stimulation for myself and the student group?
- What are the constraints on my choice of options?

Selecting appropriate teaching procedures

We suggest there are options in the following categories, all of which may be employed at some point as part of lifeskills classroom sessions.

Presentation

Lectures. Perhaps the oldest of all teaching methods can still have a place if the speaker is skilled, the time is right, the method fits the subject, the group is interested and is able to listen and concentrate, and it is not used too repetitively or exclusively. The biggest danger we see is that it can preclude participation for very long periods. This can be reduced by dialogue and questions, but we would guess that the most any group is likely to be able to take without the lecture being interspersed with something else is 20–30 minutes.

Lecturettes. Mini-lectures can be used very effectively in 10-minute bursts to introduce ideas as a basis for group activity or to give a theory input that links group learning. As a change from teacher's voice, some students may be able to contribute their own ideas in lecturette form from time to time. This can share the responsibility and the effort, and can offer opportunity for skill development.

Micro-teaching. A teaching point is made; this is discussed or analysed in small groups. They report back their discussion; the teacher deals with points raised. He then introduces the next teaching point, the group splits again and the process continues. It can take longer to teach all that one wants, but it is likely to mean that each point is really understood.

Debates. These can be extremely useful or a complete flop and are mostly somewhere between. Asking groups to give opposing views on a particular topic can be involving and stimulating, but the competitive element can mean that good ideas are casualties in the battle and learning becomes less important than winning. However, having to prepare material for debate can help clarify the ideas of those who have to do that.

Stimulus materials. These can be used to provide an initial input as an introduction to group activity. Films, video excerpts from television programmes, sound recordings from radio broadcasts can be very effective methods of giving information efficiently and with high impact.

Demonstration

Showing. This involves demonstrating what one is trying to teach slowly, step by step, or using somebody else to demonstrate while one is explaining.

Coaching. After explaining the learning stages, the teacher takes the learner through a performance of what she is teaching, giving tips as she does it.

Rehearsing. The learner practises to prepare for what he is going to do. Practice can produce familiarity with how the event might be and give the confidence to face it. During rehearsal, feedback can be given and correction and adjustment made. Using a closed-circuit video system so that learners can see and hear themselves in rehearsal can be very powerful as a teaching device.

Group learning

Skills practice. The learner has an opportunity to practise skills in front of other learners and receives feedback and has further chance to practise. Other learners can have their turn.

Discussion. This is a more usual form of learning device. It can lose much of its effectiveness if it is imposed without any clear guidelines of structure. With an experienced group there are likely to be no problems; with a less experienced group they will need a clear definition of what they are meant to be doing, a list of stimulus questions (written up) to guide their discussion, and probably some guidelines on how to proceed, e.g. two minutes for everybody to jot down ideas, then each person in turn can have up to two minutes to present her ideas to the group without interruption. (This equal-time technique is a way of demonstrating that everybody's contribution is of value.) Once everybody's initial views have been presented, discussion can follow. The discussion can end with a few minutes in which the group decides what it will report to the larger group about its discussions. Group members can rotate roles of chairperson, recorder, presenter, etc., if those functions need to be allocated.

Panels. Given time for panel members to prepare their views on a particular topic, this can be a useful way of getting a wide range of views on an issue. If students are members of the panel, it also gives them a chance to fill a teaching role, and that can be valuable in itself. The problem sometimes is that, while there is high participation for panel members, the majority in a group may be inactive for long sessions. With a confident group this can be overcome by using a 'touch-panel' technique: any member of a group is allowed at any stage to take the place of any panellist simply by touching the shoulder of that particular person, who then has to leave the panel and be replaced by the newcomer.

Seminars. These are group discussions led by a teacher or somebody with particular expertise or experience (parents or members of the community, representatives of organizations, etc.). Their success will depend on the expertise of the teacher/group leader and her ability to get group members involved and avoid lecturing. Observers, or recording and replaying group sessions, can assist the achievement of balanced participation.

Brainstorming. This is a technique for extracting a great many ideas from a group in a short time. The group is given a topic, a question or an unfinished sentence to focus upon. For five or ten minutes, members of the group say anything that occurs to them on that topic and a recorder writes up on a blackboard or a flip-chart anything that is said, however irrelevant, silly or challengeable. During that time there is no discussion, as the purpose is to produce ideas in volume and variety. Nothing is censored or evaluated during the brainstorm, and everything that is said is written up. At the end of the brainstorm members have a chance to elaborate on their comments and to challenge and discuss all the ideas produced.

Buzz-groups. These entail a device designed to energize group members after spells of inactivity. After listening to a lecture or some other input, members are asked to turn to their neighbour and share their views or impressions for five minutes before asking questions. Another version would be to have small discussion groups of four to six people with no leader, who share their views with each other for five to ten minutes. Brief reports from buzz-groups can be brought back to a general session and these can be a useful guide to what has been heard, understood, or not grasped or disagreed with.

Specific task groups. A group is given a specific problem or topic to focus upon and produce an answer or various options relevant to the teachingPlearning objectives. This can be an efficient way of breaking up tasks or topics that are wide-ranging. Different groups can deal with separate components of the task or problem and combine or exchange their results at the end. Not everybody has to tackle the same work and, therefore, a complete range of tasks can be carried out in a shorter time.

Teaching/learning groups. One of the most effective ways of learning something can be having to teach it to others. Groups can be asked to teach skills or present information to other groups. Besides clarifying for themselves what it is that they have to teach, they are required to design an exercise, demonstration, or teaching programme to teach that to the other group. This can produce appreciable activity and involvement and can be very stimulating and entertaining. Learning 'exchanges' can be arranged between groups so that giving and receiving is established as the norm.

Individual learning

As preparation or follow-up to group sessions, members can be asked to do individual work. This can include background reading if this is appropriate to the ability of the group and the leader is realistic in his expectations. It can be too easy to hand out recommended reading lists which impress everyone but the recipient, who simply feels overwhelmed and guilty because she does not know where to start, or hasn't the amount of time that seems to be required. Other possibilities are for members to carry out interviews or surveys to collect the views of others relevant to whatever is being studied. Researching newspapers at home or watching television programmes that are scheduled and may contain relevant information can be other ways in which individuals can link classroom activities with other learning sources. Individuals can actually co-operate with each other in this, by operating a 'buddy-system'. Two people agree to support and be resources to each other. This means they will each work independently but will exchange and pool anything they find out or learn. They can divide up tasks and save duplication; they can act as consultants to each other and help each other with advice; they can encourage each other to do more or spur each other on to meet deadlines, etc. Comparing notes, planning work, exchanging learning can happen between 'buddies' at times like tutor-time or registration time.

Structured experiences

Role-playing. This involves a technique that allows for skills practice and an exploration of ideas and feelings in what is a simulation of a real-life experience. Individuals can be given or choose particular roles which are then performed, scripted, or ad-libbed. Often the more over-prepared, complex, or structured the role play, the longer it takes to set up and get started, and the more likelihood there is of a breakdown occurring because someone forgets a line or a stage in the proceedings. With experience, groups and teachers can switch into the technique easily and skilfully. Entire situations can be role-played or just the most significant parts. Using role-reversal, individuals can experience roles that are not usually available to them. Indeed, the same person can experience several aspects of the same situation (e.g. a student could play himself, his father, and his teacher at different points of a role-play about home–school contacts), in a multi-role-play session. In any case, careful preparation, management, and processing is essential for success with role play. The process stage gives an opportunity for participants to explore the experience and extract the learning for them from it.

Drama. Drama involves perhaps more structuring than role-play and usually requires more time. Group members can be required to take part in a piece scripted by the teacher or somebody else to present a particular teaching point, or they can be asked to devise a drama to highlight a given teaching point. All that was said about role-play is likely to apply to drama also. To allow greater opportunity for participation, those observing the drama can sometimes be allowed to join in by replacing a particular actor (using the shoulder-tap technique!) or simply by entering the drama as a new character when they see an opportunity. It is again true that the effectiveness or otherwise of drama as a teaching/learning technique will be decided by the skill of the teacher and the group in drawing out the learning for themselves in a follow-up process session.

Case-study. This involves the use of a detailed description of an event, a character, a situation, or a problem that is related to teaching points one wishes to make. It can be real or contrived and is usually followed by a group discussion with the teacher involved, or the teacher may stay out of the group and draw out the learning from a group report-back at the end. The same case-study can be given to a variety of groups and the results compared, providing, as it will, a whole range of possible views or alternatives. This method can be used very usefully in problem-solving as it can use the whole group as a resource on a particular issue and provide a variety of possible solutions from which to choose.

146

Critical incident. This can be simply a brief introduction to an incident that the group has to think through and suggest alternative outcomes to (e.g., the teenager arrived home from the disco two hours later than the time she had been told to be in by went into the house and found her father waiting up for her). A discussion follows, in which the group examines possible background to the incident, the possible feelings and thoughts of the characters involved, various dialogue exchanges that might occur, and possible outcomes to the episode. Again, the same 'incident' can be given to different groups who can exchange findings after their separate discussions.

Exercises. Exercises can be a group activity which produces learning about the group itself or the topic to be learned, or it can be a simulation of a real-life situation, which provides learning to apply to the real situation. Exercises are many and varied and exist in prepared form in many publications, or they can be designed by the teacher or group. One of their main strengths is that they encourage active involvement of all participants in the learning experience. Typically, an exercise will have a clearly defined objective and will involve individuals in doing some individual or group work, which is then discussed or evaluated by themselves or with the teacher. Any exercise session, we believe, should always conclude with a general session in which teaching points are summarized and participants' reactions checked out and processed. We also believe that a teacher should not run an exercise with a group until she has experienced it herself as a participant, or at least has participated in a very similar exercise. The danger with exercises is that they are easy to 'inflict' upon a group, and it happens too often that no rationale is given for doing the exercise, nor are the learning points for the participants drawn together afterwards. If this happens the exercise can seem like a pointless game, and real learning is less likely.

Games. There is an increasing number of educational games available for use in the classroom. Card games, board games, etc., can provide interesting, lively sessions and learning as well. They can be used as a change from other forms of learning and can occupy groups purposefully during awkward times like registrations or wet break-times. They can provide learning and contribute to building the right learning climate.

Selecting appropriate teaching structures

Consideration of which teaching procedures one will employ from the range of possibilities above will lead naturally to which physical arrangements one will use to organize the group session in the classroom. Some choice of procedures will automatically dictate group structures (e.g., games involving six players, or an exercise to be done in fives) but others will permit flexibility. We see that in the design stage one is addressing the questions:

- How will I physically arrange my student group?
- How will I use myself or other staff during the session?

The options we see are presented in the checklist in Fig. 5.7.

Fig. 5.7 Teaching structures: options to consider

Whole group. It can sometimes be appropriate and effective to teach or work with the whole class at once.

Small groups. It can fit the task and teaching/learning objectives to divide up the whole group into a series of small subgroups, each with four to ten students.

Pairs. Each person can work with one other partner for some or all of the session; with odd numbers the teacher can make up the numbers or there can be one trio. This can give high participation, if it suits the teaching objectives.

Trios or quartets. Again, these invite great participation and offer variety.

Fishbowl. One group works while another sits around them and observes how they work. Observation data can be used as feedback for the working group. Typically, the groups would then change round.

Circle. The whole group, including staff, is arranged in one large circle. This gives a chance for everybody to make eye contact with each other person, and staff are able to do the same.

Horseshoe. A group sits in a semi-circle with an open space at one end in which the staff sit or stand, or where there is a blackboard or flip-chart on which the group can focus.

Rows. Rows in which people sit looking at the backs of heads are for theatres or lecture sessions, and are likely to be used only rarely in group teaching/learning sessions.

Fig. 5.7 Teaching structures: options to consider (continued)

Table group. A group sits or works around a table, which can be useful when materials are involved and need to be available and visible to all. In a discussion group the table may act as a physical and psychological barrier between group members.

Inter-group. Competition is set up between subgroups engaged in a similar task. This can develop a feeling of unity within each group and the rivalry can be very energizing. Sometimes, however, the rivalry can produce division in the larger group, and this may need to be carefully monitored.

Three-ring circus. Three or more groups are engaged in different activities simultaneously. They complete their different tasks at the same time and then change activities. The procedure is repeated again so that each group performs each activity in rotation.

Options groups. A range of activities is outlined and individuals opt for the one they prefer. A group then forms on the basis of choice of option and the chosen activities are undertaken by groups simultaneously.

Self-select groups. Groups form on the basis of individuals choosing with whom they would like to work. Such groups are likely to have higher trust levels than those groups randomly selected or directed. Changing groups can give opportunities of building relationships in the larger group, as more people have more chance to work with a wider range of others.

Staff involvement: options

Single teacher/leader. The teacher co-ordinates or facilitates the whole group and acts as a link between subgroups or a focus for the whole group, giving inputs or drawing out learning, managing time, making up numbers if groups need one more member, etc.

Joint teacher/leaders. Some teachers can combine groups and then have the advantage of being able to co-lead sessions. This can offer more variety in teaching style in allowing inputs to be given in turn, in allowing dialogue and interaction between the two which

149

Fig. 5.7 Teaching structures: options to consider (continued)

serves as a model for the group. It can also allow for a division of labour; e.g., one teacher 'fronts' the session, giving instructions and linking activities, while the other monitors the people in the group, encouraging, supporting, inviting participation, and checking out reactions of group members.

Team-teaching. With more teacher/leaders, there are obviously more options. Tasks can be shared, different expertise can offer more varied activities, more options become available in how student groups can be structured; e.g., one teacher may take a very large group for a film or video input while four others on the team work with small subgroups on more personal or intensive issues.

Teacher as consultant. The teacher or group leader is available in an advisory capacity to groups who are working on tasks on their own. The 'consultant' can be sited centrally or can wander around and move into subgroups when invited.

Teacher as participant. There is a real opportunity with group sessions to lead by example. For the teacher to be seen participating—actually doing what is required of everybody else—can really help to build trust within the group. Some would debate whether the teacher is ever *just* a participant, because her presence in a group is likely to be much more powerful than would be that of any other group member. Teachers sitting in as members of groups therefore do need to be aware of the power they have and should attempt to reduce its impact in whatever way is appropriate. The presence of the teacher as a group member can also be significant in subgroups, which may need more control, encouragement, or attention than others.

Selecting appropriate teaching materials
Teachers will be very familiar with the 'tools of their trade' that we list as teaching materials, but we set them out (Fig. 5.8) in the belief that most of us tend to stick to our well-tried favourites and it can, at the design stage, be appropriate to consider the range.

Fig. 5.8 Teaching materials checklist

Films. Films require good forward planning to order, can be expensive, and do require total blackout (which might disqualify their use with some groups!) and some equipment know-how in the teacher or student group. Despite all that, if you can get the right film to suit your purpose it can make a very useful impact as part of a group session to stimulate or support group discussion.

Video systems. In our experience, video systems are often under-used. Television output in schools broadcasts, and in general audience slots, can provide excellent stimulus material which can be recorded and 'banked' until required. If a school or college is particularly well equipped and a video camera can be available with the recordep and the monitor, then one has the opportunity to video-record groups at work, which can be excellent as a source of feedback for that group later. In using such a method, of course, one needs to be open with the group about what one is doing and the use to which it will be put. Any school or college not in the happy position of owning a video-camera may be able to persuade a parent/teacher group to raise some funds to purchase one; or the student group itself could form a task group to devise ways of raising the appropriate amount. In our estimation it provides such excellent learning possibilities that it is well worth the investment.

Overhead transparencies. These can provide bright, clear display of teaching points or relevant information and have the advantage of allowing build-up of information stage by stage. Good overhead transparencies can be kept and used repeatedly, which is a way of avoiding recurrent preparation. It is not easy, however, to keep very much material visible at the same time and this can be limiting.

Slides. Again, slides can make high impact but can also require much preparation and a longish time in darkened rooms. They can be the basis for some very low-activity sessions for the student viewers, and they do need the teacher to devise ways of involving the audience or frequent breaks for buzz-group interludes.

Sound tapes/cassettes. These can provide good stimulus material, but in the age of television they tend to be low-impact and have to

---

Fig. 5.8 Teaching materials checklist

---

be very good to be useful. They could be useful as a means of a group reviewing one of its own discussions to check out how the group functioned. A group can also use a cassette recorder to keep a permanent record of findings, conclusions or reports to other groups, which can be easier than keeping written records. Finally, a cassette recorder can give a group the possibility of interviewing others in the community as basic research for their own group work.

Questionnaires. Again, questionnaires can require significant amounts of preparation and review, but they can produce useful data. Students tend to be interested in views and opinions held by their peers and it can be a useful activity for a group to design and apply its own questionnaire and then review and discuss its findings. This is the kind of activity that will require co-operation and good communication within the group, so there are likely to be some additional benefits to using it.

Handouts. Handouts are sometimes a substitute for teaching. It can be tempting to believe that if we give out information on a handout we have taught, and the group has learnt. Too often this is not the case, as handouts are put aside and never returned to. The problem is that handouts can contain too much information and can seem overpowering. The language is often appropriate to the writer of the handout, but can be too advanced or full of jargon for those who have to read it, and often the layout can impede the learning by packing too much information on to a page in tight typescript, with few headings or ways of identifying the main points. If handouts are to be used, they do need careful preparation and design—and, rather than just being handed out, should be talked through and a chance given for checking understanding with the recipients.

Worksheets. Setting out tasks to be undertaken by the group or individuals and giving relevant background information can be very useful in structuring the work of a group. Again, they can be sometimes a substitute for teacher–student contact, because they can be used to give the student group work to do while the teacher has to deal with registers, reports, or any of the non-teaching tasks
152

Fig. 5.8 Teaching materials checklist

that are increasingly part of the job. Good materials enhance teacher–student and student–student contact rather than reducing it or replacing it.

Student materials. Part of our design stage should be to ask what materials may be needed during the session by the students. In doing group work, one may wish to avoid students' having to carry around cumbersome equipment like bags and books which can be a distraction, or just get in the way. It can, however, be frustrating to be free of such encumbrances and then find that one is in the middle of an exercise requiring participants to jot down a few points. It will help, therefore, to be clear at the start of a session about what students will require by way of materials during the session, and with some groups it will be important to have spare pads, pencils or whatever, as inevitably somebody will arrive without what is required.

Flip-chart sheets, masking tape and felt-tip pens. We would recommend the acquisition by all group leaders of good supplies of sheets of newsprint, marker pens and tape which will stick up wall charts without marking the wall. This basic survival equipment allows groups to record their work on flip-charts and the teacher to write up questions and instructions during sessions. We like to see rooms full of flip-charts produced by working groups, which conveys purpose, achievement and ownership of their own work. We suggest that discussion groups always keep a visible record on a flip-chart of the main points of their discussions as they go along, or else have some time at the end to list their views or conclusions, again, on a flip-chart, so that their ideas do not 'get lost'. This also enables easy reproduction of a group's work for later distribution back to that and even other groups.

In the light of using and seeing others use the teaching materials listed, we would like to offer the following suggestions.

Don't let the materials become the primary focus. We can become so excited by materials, methods, or technological slickness that we place more emphasis on those than on the students involved. We should be able to justify everything we use in terms of our teaching objectives, climate-building and appropriateness to the student group.

● Try to minimize dependency on technology. Video equipment goes wrong; slide and movie projectors have cables that people trip over, bulbs that blow, slides that get into the wrong order or turn back to front, etc. We are not saying do not use them; we do say be really sure that you need them.

● Ensure you have a sound rationale for surveys, questionnaires, etc., and that their value is demonstrated to the group who put the work into providing the answers. There is nothing so devastating as being unable to answer the student challenge, 'Why are we doing all this?'

● Some secretarial help and access to a duplicating machine or photocopier are likely to be tremendous assets, as groups produce work on flip-charts and need to have a copy later to retain individually.

● Keep handouts up-to-date. It is tempting to use handouts once produced, for subsequent sessions, but information does need updating and some groups may need different quotes, language or lay-out than other groups.

● Consider the possibility of developing a resource assistant or assistants from among the student group. Our experience suggest that there is much untapped technical expertise and organizational ability in many student groups, and it can be very developmental (not to say extremely valuable to staff!) to promote the use of such skills.

Some final design questions

At the end of the design stage the following should be our focus questions.

Are my proposed teaching procedures, structures and materials compatible with each other and with m teaching/learning objectives?

If we design a teaching session in a very detailed way, we can sometimes consider the different design areas independently, and we do need finally to be sure that they all 'hang together' and make sense, so that, for example, the teacher will have the group facing him for inputs and not sitting in small groups with their backs to him, and if handouts need to be read there will be time to read them. Ensure that therd will not be such a variety of form and method that participants finish up feeling dizzy and confused. The design stage can transport the designer into the realms of exciting possibilities, which can sometimes translate very badly

154

into reality. Remember, therefore, that designs will come to fruition at some point and you will have to manage the event and students participate in it, so designing is about realities rather than fantasies. What we build into our design should also be consistent with what we want to teach. Lecturing a group for half an hour on 'How to Make Relationships', then asking them to write about it for the rest of the session, without speaking or having a chance to exchange their own experiences, is likely to be a case in which the medium contradicts the message. Attempting to teach democratic decision-making in a heavily autocratic way is also likely to be just as inconsistent. We may teach more by what we do than by what we say.

Do I find the prospect at this design stage interesting and stimulating and is the student group likely to do so?

I am much more likely to teach effectively if I am excited about the content and method. Boring old subjects and routines are likely to induce apathy and indifference in teacher and student alike. Therefore, if I can introduce variety into teaching by way of new topics, or trying out new approaches, then I am likely to increase my own energy for the work and probably that of the students also. There is a balance to be struck between the old subjects taught in old ways and innovation for its own sake. The balance is in teaching what can be shown to be relevant, in ways that are different but not freakish or gimmicky, and in which variety is used for the energy and expectancy it can create. It is useful to remember that even new methods of education can become boring if they are used relentlessly and repetitively. Vary the menu and keep the appetites alive!

Do I have a presentable rationale for each stage of my design?

We are likely to learn more if we are convinced of the relevance and purpose of what we are studying. Therefore, the more the teacher is able to justify each activity to the students, and its contribution to identifiable learning goals, the more likely it is that the learners will be committed and motivated to participate. Unless we can present our rationale, and have it accepted, it can appear that we are just time-filling, playing games, or putting students 'through the hoop' for our own entertainment. So think through how you will present your reasons for the different stages of your design.

Have I considered timing, sequence, and flow in my design?

In designing each stage of a teaching/learning event it can be easy to miss out on how well the pieces will interlock and what the 'whole picture' will look like. In reviewing the whole design one can ask the following questions of it.

● Will the teaching/learning objectives be presented, and acceptance of them sought, at an early stage?

● Does each stage suggest a flow and sequence in terms of teaching points being made and activities undertaken by the groups?

● Will what the groups are asked to do fit the time they have and the stage they are at?

● Are there built-in summary stages so that learning occurs in clear progression?

● Is student participation balanced with teacher input and an opportunity to review or process activities?

● Is work intensity balanced by breaks or lighter tasks?

● Will the content and method suit the group and the time of the event?

● Do I have alternatives for each stage if it becomes inappropriate?

● Will the style of beginning and ending the session match how the group will be to start with, and how I would like them to be at the end?

Good beginnings make a great deal of difference to sessions. Settling a group in, starting together, introducing warm-ups or ice-breakers, or having a method of making an early impact which grasps the interest of the group obviously will create a better climate for what follows. Having individuals drift in late or begin to give attention when they have finished other tasks, or making such a low-profile start that few are aware of what is going on, is likely to impair work later. People can find it difficult to move straight into deep, serious, and intense work and will need time to build up to that, and structured work can lead them there. It is also difficult to be deep and serious all the time, so changes of mood can help. A session of light relief, if it is appropriate, can provide a real break after some serious discussion. Moving around after sitting, a chance to talk after listening or watching, being quiet after a great deal of talk and noise can all give variety and renew energy. It can be very useful also to work out timings for each stage and each activity and to build these in to your design, so that it is clear that what you plan to do fits the time you have. Also, it can be very helpful to have alternative activities to fall back on if any particular one appears inappropriate at the last moment. Having options can help the flexibility that is a mark of a skilled teacher/group leader.

There are some obvious traps to be wary of in designing sessions. Films or lectures after lunch are clear invitations to go to sleep, as is any amount of passivity on a Friday afternoon, or at the end of a long day. People do not learn if they are tired, and we need ways to keep them involved and yet refreshed by new ideas and activities.

Closing a session also requires sensitivity and skill. Summarizing the learning or having somebody else do it, checking out reactions, reviewing any promises of action or follow-up, making groups aware of where they go next and of any preparation for next time, and making sure the final mood is a positive one are all likely to be important in drawing a session to an effective close.

We have spent a great deal of time in considering the design stage of teaching/learning events and we make no apologies for that. We think that the more thought and awareness is put into planning what and how one will teach in a session, the more effective that session is likely to be.

5.7 Preparing for the session

The time between planning and designing one's teaching event and actually running the session can be crucial to its success. Good schemes and designs are in themselves not enough; they have to be turned into actual happenings, and at the end of the design stage one is likely to be left with an amount of preparation. This preparation will require some definite action plans to ensure it is not overlooked, and we think those plans can be made by completing the checklist in Fig. 5.9.

Fig. 5.9 Preparation checklist

As a result of my design, do I need:
to book or make any room arrangements?
If so, what? _____
Who will do it? _____
When? _____

To obtain any additional equipment for the room?
If so, what? _____
Where will I get it? _____
When? _____

Fig. 5.9 Preparation checklist (continued)

To prepare any visual aids?
If so, what? _____
How will I do that? _____
When? _____

To prepare any materials for the students?
If so, what? _____
How many copies? _____
How will I do it? _____
When? _____

To communicate any information regarding the session to colleagues, students, anybody else?
If so, what? _____
To whom? _____
How? _____
When? _____

To enlist the help of anybody else?
If so, who? _____
To do what? _____
When? _____
How will I ask? _____
When? _____

To obtain any additional information or check on anything myself?
If so, what? _____
From where? _____
How? _____
When? _____

To make any changes in the layout of the room I will work in?
If so, what? _____
Who will do it? _____
When? _____

Fig. 5.9 Preparation checklist (continued)

Are there any implications in this design for the system I am working in?

If so, what? _____

Does that require any action from me?

If so, what? _____

When? _____

Is there anything else I need to do between now and the teaching session?

If so, what? _____

When? _____

Enlisting help, or delegating tasks skilfully if one is in a position to do that, can contribute to setting the stage for effective teaching, and any time given to preparation is likely to be a sound investment in contributing to smooth-running, less stressful sessions for all involved. Having identified and carried out all preparation tasks, one will now be ready to face the group and conduct the event.

5.8 Managing a group session

When all the planning, designing and preparation are over comes the chance at last to work face-to-face with the students in the classroom. We thus enter a whole other skill area which we will describe as 'managing skills', and identify under the following sub-headings:

1. getting started;
2. climate-building;
3. leadership behaviour;
4. observation of groups;
5. coping with difficult members;
6. closing a session.

Getting started

Teacher effectiveness is usually always measured in the ability to teach and manage student groups in the classroom, on the so-called 'coal-face'. Walking through the door is indeed very often the moment of truth, when the quality of what one has given time to preparing will be tested. Its success or otherwise will rest upon the teacher's face-to-face skills with the students.

Once through the door, there are tasks to be addressed.

159

Getting attention

If you are there first, prepare to receive the group and indicate where you wish them to sit. If they are there first, announce that you wish to start and explain that you would like them to sit in the appropriate places. Depending on how one wishes to operate, there will be a series of seating options to suit various purposes (see Fig. 5.10). Once the group is in position and attending, the session can get under way. If it is the first session of a new programme, then some contract-building will need to be undertaken. If it is not the first session, then it may suffice to identify clearly the objectives for the session and how it is hoped to achieve them. Whether one is able to make such a clean start will, of course, depend on:

1. whether the group has any 'unfinished business' or 'baggage' carried in from other sessions: if it has, then there will need to be time to 'clear the air' before they can settle down to work;
2. whether one has all the equipment and materials to hand that one will need for the session: if not, the first task will be to deal with that.

Most sessions will benefit from a warm-up activity (unless the group is 'high', and needs a 'cool-down' activity). This can be a short activity related to the content, which gets the students involved; e.g., 'This session we will be dealing with the skills of making decisions. We all have to make these at some time or another, and to help us realize that I would like you to turn to the person next to you, and you have two minutes between you to try to remember as many decisions as you can that you have made in the last week.'

Having clarified objectives, established or reiterated group ground rules, presented a menu for the session, and helped the group to focus and get involved, one is in a position to move on.

Teacher modelling

From the moment the teacher enters a room to teach a group, he is communicating with them. Before he says a word, the students' first glances will be assessing mood and outlook from the way he dresses, walks, looks, etc. Students are very perceptive of 'where one is', and so the way the teacher presents himself from the start will have an impact on them. If he is confident and relaxed, he is likely to put them at ease; if he is tense and edgy, then that also can spread to the group. So as soon as the teacher enters the room he is teaching and creating, or failing to create, a learning climate. His

Fig. 5.10 Seating options to suit various purposes

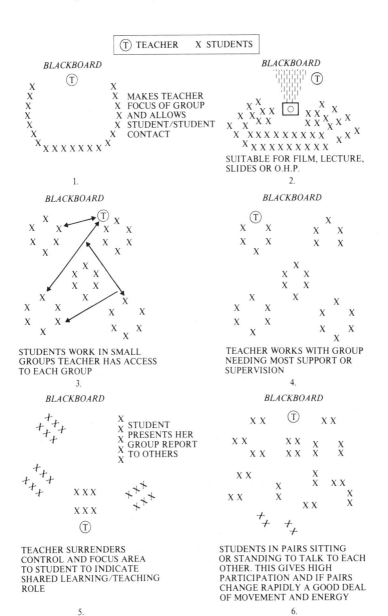

greatest resource therefore is himself, and the effective teacher is likely to be making a very conscious use of himself in every session.

An immediate possibility which can help enormously in developing trust between the teacher and the student group is for the teacher to lead off with anything he is asking others to do, or to give information about himself to encourage group members to do the same. In the first case we have the teacher modelling leadership by example, which is always more convincing than asking a group to do something then sitting back and observing. In the second, we have the teacher using significant personal information *appropriately*, as a contribution to a more genuine contact with those he is teaching. It is clearly established (Derlega and Chaikin, 1975) that, if one individual is prepared to disclose information about thoughts, feelings, experiences, hopes, fears, etc. (i.e. things about herself other than merely safe biographical facts) in amounts and at levels that do not offend or dismay those present at the time, then the likely effect will be to encourage others to do the same. Relationships develop as people get to know each other better. It can involve a risk to disclose personal information about ourselves, but if we are prepared to take that risk we will probably find others are more prepared to do the same, and it is likely that trust will begin to be built. Trust does not happen accidentally; it has to be created by people behaving in open genuine ways. It is unlikely that students will learn to trust a teacher who risks nothing himself, and hides his humanity behind an impenetrable facade of his professional role, keeping himself remote from them. The teacher, then, can begin by modelling the behaviour he would wish to develop in the student group, and the way he operates will help to develop norms within the group.

Building a positive climate

Establishing a conducive climate—an atmosphere in the class-room in which openness and confidence are the norms and an optimum of learning can take place—is likely to be the main task of the teacher in any session. The way the teacher behaves will be highly significant in encouraging or impeding such a development, but there will also be many other relevant factors, which we indicate in Fig. 5.11.

Fig. 5.11 Factors that can affect the development of a group (class) climate

Negative climate	*Positive climate*
Style of leadership is inappropriate for task and group.	Style of leadership (autocratic; *laissez faire;* democratic) fits task and group.
Task of group or purpose of session is obscure, not communicated or not fitting abilities and interests in group.	Task interests group and they feel competent and willing to deal with it; purpose, objective, method, and conditions of work are well prepared and clearly communicated.
Procedures are not in keeping with the objectives or are unsuitable to the group.	Method of procedure is consistent with the objectives and is well matched to the group.
Group size or composition is ill-judged or unsuited to task, objectives or methods.	Composition and size of group is appropriate to content and method.
No recognition is given to what members may be 'bringing in' (feelings of excitement, resentment, etc.—'unfinished business' left over from previous activity).	Opportunity is given for 'baggage' ('unfinished business') to be cleared, and members are allowed time to make the transition and settle in.
No attempt is made to build contract with group regarding content and method (what it will be relevant and useful to do and the most acceptable way of working). Rationale is not presented for work, nor are ground rules agreed.	Clear, acceptable rationale for content and method is presented; contract is established and understood; ground rules are agreed and applied.

Fig. 5.11 Factors that can affect the development of a group (class) climate (continued)

Negative climate	*Positive climate*
There is a vagueness of purpose, or lack of clarity about what is required to pursue it.	There is a clarity of purpose and well-defined routes to its achievement.
Individuals or small groups dominate others; participation and influence is unbalanced.	Participation is distributed evenly; everyone is involved and influence is shared; there is no attempt to dominate by any member or group.
Conflict is 'buried' or allowed to escalate.	Conflict (if present) is brought out and dealt with.
Teacher requires students to take risks while not apparently risking anything himself.	Teacher leads by example, modelling what he is inviting students to do.
There is a low trust level; group members feel ill at ease or feel the need to be defensive.	Trust exists within the group; members feel they can say things about themselves without needing to fear that this will be ridiculed, rejected, or used against them subsequently.
Teacher is tense, anxious or not convinced about what or how he is teaching.	Teacher confident of his skills and the content of his teaching; he presents calmly and is sufficiently relaxed for students to feel the same.
Teacher is not alert enough to dynamics of the group or skilled enough to deal with issues arising.	Teacher has necessary observation and group management skills.

Fig. 5.11 Factors that can affect the development of a group (class) climate (continued)

Negative climate	*Positive climate*
Lightness not present; pace is monotonous or ponderous; humour is lacking or its type is inappropriate.	Session blends serious work with light relief or changes of pace. Humour lightens the session and is shared in by the whole group.
Over-competitive or win–lose approach by members divides the group.	Co-operation and problem-solving are the norms by which the group operates.
Over-critical, heavily judgemental, or aggressive behaviours predominate. Negative feedback is much in evidence.	Accepting, non-judgemental behaviours are employed by teacher and group members. Skilled feedback is used effectively.
There is a lack of predictability in teacher/leader behaviours. Leader's motives are not clear; group are unsure of what they might be asked to do, and feel manipulated.	Teacher/leader behaviours are clear and open. There are no hidden agendas or 'nasty' requirements. Teacher is consistent and behaves predictably.
'In-groups' or 'pairing' develops. Teacher relates particularly to one or two subgroups or members.	Group relationships are shared. Group functions well together but also relates to other groups. Teacher's attention is evenly distributed.
Specialist or jargon language excludes some members.	Language used is appropriate to the task and the group.
Feelings and reactions of group members are not monitored or checked out—teacher assumes he knows how members are feeling.	Leader is sensitive to what group members are feeling and experiencing and checks out his assumptions appropriately.

Fig. 5.11 Factors that can affect the development of a group (class) climate (continued)

Negative climate	*Positive climate*
Silence occurs frequently and becomes threatening or creates awkwardness.	If silence occurs it is used positively, for thought and reflection.
Group decisions or action plans are not clear or are not followed through. Members do not carry out promised action or feel any need to account to the group.	Decisions taken represent group views and wishes. Responsibility for action is clearly allocated and members carry out agreed tasks and report back.

Physical factors that can affect climate

Too much, too little, or badly used space gives group members feelings of being 'lost', 'crowded', or 'divided'.	Space available is appropriate to the group size and is used in a way that produces feelings of easiness and closeness.
Seating is uncomfortable or is placed inappropriately so that members find concentration difficult or feel out of touch or disregarded.	Seating is comfortable and gives group members feelings of equality and sharing. It is arranged so that eye contact is possible between the teacher and all group members and between the members themselves.
The general environment is dull or cluttered, and looks uncared for and unwelcoming.	Surroundings are bright, clean, and well cared for. Rooms seem pleasant and welcoming without being uncomfortably ostentatious.
Other users of the work area produce expectations or provide connotations that are negative for the group members.	Work area has pleasant associations for those working in it; expectations and 'vibrations' are therefore positive.

Fig. 5.11 Factors that can affect the development of a group (class) climate
(continued)

Negative climate	*Positive climate*
Teacher is not easily accessible or contactable by group members or adopts position inconsistent with leadership style.	Teacher is readily available and gives the appropriate messages about his chosen style.
The work of the group is impeded by frustrating interruptions or distractions.	Group is secure from outside interference and is thus able to work without interruption.
Work area is inadequately heated or ventilated and therefore those working there feel ill at ease.	Work area is warm, airy, and comfortable.
Time of session is badly judged or ill-chosen; too much or too little time allowed for work allocated; session occurs when members are tired or overloaded.	Time of event and amount of time available are suitable to all and appropriate to the task.

External factors that can affect climate

The system within which the groups are working has firmly established norms that intrude into the work of the group; or the system reacts negatively to results of the work of the group.	The norms in the system are compatible with those that develop within the group. The system can and does accept the outcomes of the work undertaken in the group.

Some of these factors have been dealt with fully in the design stage; those referring to appropriate leadership skills will be further developed later in this section; and the remainder we would like to comment upon here.

Conflict
In groups that work genuinely and openly, there will be occasions

167

when participants will differ deeply over ideas that are strongly held. To experience deep differences, openly demonstrated, can be uncomfortable both for those involved and for those observing the process. For that reason, conflict is often regarded as something to be avoided at all costs. Such thinking may not be the most realistic or constructive way of regarding the matter, however. We would regard the most useful attitude and approach to conflict is to recognize it as a reality and to teach that:

1. conflict may be inevitable in most situations in which people honestly and openly exchange ideas and give their personal opinions, or work together for any length of time;
2. conflict is likely to be uncomfortable for those involved or witnessing it, but the consequence of it need not be destructive. Conflicts resolved can produce a more unified and co-operative group as a result.

One danger with conflict is escalation, in which the real issue gets lost in wider-ranging and more personally abusive expression. This development can produce such hurt and bitterness that recovery of the relationship becomes very difficult. The other danger is that conflict is 'buried'. In trying at all costs to avoid the discomfort that conflict can bring, group leaders or members jump in to pacify any situation as soon as it looks like becoming tense. This can result in genuine feelings and ideas being suppressed and 'buried'. The problem then is that, unless real issues are brought out and dealt with, they are never cleared, but remain in operation below the surface and are very likely to interfere with subsequent work in the group. Conflict then needs to be managed by:

1. helping members to express feelings constructively;
2. encouraging real listening by members to each other;
3. inviting those who are differing with each other to examine common ground or to look for parts of the opposing opinions that they can agree with, rather than rejecting differing views indiscriminately;
4. requiring those with opposing views to become very specific about what it is they have difficulty with in each other's arguments;
5. pointing out how we can differ with another's point of view without extending that into personal abuse, and demonstrating the difference between those two behaviours;
6. teaching negotiation and compromise in which parties identify what they can agree about, what they cannot agree about, and what they will each do to reduce the possible difficulties as they

continue to work together, i.e. personal contracting to rebuild working relationships, rather than allowing disagreements in some areas to destroy many other possibilities.

The teacher can make a very significant contribution to the learning about conflict by presenting and modelling the view that conflict can be a growth point. Out of difficulties and differences can come energy, and if that is managed and channelled and the moment of crisis is worked through, then real gains can result in the form of even stronger contacts than previously existed.

Participation

If groups are to sustain the interest and involvement of their members, then participation by each and every one is likely to be highly significant. Achieving a balance in participation then, can be an important contribution to the maintenance of involvement and commitment. Members may not perform evenly all the time, and on some occasions it may suit individuals to present a low profile. That is fine as long as that is the way the individual chooses to be and the rest of the group members accept it. It remains important, however, for groups, overall, to achieve and balance the involvement of their members.

Each individual will have his own personal style of group membership. Some will be more extrovert than others; some will naturally display a greater range of leadership behaviour or play a more prominent part than others. We do not say that each member of a group should contribute exactly the same amount as each other member in every session. We do recognize that a person who says very little can in fact play a significant part in what the group achieves by listening carefully to others and making relevant or supportive comments from time to time. At the same time, someone who says a great deal is not necessarily operating in the best interests of the group, because he may simply be promoting his own point of view and being insensitive to others. Participation therefore needs to be measured both in terms of the *amount* and the *nature* of an individual's contribution. The group leader will have to monitor both the verbal and non-verbal behaviour of every individual member if he wishes to assess his or her involvement. An overall objective, if that leader wishes to retain every member's interest and commitment, should be to maintain some balance in the contribution made by each individual. It is likely that those who do not experience involvement will, eventually, decide that there is little value for them in membership of that group.

169

Opportunity can be given for personal development by a teacher giving feedback to individual students on their personal style in groups. On the basis of such feedback, an individual student might decide to experiment with new behaviours, which would enable her either to increase her influence on the groups she works with or to reduce it, if that were appropriate.

Humour

A major factor in whether individuals enjoy being part of the groups they work with can be the presence of humour in the group. 'A group that laughs together stays together' is probably over-simplistic, but it does suggest, quite rightly, that people who enjoy the time and the work they share together are much more likely to want to continue to be part of that group and that work. Humour can ensure that people can enjoy an experience together; it can be an 'ice-breaker' that encourages people to relax and settle in; it can, if used appropriately, lift tension that can build up as groups undertake serious or difficult work; and it can be the expression of a common, enjoyable, shared experience that can weld members of a group more closely together. Those are the possibilities in humour that is used appropriately. Humour used inappropriately can achieve the opposite of all those benefits—it can be hurtful, offensive and divisive—and it may be useful to focus on some of the differences between the two types. Humour that is used creatively in groups is likely to meet the following criteria.

● It will be of the type that all members of the group can share in. It will, therefore, not be built on 'in-jokes', which amuse those in-the-know but irritate others. It will not be some members laughing at the expense or misfortune of others, because that could be divisive. It will not be based on subject areas that offend the values or beliefs of some group members; e.g., racist or sexist humour can be extremely offensive to some and can cause such strong antagonism that it can severely damage group unity.

● It will be well timed and not constant. Humour that replaces the work the group has been set can become irritating or frustrating eventually because the group will fail to achieve its objectives and some members could become resentful of that. Humour, then, should 'lubricate' the group's work rather than 'clogging the mechanism'.

● It will not seem offensive to outsiders. Groups that become very close and are seen to be greatly enjoying themselves can sometimes produce dynamics of which they are unaware. 'In-groups', by their existence, can create 'out-groups', people on the outside, looking in, but not being able to share the experience. This can cause resentment, especially if the group's humour or laughter seems to be directed at the outsiders. So sensitivity to other groups should be part of the togetherness enjoyed by any group.

A teacher who is able to use humour obviously has a highly significant skill, but again, awareness will be required of its nature and style. It is easy when working with students to entertain many at the expense of a few. In many groups, particularly in schools, there is some unfortunate person who becomes the butt of the group jokes or criticism, and groups can give this individual a very hurtful time, which can be destructive to the person's self-esteem. The teacher should be careful not to fall into the same pattern, no matter how much the majority might enjoy it. Jokes can create norms and stereotypes that erode the worth of individuals, and it is the opposite of this that lifeskills teaching would be trying to establish. Rather than humour based on denigration of others, perhaps the teacher's safest model is to be prepared to laugh at himself. A willingness to do this can indicate a wish to avoid the use of the professional facade behind which it can be tempting for teachers to hide significant parts of their personalities from their students.

It will be important, as groups increase their awareness of how they function and work together, to help them examine their use of humour alongside consideration of all the other factors in their group interaction.

Win–lose

Groups become very keen on achieving objectives and attaining successes, and doing so can give a sense of purpose and power that can energize and unite group members. Sometimes this wish to achieve produces elements of competition with other groups which a teacher can use to advantage, because it can stimulate interest and energy. However, in helping groups to understand the way they work and the implications of that, a teacher should help them to appreciate some of the dynamics in winning and losing.

Success is important for each of us, bringing, as it is likely to, increased self-esteem and confidence, on the basis of which we can go on to achieve even more. Sometimes, however, success is attained to the direct detriment of others. Sometimes we 'win' by ensuring that somebody else 'loses'. That moment of triumph may feel very good for us, but for the 'loser' it can be a negative experience which can turn into harmful loss of self-esteem and resentment against the 'winner'. Therefore, inter-group competition between subgroups needs to be monitored carefully, in case it produces dynamics that damage total group unity. If some do need to 'win' some of the time, then it may be important to find ways in which others can redress the balance on other occasions.

As well as building awareness of the effects of rivalry between groups, the skilled teacher can help groups to understand the possible outcomes of internal rivalry between members of the same group. It is possible within a group for 'win–lose' situations to arise. This happens when a group member or members pursue their views, opinions or preferred course of action so singlemindedly that they ride over all opposition. If this occurs, then they can finish feeling satisfied themselves, but having alienated others in their group. As a result of this, what can happen is that the 'losers' feel so resentful that they feel less enthusiasm for future sessions, less inclined to co-operate on future tasks; and they may even be so upset that they will 'sabotage' what the 'winners' may want to achieve subsequently. 'Losers' may need to re-assert themselves to such an extent that group unity is destroyed.

A teacher may help groups therefore by increasing members' awareness of the desirability of achieving objectives without alienating individuals *en route*. Being able to perceive when 'win–lose' situations are beginning to arise is the first task. Being able at that point to adjust positions and work for 'win–win' outcomes is an important skill to develop in group members. Majority decisions or agreements are tempting to go for, but they may often be less of an achievement than consensus, in which everybody feels they have been involved, considered, and have gained something of what they wanted.

Leadership behaviour

The lifeskills approach places enormous importance on the role model offered by the teacher in the classroom. There are a great many versions of what exactly a 'good teacher' is and we would like to identify here the approach to teaching and group leadership that is most compatible with the objectives of increasing personal competence generally, and working for the empowering of those whom one is teaching.

The teacher will be visible to students mostly in a leadership position in the classroom, and what we would like to outline are the kind of teacher/leader behaviours that are most consistent with

172

developing interpersonal skills in students and working for their empowerment.

We are placing great emphasis on behaviours—the things that a teacher says and does—because that is what will be significant for the students. They cannot read the teacher's mind, or telepathically tune into her beliefs or intentions. All they can do is observe what she says and does and make assumptions on the basis of that. Therefore, a teacher needs to turn her beliefs into actions, and ensure that these communicate whatever is central to what she wishes to teach.

We see that the teacher/leader's task is to *convey* to her students that:

1. she is genuine herself;
2. she believes in the students' importance, significance and potential;
3. she believes in their individuality and uniqueness, in their being different from her and from each other;
4. she wishes to help them to develop their potential, and she to develop her own, by increasing skills and acquiring new ones;
5. she wishes to increase their responsibility and capacity to influence their own lives and situations they are part of;
6. she sees everybody in the group, including herself, as a potential teacher/learner and wishes to work in ways that underline that;
7. she believes in giving the kind of help that will enable people to do things for themselves rather than the kind that can disable individuals by removing the need for personal initiative and self-direction;
8. she values personal autonomy used sensitively and with respect for the autonomy of others; independence within a framework on interdependence;
9. she sees herself as responsible for creating learning situations in which students can most effectively educate themselves; that is, her responsibility is directly related to theirs;
10. she wishes to help them search out and find their own understanding of themselves and their lives; to examine a range of values and to own those that have meaning for them; to ask questions and find answers that are theirs and not simply those that she may give; to begin to take charge of themselves and be responsible for their own development.

Given those tasks, the teacher will need to become specific about the behaviours she can use in the classroom which will be consistent with those intentions. Aspy and Roebuck (1977) have very clearly identified the teacher behaviours that are significantly related to student learning and motivation. It is clear from their research and our own experience that it is in situations in which a high level of interpersonal skill is demonstrated by the teacher that students learn best and present fewer behavioural difficulties. Consequently, we regard the guidlines we offer on teacher behaviour to be relevant not only to teaching in lifeskills sessions, but also as the basis of effective teaching and learning in any subject.

It is apparent, and the research confirms it, that people learn and prosper best in environments in which:

1. they are respected, valued and regarded as important and significant;
2. they feel they are understood and accepted rather than judged;
3. the people they relate to are genuine, real people who are not playing a role or manipulating them.

How then can the teacher create those necessary conditions in her classroom? We list below the behaviours that, in most situations, are likely to convey those vital messages. Teachers and their own groups may wish to produce their own versions of these lists.

How we might convey respect

● By taking trouble to consider the students and find out their interests and preferences, rather than simply imposing ours.

● By observing agreements or promises made, unless changing those can be justified and explained.

● By listening actively, being receptive and responsive to student opinions and ideas; asking questions that encourage thought and expression rather than giving answers oneself.

● By spending time with people when one has a choice, taking an interest in them as whole people rather than merely as students of one's subject.

● By recognizing and valuing student effort, involvement, and contribution and demonstrating that one does so; praising and strength-building.

● By looking positively at others and emphasizing what they do well rather than focusing on the negative; this can make a very real contribution to student motivation and achievement.

● By sharing power and influence, not making decisions for others but allowing them to make them for themselves; acting on

174

their decisions, not dominating a group by doing most of the talking or being keen to demonstrate one's expertise or greater experience.

• By disagreeing if one genuinely has to do so, but distinguishing between disagreeing with ideas and rejecting the person who has them. Therefore, disagreement should be allied to validation in other behaviours of the person with whom one disagrees.

• By avoiding negating or devaluing the person, ignoring, belittling, ridiculing, being sarcastic or putting him down.

• By showing warmth in one's words and behaviour towards the person.

• By not being condescending, patronizing, or talking down to one's students.

• By using appropriate language that does not exclude the person—jargon or 'expert' language can shut out others.

• By using people's names rather than the depersonalized 'you'.

• By taking trouble in preparing and presenting work for students, welcoming their participation and valuing the work they do.

• By helping without 'taking over', contributing without requiring ownership or most of the credit for any success.

• By not getting work done at the expense of the people doing it, regarding their welfare as a priority.

• By ensuring a welcoming, comfortable physical environment.

• By keeping to time, not keeping people waiting.

• By not prying or imposing, accepting a person's decision to do what she is comfortable with, at a pace that is appropriate for her.

• By asking them what makes them feel valued and making those things part of one's behaviour towards them.

How we might convey understanding

• By focusing on a person's feelings and not simply on his words, asking oneself how the person is feeling and experiencing the situation; by recognizing that the other person is different from us and will see the world differently; by trying to see things from the other person's point of view and showing in the comments we make that we are making this attempt.

• By asking a person's point of view—what she thinks, feels, prefers—and giving attention and status to her unique experience.

• By sharing one's own experience, which may be similar to the other person's, in a way that suggests you have something in common despite your personal uniqueness.

- By not making assumptions that you know what people are thinking, feeling, or would prefer, but checking out with them by asking.
- By acting on the basis of another's wishes, giving their preferences priority.
- By asking about their thoughts and feelings rather than simply asking questions requiring a factual response.
- By avoiding issues that may be sensitive for the other person, if he does not wish to raise them.
- By avoiding putting people in situations that would cause them loss of face.
- By giving extra time and attention on occasions when people have experienced something significant for them, to listen or share in their special happiness or sadness.
- By taking special trouble to do something that is important to the other person.

How we might convey genuineness

- By speaking openly and appropriately about ourselves, not pretending to be what we are not.
- By admitting weaknesses or mistakes, not presenting ourselves as omnipotent.
- By saying we do not know when asked a question we cannot answer, rather than attempting to cover up the gap in our knowledge.
- By being consistent and honouring contracts and promises.
- By avoiding unpredictable behaviours which could be uncomfortable or produce anxiety for others.
- By practising what we preach; by ensuring that our behaviours match our words.
- By being open rather than defensive or secretive.
- By confronting difficult issues if principles or values are at stake.
- By avoiding playing games or roles or hiding behind a facade that does not represent our real feelings, opinions, or preferences.
- By respecting confidentiality when somebody trusts us with information she does not wish others to know.
- By not discussing people with others in terms one would not be prepared to share with the people themselves.
- By acting in the interests of others when there is risk to oneself, or regularly 'taking trouble' to help others.

Translating the above possibilities into teacher behaviour in the classroom is obviously a different task for each teacher in each teaching situation, but the evidence is clear that, if these features became the norms of teacher–student contact, then there will be real gains in so many areas.

Observation of groups

As well as modelling the relationship-building skills he wishes to develop in the groups he is working with, the teacher is likely to require a high level of observation skills to monitor how those groups are working. Group leadership involves skilled perception of, and sensitivity to, the individuals within the group; and a teacher, besides using these skills himself, should also hope to develop them in the students. As the teacher operates mostly in an overall leadership role, he can use opportunities to give leadership positions to students in subgroups and even from time to time over the larger group. As they learn leadership skills, students will develop awareness of the difficulties of that role and this awareness may make them more receptive and appreciative as group members.

As well as the specific teaching objectives which are to do with the content of sessions, the teacher can hope, as a spin-off, that students will learn about leadership and about the processes and dynamics of groups at work. This learning will be transferable to other situations and we regard it as of major importance—so much so that we would recommend that the teacher should not simply hope that it will occur incidentally, but should directly introduce leadership and group observation opportunities for the students.

On the subject of leadership, this could involve teacher and student discussing at some point the following questions.

- What is good leadership?
- What different kinds of leadership are required in different situations?
- How can leadership be shared in a group?
- What kind of help and support does a leader need from her group?
- What kind of help and support does a group member need from a leader?
- If each member of the group wanted to be more of a leader, what behaviours could she use to help this happen?

In this way the teacher and the students can begin to consider some of the dynamics of groups at work and students can begin to appreciate what they need to be sensitive to as they work together on different tasks.

Awareness of group dynamics can begin to be taught by the teacher's giving time at the end of a session to consider some of the things he has observed as the groups worked. He is teaching that a group operates at two levels:

1. There is *what* the group is doing (i.e. the group's 'task').
2. There is *how* the group is working (i.e. the group 'process').

Therefore, at the end of any piece of group work there is an opportunity for members to focus on:

● What can we learn from the content of that session?
● What can we learn from the way we worked together?

In the early stages of developing student awareness, the teacher can begin by considering with the group the following basic process questions.

● Did everybody participate in the group's activity?
● Did members listen to each other?
● Were there examples of members supporting, helping, each other?
● What can group members be pleased about in the way they worked together?
● If they were to repeat the session, is there anything they could change to improve how they worked together?

As students become more aware and sophisticated, the teacher can begin to invite them to take turns observing their groups at work. He can help them to look for what he is looking for as he works with groups. This is likely to cover:

1. participation;
2. influence;
3. individual styles;
4. decision-making;
5. the work and the people.

Participation
● What are the signs that people are involved/not involved/excluded?
● Who participates most/least? Are there any apparent reasons for this?
● Does participation vary? Do individuals 'drop out' as the group works?
● Are any members silent? How does the group deal with these?
● Who talks to whom? Do members 'pair up', or is interaction distributed?

- How much do individual members:
  — give information to the group?
  — ask questions?
  — respond to what other members say?
  — agree with the comments of others?
  — disagree with others?
  — praise, support, or encourage others?
  — criticize others?
  — invite others to speak?
  — interrupt others who are speaking?

Influence

- Which members seem to influence the group most? Whose ideas or behaviours seem to be most important to others? Who is listened to most? Whose suggestions are followed?
- Does the group have an appointed leader? Is that leadership accepted or resisted? Are there other leaders in the group? How do they display leadership? Who accepts their leadership? Does leadership change as the group works? Is there rivalry for the leadership? How does the group react to this?
- Does the group appear resistant to, or unaware of, any particular member's or subgroup's ideas and contributions?

Individual styles

- Does anyone attempt to impose ideas on the group or push others to support his views or decisions?
- Does anyone attempt to block the ideas of others? How is this done?
- Who co-operates with others or tries to get members to work together?
- Does anyone seem to look for ways to differ from the rest of the group or to seek conflict?
- Does anyone avoid conflict or any signs of disagreement; smoothing over problems or changing the subject when difficulties occur?
- Does anyone seem to specialize in either positive comments or negative comments, praising or criticizing others?
- Does anyone seem uninvolved or ready to agree with anybody without seeming to have strong views of his own? Does anybody wait to be asked before offering comment?
- Does anyone seem particularly helpful in solving problems that arise, in considering the views of others, in helping the group to work together?

179

Decision-making

- Does the group make any decisions? If so, about what?
- How does the group make decisions:
  — by majority decisions?
  — by a minority overruling others?
  — by working for unanimous agreement?
  — in other ways?
- Does decision-making, if it happens, divide the group? Do some seem to 'win' and others 'lose'? How do the 'winners' treat the 'losers' and vice versa?
- Does the group seem united at the end of its work?

The work and the people

- Did the group accomplish its task? If not, why not?
- Did the group stick at its task or was it side-tracked from time to time?
- If the group did achieve its task, who and what helped it to do this?
- Did the group have an agreed procedure, or did members make suggestions about how to work as they went along?
- Did anyone keep a check on progress by summarizing from time to time, indicating what had been dealt with and what remained to be done?
- How aware of each other were group members as they worked together? Did they use each others' names or refer to each other? What were the signs, if any, that they were listening to each other?
- Did members support, encourage, praise each other? Did members criticize each others' ideas or ignore them? Was any member personally abused or put down? If so, what were the effects of these behaviours?
- Were there any behaviours that drew group members closer together as a group or any that seemed to divide them?
- Were there any indications of the feelings of group members? Did members seem interested, bored, involved, withdrawn, angry, irritated, happy, excited, warm, friendly, defensive, shy, competitive, etc? Did members express positive or negative feelings? If so, what were the results of that?

On the basis of such analysis, teachers and students will be able to become a useful resource to the groups they observe and to the members of those groups. They will be a source of feedback to the whole group and to individuals within the groups. Again, by modelling how to give feedback, the teacher will be teaching the students some very important skills. We think feedback is essential in helping groups and group members learn more about how they operate and about themselves individually. We also think that that feedback has to be given skilfully. This will more likely be achieved if the following rules are observed.

1. *Feedback should be offered rather than imposed.* The teacher or observer is there to assist the group and its members; he is not there in a God-like role, sitting in judgement, deciding what is right or wrong. He can *offer* his observations, but may not tell the observed what they should or ought to have done or not done. Feedback should be offered in a way that leaves the recipients with a choice of whether to accept it or not.

2. *Feedback should be descriptive rather than evaluative.* The observer can describe what he saw and heard. Terms therefore such as 'that was good/bad/awful/terrible/brilliant/destructive, etc.' are interpretations or assumptions made on the basis of observed behaviours and are better avoided. The observer is not making a psychoanalytical assessment of the group or its members, and should offer descriptions of what he observed rather than his assessment of its underlying meaning.

3. *Feedback should be specific and should refer to features or behaviours that can be changed.* For a group to be told they displayed a great deal of 'teamwork' may be very encouraging for them, but it is not as helpful possibly as being told what they did that was labelled 'teamwork'. If the observer can be specific and say, for example, that he saw members sharing out the task and all getting involved, that they gave each other help and support as they worked, that everybody kept in touch with each other rather than doing his own thing, etc., then the group can identify features they can repeat on other occasions. It is also not very useful to give feedback on matters over which people have no choice. For a group to be told it is too small or it would have been better 'had they had more comfortable chairs' is not helpful if they had no choice.

4. *Feedback should emphasize the positive rather than the negative.* There is a tendency in our culture to focus on the mistakes that people make rather than praising what they do well. We would like to challenge that trend and emphasize strength-building as an approach to education. To be told what one does well, to have that strength reinforced, is likely to establish that behaviour in one's repertoire and contribute to the development of a positive self-concept. Recognizing one's strength is likely to give one a

181

sound basis on which to develop others. If positive feedback is given, one is much more likely to listen to, and be able to use constructively, any negative feedback there might be.

5. *If negative feedback is given it should include a positive suggestion.* It is sometimes easy to criticize another's behaviour or performance. If one is to do that, then we think it is helpful not simply to point out what one observed that was not useful, but also to add what the person might have done instead. In this way, one is turning the negative into a positive, which the recipient may be able to use on another occasion.

6. *The person giving the feedback should take responsibility for it and the feedback should be checked out with others.* Sometimes it is possible to suggest in the way we speak to others that we are in a position to give an objective, detached judgement about them. We may say, '*You* are unfriendly' or '*You* are sarcastic', etc. By beginning our statement with '*You are* . . .' we suggest that the judgement is accurate, infallible, true of other times and other places, and shared by everybody else. In fact, all we may be entitled to say is that that is how *we* experienced that person at a particular time. Therefore, it can help to begin feedback with the word '*I* . . .' (e.g. '*I* heard you reject Jim's request for help and I thought that was unfriendly.') I can only ever speak for me, and any feedback I give, therefore, or any feedback anybody gives, should be checked out against other people's views or experience. It is also useful to recognize (especially when we write school reports!) that any feedback given is likely to say as much about the giver as it is about the receiver. Any statement I make about another person will also say a good deal about my personality, values, anxieties, prejudices, etc.

Feedback skilfully given, gives individuals more information about themselves and more options on choosing behaviours that will achieve what they wish to achieve. Through feedback, groups and individuals are helped towards greater awareness of themselves, and it should therefore become an integral part of group work. Each group, and each group member individually, at the end of a session should be able to identify:

1. what I/we liked about the way I/we worked in that session;
2. what, if anything, I/we might change if I/we were to do the session again;
3. one thing I/we will remember next time we work together.

To help students develop more awareness of how individuals

and groups function, the teacher/group leader can introduce a simple observer's checklist such as that in Fig. 5.12.

Fig. 5.12 Observer's checklist

Group _____ (Name or number)

Group task _____

Time and place of session _____

	Names of members								Totals
Behaviours observed									
Suggesting ways of working									
Giving information									
Asking questions									
Agreeing with or supporting somebody									
Disagreeing with somebody									
Personal criticism or conflict with somebody									

Inviting somebody to comment									
Interrupting or shutting up somebody									
Summarizing what has been said or achieved									
Use of humour									
Individual totals									Group total behaviours

In using a checklist like this, the observer will write the name of each group member at the top of a column and watch the group at work. As each person speaks, the observer decides into which category the person's comment most fits and puts a small mark (/) in the appropriate space. More sophisticated checkmarks can be used as observers become more experienced, e.g., X for a comment lasting more than 30 seconds, O for one lasting longer than a minute, etc. It is better, however, to build up observation skills in the students gradually. For beginners, it could suffice simply to list the names of group members and place a tick next to a name each time that person speaks. This would indicate the proportion of contributions made by each person against the total for the group.

The more advanced version of checklist can be a useful source of feedback for group members because it can show:
1. the amount each person contributes verbally to the group session;

2. the style of that contribution (e.g., a group member can find out how much she gives opinions as against asking others to speak, how much she supports rather than criticizes, etc.);
3. how balanced participation is in the group;
4. whether the group is supportive rather than critical;
5. how leadership was exercised and by whom (there can be a very useful discussion with the group as to whether some of the behaviours on the checklist would be more the responsibility of the leader than anybody else);
6. the proportion of contributions that were to do with the task, against those that are to do with members' relationships with each other (again, the group should consider which of the behaviours contribute to getting the job done and which to helping and involving each other).

On the basis of this information, groups and individuals can decide whether and what they might want to change about the way they work. Seeing a whole series of such checklists, a person can probably see consistent patterns of her contribution which can be described as a personal style; e.g., one person may realize that almost every contribution she makes is to give information. Rarely, if ever, does she ask questions or invite another member to speak. Being aware of that, she may want to experiment and introduce some of those behaviours. It is important to remember that there are no rights or wrongs indicated on the checklist. All the checklist does is indicate certain behaviours that will have an effect on the group and its members. It will be for each member to ask:

- Am I happy with the way I work in groups?
- If so, fine! If not, what would I like to change and how will I do it?

The group can face the questions:

- Are we happy about how we work as a group?
- If so, fine! If not, what would we like to change and how do we do it?

Coping with difficult members

Sometimes teachers are reluctant to start group work because they foresee the difficulties that certain individuals will create in the group situation. They look at the possibilities and decide 'It will never work with that student!' They may be right! There is never an approach that will work for everybody. We do maintain that there are tremendous gains to be made for the majority in this style of work, but there will remain a small minority of students whose

185

behaviour, on occasions, in some groups, will produce difficulties. There is no blueprint to come to the rescue in every one of those situations, but we hope there can be some benefit in considering here the types of group member who is difficult to cope with and some of the options that it might help to think about to help cope with those difficulties.

Some preliminary thoughts

● When labelling a member of your group as 'difficult', what do you actually mean? What actually happens? Can you describe the behaviours being used, and the frequency and regularity of them? (i.e., is the person often like that, or on just some occasions, with some people, in some places, doing some kinds of work?)

● Whose problem is it? Describe the effects of the 'difficult' members' behaviour on:

— *yourself:* how do you feel? How do you respond and behave? Is there anything you or anybody else does that seems to cause or reinforce the difficult member's behaviour? Would any change in *your* behaviour help at all?

— *other group members:* do they seem to experience difficulties from the member in question? If so, what are these? How do you feel and react? (You may need to check this out!) Do they seem to be hurt or damaged?

— *the group task:* does the difficult member's behaviour prevent the group achieving its task, or is the effect limited, irritating rather than a major hindrance?

— *the difficult member himself:* is the person gaining or losing by the behaviour? There is likely to be a reward or a 'pay-off' for all our behaviour, even though what that is may not readily be apparent (e.g., some students will risk and invite the direst punishments because that will bring attention and notoriety, which for them is preferable to being ignored or discounted). If we can recognize what the pay-offs are for the difficult member, we may be able to deny him them, or possibly to find another way of his getting what he wants without having to be disruptive.

● What would you like to change? How would you like things to be different?

— Can you establish with the individual what it is specifically that you would like him to do differently?

— Can you offer help towards that change and find reasons, in

the person's own interests, that might make him willing to attempt the change?
— Can you change any of your own behaviour in a way that could help that person?
— Can the group he is a member of make any changes that would help him?
— Can a contract be established which will identify what is required? Who will do what, and at what stage will progress be reviewed?

It is sometimes helpful to consider, when labelling somebody as 'difficult', that there will be occasions when others experience *us* as that. Some people seem to be more generally difficult than others, but we will do well to realize that each of us is potentially or actually difficult to others sometimes. When we are describing somebody as 'unco-operative', we might dwell upon the times when we are reluctant to co-operate with others. What is it that results in our behaving in that way on that occasion? If we can be aware of the factors that influence our own behaviour, then these may be clues to understanding the behaviour of others and to avoiding creating situations that may trigger off difficulties. It can also help to realize that sometimes other people are like they are because we are like we are. Their behaviour can be a reaction to things we say or do not say, do or do not do. It can help to promote changes in others, therefore, if we are prepared to analyse the effects of our own behaviour and to adapt some of them if it will help.

However, it is likely that teacher/group leaders will continue to experience difficulties with some types of students, and we would like to consider in Fig. 5.13 what those types might be and what optional responses might help. It is important for the teacher/group leader to be aware of the balance to be struck between the welfare and development of the individual, the welfare and development of others in the group, and the importance of achieving the group's objectives. In attempting to link all of those responsibilities, it is likely at some point to be difficult to reconcile all of them. Sometimes one group member may behave in such a disruptive and damaging way that other members, or the group tasks, suffer to an unacceptable extent. At such a point it is likely to be necessary to exclude that member, until such time as he changes the behaviour that is causing the difficulty, so that other members of the group are not damaged or continuously frustrated in what they are reasonably trying to achieve. The teacher will need to do further work, giving specific feedback and identifying how the person may rejoin the group when specific behavioural conditions are agreed between the person, the teacher and the group.

Fig. 5.13 Coping with difficult group members

Difficult type of group member	Possible ways of coping
Silent	— Have equal/shared time exercises. — Pair with friend or place in group who will provide support and encouragement. — Give preparation time so that he has time to think and work out something to say. — Direct questions to him or invite him to comment directly. — Give feedback out of group and check out reasons. Respond appropriately to any difficulties. — Support any contribution as an encouragement. — Make task more relevant to him. — Accept his silence if he is happy with it and that is how he wants to be. — Give time for him to build up confidence.
Too talkative or dominant	— Avoid eye contact. — Share time in group. — Give a task, like recording, or writing up on flip-charts, etc., to reduce talking time. — Give feedback. Use observer's checklist to support. Praise willingness to contribute, but point out effect of reducing the contribution of others. Invite individual privately to give less himself and encourage others—i.e. a leadership role. — Pair or place in group with others of similar style so that they will cancel each other out.

Fig. 5.13 Coping with difficult group members (continued)

Difficult type of group member	*Possible ways of coping*
Bored, withdrawn	— Introduce participatory exercise or procedure. — Vary the 'menu'; include features that might appeal to him. Let him choose topic. — Give a task—observer, recorder, timekeeper, etc. — Offer optional work; make attendance in group a matter of choice. — Give feedback; check out feelings and reasons. — Pair or group with friends. — Provide stimulating, lively teaching materials or procedures. — Take any opportunity to support any indications of involvement.
Aggressive	— Identify specific issues that may cause this. Focus on the reasons for strong feelings. Talk it out. Let him 'get it off his chest'. Adjust anything causing difficulty if that is appropriate. — Give feedback afterwards; point out effect of behaviour on others. Say what would be preferable. — Avoid retaliation and escalation. — Employ ground rules which 'outlaw' aggressive-type behaviours. — Place in group with teacher. — Teach conflict resolution strategies; invite the person to begin comments to others with something positive. — Exclude from group if difficulty continues and other members of the group are being hurt.

Fig. 5.13 Coping with difficult group members

Difficult type of group member	Possible ways of coping
Reluctant attender	— Give option of other work. Make attendance in group voluntary. — Allow some choice in what the group undertakes. — Use warm, friendly behaviour; give the person support. Encourage other members to do the same. — Check out with person why there is reluctance. Find out whether the person's 'needs' can be met by the group. — Give the person some task or responsibility. — Allow to work with friends.
The 'clown'— causes disruption through inappropriate use of humour	— Confront the behaviour. Give feedback on behaviour and its effect. Be specific about how the person might behave more appropriately. — Use group members as a source of feedback and agree on ground rules that 'outlaw' disruptive behaviour. — Have group discussion on the use and misuse of humour. — Be patient. It may take time for a person to change behaviour pattern. — Place in group that will not reinforce the behaviour by providing an audience.
Less articulate	— Allow time to gain confidence. Build confidence by encouragement and supportive behaviour. Encourage group to do this. — Select appropriate topics and methods; more active than verbal work can help. — Ensure that language used in group is appropriate. Place with similar types.

Fig. 5.13 Coping with difficult group members (continued)

Difficult type of group member	*Possible ways of coping*
	— Give time to prepare. Help with preparation. Work one-to-one on skill development outside the group. Use shorter sessions to reduce pressure.
Shy	— Place with friends. — Avoid over-attention, but encourage by supporting contribution. — Work one-to-one afterwards, encouraging the person to experiment with making small contributions to begin with. — Allow time for person to develop confidence.
'Distracter'	— Give feedback on behaviour and its effect, and indicate specific changes that the person might make in behaviour. — Provide alternative to presence in group. — Place in group that is unlikely to reinforce or welcome distraction. — Place in group with teacher, and seat in position that allows most supervision. — Identify how the person could improve behaviour step by step. Reward each sign of progress. — Remove potential sources of distraction in physical setting. — Exclude, if effects are severe for others, or employ 'sin-bin' (miss a session) method from time to time.
'Teacher's pet' (always trying to please or get teacher's attention)	— Give person attention at other times, but give feedback on how behaviour is sometimes inappropriate. — Place person in group in which teacher is not available.

Fig. 5.13 Coping with difficult group members (continued)

Difficult type of group member	Possible ways of coping
	— Ignore behaviour and it may eventually go away. — Reward signs of independence and encourage contacts within peer group.
Especially vulnerable (individuals at risk from time to time)	— Place in most supportive group and situation. — Avoid topics or procedures that may highlight person's 'risk'. — Provide alternative activity at sensitive times. — Place in group with teacher/group leader. — Have clear ground rule so that group members do not have to do things which they prefer not to do.

Closing a session

As a culmination to managing (a) the task, (b) the group, and (c) the time, the leader will need to ensure as the session concludes that any learning or achievement is consolidated and that group members have a sense of having reached an acceptable and satisfactory stage of conclusion if not of the completion of all they are working upon. This is likely to be achieved if the group leader gives attention to the following:

● The group should be kept informed of the time remaining at various stages during the session, but particularly during the last fifteen minutes.

● The group should be helped to focus on its objectives for the session so that members are aware of what has been done as well as of what remains to be done.

● Time should be allowed at the end of a session for tying-up loose ends, so that students experience a collective, controlled final stage, rather than a fragmented, ragged disintegration of the group and the session.

The loose ends are likely to be neatly tied if the following things are done:

● Group members should be given some time to focus on what has been learned, gained or achieved during the session. The leader, or a group member, may give a summary which focuses on the main points, or members can be asked to work in pairs for a couple of minutes to exchange their own review of the session. The summary or review can be structured to cover what was learned from *what* we did (the task) and what was learned from *how* we did it (the process).

● The action required as a follow-up to the session, and individuals who will have the responsibility for it, should be clearly identified.

● Notice should be given, if appropriate, of what the next session will involve and what preparation members may need to make for it.

● Any 'unfinished business' (work which is incomplete or issues raised but not dealt with) should be recognized and an indication given of when and how this will be dealt with.

● Time should be given for members to comment upon or give reactions to the session if they wish to do so.

● Individual members who have a co-responsibility for work arising from the session should have time to make their arrangements with each other to undertake that.

● Members should have a chance to 'check-out' or clarify anything about which they are unsure.

● Members should have time to think about what follows for them immediately after the session, so that they can focus on what they may require or what may be required of them by whatever is next on the timetable.

Finally, it will help enormously to close a session on as positive a note as possible. If the leader is able to comment, *genuinely*, on what has been achieved, on strengths observed in the group, on signs of progress or development, or, indeed, any positive feature of the session, then to focus the attention of the group on this is likely to have a reinforcing, encouraging effect on the members and invite similar, or even higher, standards of achievement in subsequent sessions.

5.9 Stages of group development

Sometimes difficulties occur within groups working together that are not simply due to individual students being awkward and disruptive. As they learn to work together, students will develop new skills and will experiment with those skills. In this way, the teacher/group leader will be able to introduce more and more sophisticated work as the students become more experienced. Along the route to becoming experienced, however, groups, as distinct from individual members, are likely to pass through definite stages, which will be identifiable by quite definite features.

The stages will probably approximate to the following (Tuckman, 1965).

Stage 1: The 'forming' stage
The students may:
— attempt to define the nature and boundaries of their task;
— grumble about features of the task or the setting;
— attempt to intellectualize or begin to talk about irrelevancies;
— exchange information;
— do little real work;
— appear suspicious of the task or each other;
— test relationships with teacher and each other;
— be dependent on leader;
— attempt to organize each other;
— participate hesitatingly; get involved or withdraw.

Stage 2: The 'storming' stage
The students may:
— begin to question the value of what they are doing;
— challenge the teacher/group leader, the work and methods;
— begin to display hostility, aggression, or frustration, and experiment with these behaviours;
— resist work that involves self-disclosure, and appear defensive;
— display tension, rivalry with each other, opposition, rebellion, and argument;
— become either very active or passive.

Stage 3: The 'norming' stage
The students may:
— begin to be more open with each other and invite each other to be more open;
— begin to express feelings constructively;
— begin to redefine the task and help rather than hinder the work;
— ask and give opinions and decide the value of contributions in terms of achieving the task;
— begin to feel like a group and be clear about how they will work;
— develop special relationships;

— co-operate more and give mutual support;
— be clear about leadership and cease to challenge;
— become concerned about unity and consensus;
— develop an in-group feeling which reduces interest in what is going on elsewhere.

Stage 4: The 'performing' stage
The students may:
— really pursue the task and work keenly and effectively for its accomplishment;
— contribute highly and invite each other to do so;
— show greater insight into and understanding of their task;
— not deal with interpersonal issues, as these have been resolved or placed second to the task;
— feel safe, confident and certain of 'where they are' and what they are doing;
— work very effectively and make real achievements.

A teacher/group leader aware of these stages will be able to monitor the development of groups he is working with and help them to work through the difficult, formative stages. With patience and skill, difficulties that arise can be dealt with and groups can be helped through to the stage in which members can experience the satisfaction and pleasure of being part of a fully functioning group.

It will be important to build in the possibilities of success and achievement to assist the group's development, as experiencing these will weld the members more closely together, more quickly. The teacher should ensure that within each session groups can recognize some accomplishment, can make a significant contribution to maintaining motivation and a sense of purpose.

In recognizing the stages, the teacher is less likely to become discouraged if, at times, little progress seems to be being made by his groups. Patience and persistence at those times, encouragement and support for the groups that are struggling, helping them to understand any difficulties and to remedy them, is likely to bring its reward for the teacher in the pleasure that comes from seeing development occur as a result of her skills and efforts.

5.10 Following up a group session
The effective teacher/group leader's task is not complete with the end of any group session because there is likely to be some follow-up work to be done. It will be important to ensure that this is done if group motivation is to be maintained; it can be very

discouraging for groups to put real effort into producing work which is then not rounded-off or finalized. Following up what remains to be done after a group session can be a way of recognizing the value of the group's efforts and is likely to make them more prepared to invest themselves in further work. What remains to be followed up will differ with each group but the areas needing attention can include the following:

- Individual students may need to be seen as a result of issues that it was not appropriate to deal with in the group (e.g., checking out students who seem particularly subdued, or who have indicated in comments they have made that they may benefit from further contact).
- Individual students may benefit from personal feedback given one-to-one.
- Individual students about whose feelings or reactions the teacher/group leader is unsure may need to be checked out.
- Those individual students from whom the teacher/group leader might wish feedback, should be seen.
- Action plans, agreements or promises of action made during the group session will need to be completed.
- Students' flip-charts will need to be typed up and duplicated for distribution to group members.
- Student work may need assessment if that is appropriate.
- Teaching materials used by the teacher should be filed away, with additional comments made on any development or adaptation made during the session, so that these will be available for use on other occasions.
- Any equipment borrowed for the session should be returned.
- Work area will need to be restored to its former layout, or to the condition required by the next session.

If possible, the teacher should give responsibility for some of the follow-up tasks to the student group members. This will convey yet again that the work of any group involves sharing and co-responsibility.

5.11 Evaluating the work

At the end of any piece of work, it is obviously necessary to attempt to assess its value. This will mean that future work can build on its success or be redesigned to improve on what was not so effective. Evaluation will be most meaningful if it relates to the teaching/learning objectives one had in setting up the experience. The questions one has to address are therefore:

- What did I wish to teach my group in terms of information? skills? attitudes?
- Did I have any additional objective (e.g. to make the learning interesting and enjoyable, to give further experience of working in groups? What were they?
- Did I have any objectives for particular individuals in the group (e.g. to encourage a quiet student to contribute, or to give special support to a student who was at risk)? What were they?
- Did I have any objectives for myself (e.g. to become more confident in managing subgroups, to manage the timing more effectively)? What were they?
- Did members of the group have any declared objectives (e.g. to enjoy the session or learn a particular skill)? What were they?
- Were the objectives achieved?

How can I measure whether the different objectives were achieved?

By being clear about what one would regard as the criteria of effectiveness

In terms of skill objectives, one might expect students to behave in particular ways which would indicate skill acquisition. If one wished students to have learned certain facts, then one will have to decide how to check that the knowledge has been gained. Attitudinal development will most likely be judged on the evidence of behaviours that would suggest the attitudes one had wished students to have. So for each of the questions above, the teacher should be able to list the objectives pursued and write down for each one what would indicate for her that those objectives had been satisfactorily achieved.

Once one has established *what* evidence of effectiveness one is looking for, one can decide *how* one will collect it, and from *whom*.

How can I measure what has been achieved?

By observation

The teacher and others will be able to monitor behaviour of group members during and following sessions, and, if they are clear what would indicate progress for them, may be able to observe evidence of it. The behaviour of group members after a session will indicate a good deal about the way they experienced the learning. After sessions they have enjoyed they are likely to want to stay around and chat; if they have had a negative experience they are more likely to leave quickly. Whether students talk about sessions

197

afterwards, and in what terms, can also indicate what they got out of it.

There will be many clues in the non-verbal behaviour of the students to how they experience sessions. Keenness to get into class, bright, expectant expressions, enthusiasm to get started, questions about what work will be coming up next time, etc., are all likely to indicate that the work is being well received.

Apart from the teacher and the students directly involved, there can be additional sources of feedback in other staff, other students, and parents of students. They are likely to be in a position to notice changes in behaviour or attitudes in members of the student group, and may be asked to look out for these if that is appropriate, and to give feedback on any developments they notice.

By formal feedback

Feedback can be gathered systematically after a session by asking all group members to comment upon:
1. what they think they have learned;
2. what they liked about the session;
3. anything they were not happy with or might want to change.

This feedback can be collected orally or written down. Students can even be asked to rate a session on the scales shown in Fig. 5.14.

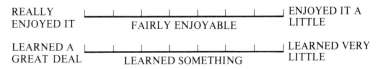

Fig. 5.14 Place a tick in the appropriate space to show how you experienced this session

If the rating is given anonymously, then one is likely to get an assessment that is not based on a wish to find favour, or on a fear of the consequences, and should therefore be a very useful guide.

By informal feedback

Casual comments by group members, other students, other staff, and parents are often very useful indicators of what kind of impression is being made by the work done in the group. Whether these comments are positive or otherwise will indicate perceptions that are around outside the group itself. There are limitations in this kind of feedback, because it will be expressed in terms of feelings, impressions or reactions of people who have not been involved in the experience themselves and may not even be in

198

sympathy with the educational objectives. It does underline the importance of contract-building with the system in which one is working so that these non-members are aware of the purpose and nature of the work. The more awareness there is, the more valuable the feedback is likely to be.

By testing

If one wishes to assess whether knowledge has been imparted or skills developed, then this may be checked by testing in some form or another if that is appropriate. Knowledge gained may be measured by oral or written test or by inviting some form of presentation by the learner. Skills acquired may be put to some test in real or simulated situations if that is desirable. Observers or closed circuit television may help the analysis and assessment of the skill performance and provide the learner with valuable feedback. A very useful test of what has been learned can be to invite the learner to teach somebody else. Having to pass on certain knowledge, or teach a skill one has acquired, is likely to be an excellent test of what one has understood or grasped.

Evaluating in stages

Evaluation carried out very soon after an educational event will have all the advantages of feedback that comes fresh from the experience, when those involved will be able to use their immediate feeling, thoughts, reactions, impressions, etc. It will also have some possible limitations simply because it is so instant. Fresh from an experience, students and teacher may have views and make responses that will subsequently evolve or change. Sometimes participants are 'too close' to an experience fully to assess its value. Immediate impressions have their worth; so does feedback given after participants have had longer to reflect, assess, practise, and test the significance of that experience. Evaluation procedures therefore should take into consideration feedback and assessment data collected at different stages after the event.

Once evaluation has been carried out, the findings may be of interest to others, e.g. the students, colleagues, or parents. If it is appropriate, and does not damage any contractual or ground-rule agreement, the teacher/group leader may find it useful to share the evaluation data with those who have an interest in the work, or who have provided feedback. Positive results will obviously be very reinforcing for all involved and the work will therefore gain credibility.

5.12 A final checklist

In using small group teaching methods, it is unlikely that any teacher will have the amount of time required to work and plan to the extent we indicate here. As teachers become more experienced they may be able to short-cut the amount of 'before and after' work that we have suggested should go into educational experiences if they are to be really effective. We agree with one teacher who, in considering the skills required to work with the small group method, said, 'It strikes me that the more "befores" and "afters" you have, the better your teaching is likely to be.' If there are to be short-cuts, therefore, they should not go beyond the point at which the session itself becomes merely a time-filler or just another item on the timetable.

We include, finally, in Fig. 5.15 a checklist which may help to reduce the task of ensuring that one has not omitted any significant step in setting up educational events involving small group work.

Fig. 5.15 Working with groups—teacher's checklist

Contracting questions

- What are my teaching objectives?
- What are the specific learning outcomes I wish for the student group in terms of:
  — knowledge gained?
  — skills acquired?
  — attitudes developed?
- What is my rationale for what I wish to teach and how will I present it to those involved or to whom it may be relevant?
- Who are the individuals or groups for whom the work may have implications and in what way can I provide for this?
- What contract will I wish to negotiate with:
  — the learning group?
  — any other individual or group?
  When and how will I do that?
- What is negotiable and what non-negotiable?
- Do I have a clear contract with colleagues, superiors, students, and parents?

Design questions

- Which student group am I designing for?

Fig. 5.15 Working with groups—teacher's checklist (continued)

- What do I want to achieve:
  — for the student group?
  — for individuals within the group?
  — for myself?
  — for anybody else to whom the work may relate?
- What do I know about the student group that may be relevant to the design?
- How will I make the work appropriate to that group?
- How much time do I have for the learning event?
- What will immediately precede and follow the event:
  — for the students?
  — for myself?
  What are the implications of that for my design?
- What will I do to produce the learning climate I require?
- How will I order and present the educational content of the session?
- What teaching materials will the session require?
- Which will be the most appropriate:
  — teaching procedures;
  — group structures;
  — sub-group composition?
- What additional equipment, if any, will I require?
- What will be the most appropriate way to start the session?
- How will I arrange the content and method of the session to give a sense of flow and variety?
- What will be the most effective way to close the session?
- Have I allocated time for each stage? Does the total match the time available?
- How will I make the most of the physical setting in which we will be working?
- What are my options if I find I need to energize the group at a certain point or relax and quieten them down?
- What will I need to do, or invite others to do, to prepare for the session itself? When will this be done?

Preparation questions

- What do I need to communicate to any relevant individuals or groups and how will I do this?
- How will I ensure I have all the necessary equipment and materials I need for the session?
- What arrangements do I need to make to the room I will work in so that it is suitable for the work I have designed?

Fig. 5.15 Working with groups—teacher's checklist (continued)

Managing questions

- What will I do to establish the appropriate learning climate?
- What will my leadership role be, and how will I ensure my behaviours are consistent with that role?
- How will I establish the contract and ground rules with the group?
- What will I need to be aware of, and do, at each stage of the work I have designed?
- What will I particularly give attention to in my observation of the group?
- What are my options if the behaviour of any group member produces difficulty?
- What rationale will I present to the group for each stage of the work?
- How will I ensure that I manage the time to best effect?
- How will I ensure that work or ideas produced by the group in the session will not be lost?
- To what will I particularly give attention at the close of the session?

Follow-up questions

- How will I ensure group action plans are followed through?
- How will I have the work produced by the group copied and returned?
- What will be left to attend to regarding:
  — returning or storing equipment?
  — putting room in order?
  — filing work or materials?
  Who will do it? When?
- What provision can I make for seeing individual students afterwards if that appears necessary?

Evaluation questions

- What will be my criteria for deciding whether the work has been effective?
- What will be my sources of feedback?
- How will I collect feedback or data for evaluation?
- To whom, other than myself, may the evaluation be of interest and, if appropriate, how will I inform them of the findings?
- What are the implications of the evaluation for future work?

Reading list

For further background and ideas on conducting classroom groups, we recommend the following books.

COREY, G. and COREY, M. S. (1977), *Groups: Process and Practice*, Brooks/Cole, Monterey, California.
Designed for group leaders with a description of appropriate behaviours with guidelines on how to deal with difficult members and how to select a group. Less classroom-oriented, but valuable information on group process.

GAZDA, G. (1971), *Group Counseling: A Developmental Approach*, Allyn & Bacon, Boston.
A basic book on group process with an emphasis on school counselling. Contains chapters on procedures for groups of pre-schoolers, children, adolescents, and adults.

JOHNSON, D. W. and F. P. JOHNSON (1975), *Joining Together: Group Theory and Group Skills*, Prentice-Hall, Englewood Cliffs, NJ.
Relates group theory to group practice by offering many exercises to be used with groups. Chapters on leadership, decision-making, use of power, problem-solving, communication within groups, the leading of discussion groups, and growth groups. Again, oriented towards a college population, but most of the exercises are adaptable.

MAHLER, C. A. (1969), *Group Counseling In The Schools*, Houghton-Mifflin, Boston.
Oriented towards secondary school groups, it deals with the nature of group counselling, the formation of the group, and the various stages of group development.

STANFORD, G. (1977), *Developing Effective Classroom Groups*, Hart, New York.
A practical guide for teachers, including activities and games designed to help students develop the skills of working together within a group development framework involving the stages of orientation, establishing norms, coping with conflict, productivity, and termination.

6. Lifeskills teaching— a guide to resources

Our original intention for this chapter was to provide a *Which?* style report on materials and books available for lifeskills teaching. Shortly after beginning the project we realized the impossibility of that task, and began to question even its desirability. What we have done instead is to provide descriptions of the resources, although we have included only items that have been positively referred to us by at least one source. Our own Lifeskills Teaching Programmes have been tested by nearly 100 teachers in schools and colleges in England, and part of that programme included a request for recommended resources which had been used to good effect by our evaluation network. We are most grateful to all those teachers that fed back information to us.

We have grouped the resources under the headings of our own lifeskills model (see page 25). In this way the gaps in provision become much clearer. We do realize that we will not have seen all possible materials, and we would be grateful if, for future editions, readers would inform us of resources they have used successfully.

Largely we have included material suitable for 14–18-year-olds of average ability level. When the materials diverge from this we have indicated in what way they differ. We have excluded resources designed for adults, although some of the resources described would themselves be suitable for lifeskills teaching with adults.

We have largely included resources that concentrate on developing awareness or, preferably, are actually intended to promote skills. Consequently resources that proffer information only—for example, choice of career booklets about specific jobs—are excluded.

We have included American resources where British ones were thin on the ground. We always indicate which are American and we do evaluate those. In spite of the differences in language and, occasionally, approach, we have found that some of the American materials, especially those designed to promote what is called 'psychological education' in the USA, are very adaptable to use here. We believe that many teachers who will want to do lifeskills teaching have the abilities to be able to make their own translations.

Sometimes we refer to a resource more than once. The full details are given for the first reference but subsequently only the title is given.

We have put the June 1979 prices for all materials, knowing that they date rapidly. This is to give a rough guide to how much comparatively the resources cost: the differences will remain, however much prices rise across the whole range.

We begin with a section on resources that are useful in general to teachers preparing to design and initiate lifeskills programmes in their schools. We end with a list of the addresses of all the publishers mentioned. This is particularly important for the American resources; these should be ordered directly and not through British bookshops, which often takes an eternity.

We have drawn an arbitrary line at 1970 for resources focused around general awareness-raising and skill development, but for items with heavy information content we rarely go back further than 1975.

Some of the large curriculum projects provide classification difficulties as they cover a variety of skills. We have placed them either in the general section or under the lifeskills heading where the main emphasis seems to be.

Source books and materials for teachers

AVENT, C. (1976), *Practical Approaches to Careers Education*, CRAC, £4.95.
A handbook of resources, practical ideas and suggestions.

BLYTHE, J., BRACE, D. and HENRY, T. (1978), *Teaching Social and Life Skills*, Association for Liberal Education, £2.50.
This is not a teaching package, but presents a set of broad aims appropriate to all social and lifeskills programmes.

BRANDES, D. and PHILLIPS, H. (1978), *The Gamesters' Handbook*, Hutchinson, £2.95.
140 games for teachers to enhance personal and social development. Some tips for running groups and organizing games in the classroom.

BUTTON, L. (1974), *Developmental Group Work With Adolescents*, Hodder & Stoughton, £2.10.

COIC. (1979), *Occupational Search List*, Careers and Occupational Information Centre, free.
An aid to careers advisers consisting of occupational titles classified according to interests and four ability levels.

C.O.I.C. (1975), *Thinking About Work*, Careers and Occupational Information Centre, £17.82.
23 overhead transparencies to be used as stimulus material for work with school-leavers.

COMMUNITY SERVICE VOLUNTEERS (1979), *Life Skills Training Manual*, Community Service Volunteers, £4.
A variety of classroom exercises gathered together under the headings of personal, family, community, leisure, and job. There is, in addition, a description of a range of teaching techniques and a collection of resource material—much of which is taken from previous CSV publications. The approach is modelled on the approach of the Saskatchewan project.

COOKSEY, G. (1974), *Pegs: The Guidance Planning Simulation*, CRAC, £14.72.
A planning board with 168 pieces representing a range of tutorial and guidance activities from which a selection must be made to produce a guidance programme. Can be used for training or in an actual school.

DAVIDSON, A. and GORDON, P. (1978), *Games and Simulations in Action*, Woburn Press, £5.95.
How to use games, role-playing, and simulation classroom exercises. Most of the games in the book are relevant to clarifying values and making relationships. Many mathematical games. An extensive bibliography under subject areas.

EIBEN, R. and MILLIREN, A. (eds) (1976), *Educational Change: A Humanistic Approach*, University Associates, £6.75.
American. A collection of readings of useful group techniques, psychodrama and role-playing, change strategies, suggestions for in-service training, and ways of creating the 'open classroom'. Valuable source book of ideas.

GORDON, A. K. (1972), *Games For Growth*, Science Research Associates, £3.20.
American. Excellent discussion of the use of games, teacher and student preparation, with an anthology of classroom games.

HAMBLIN, D. H. (1977), *The Teacher and Pastoral Care*, Basil Blackwell, £4.25.
One of the few skills-based books on pastoral care. Packed with ideas and practical tips for setting up guidance programmes and carrying out classroom-based skills development.

HAYES, J. and HOPSON, B. (1972), *Careers Guidance*, Heinemann, £2.20
A selection of self-assessment techniques, aids to job choice, and a questionnaire for assessing attitudes to women and careers.

HEALTH AND SOCIAL STUDIES CASSETTES, E.J. Arnold, £4.95 each.
Originally called Infotape, this series is designed to raise awareness and give information on some major problems facing young people—drug-taking, smoking, alcoholism, contraception, venereal diseases, violence, law and police, nutrition, hazards of modern living, human relationships, leaving school.

HOPSON, B. and HOUGH, P. (1973), *Exercises in Personal and Career Development*, CRAC, £5.00.
32 classroom exercises and three teaching programmes (of 8–10 exercises each) to raise awareness and to teach skills in the areas of sensing, thinking, feeling, and doing.

HOPSON, B. and SCALLY, M. (1980), *Lifeskills Teaching Programmes No. 1*. Lifeskills Associates, £14.95
Eight teaching programmes based on the philosophy and methods described in this book. An introduction is provided with tips on using the materials, all of which have been tested by almost 100 teachers in schools and further education colleges.

HOWDEN, R. and DOWSON, H. (1973), *Practical Guidance In Schools*, Careers Consultants, £2.00.
A practical guidance scheme for schools, outlining in some detail work that can be included in pastoral work in secondary schools.

JACKSON, R. (ed.) (1973), *Careers Guidance: Practice and Problems*, Edward Arnold, £1.90.
A collection of original articles on topics such as using occupational information, the careers library, records, assessment, careers conventions, school visits, the careers room, careers programmes.

PFEIFFER, J. W. and JONES, J. E. (1972–), *Annual Handbooks For Group Facilitators*, University Associates, £11.75.
American. A new volume each year, they are directed primarily to group leaders in industry and the social services. However, we can often find valuable ideas and techniques translatable to teaching lifeskills in schools, especially how to work in groups. Each volume has sections on instruments, structured experiences, lecturettes, theory and practice, and resources.

PFEIFFER, J. W. and JONES, J. E. (1975), *Handbooks of Structured Experiences For Human Relations Training*, University Associates, £2.95.
American. This is a continuing series. Each is packed with structured exercises, many of which can be adapted for classroom use. Particularly useful for communication skills, making relationships, working in groups, managing conflicts, and expressing feelings constructively.

PRIESTLEY, P., McGUIRE, J., FLEGG, D., HEMSLEY, U. and WELHAM, D. (1978), *Social Skills and Personal Problem Solving*, Tavistock, £4.95.
A handbook of exercises and teaching programmes designed to teach a variety of personal and social skills. Much discussion of the teaching skills required and organization of learning programmes.

SAX, S. and HOLLANDER, S. (1972), *Reality Games*, Macmillan, $8.95.
American. A compendium of over 50 games for personal growth. Oriented to adults, but still a useful stimulus book.

SCHOOLS COUNCIL PROJECT (1977), *Health Education (5–13)*, Nelson. Designed for use below secondary level but adaptable for older students. Comprises *All About Me* (£3.25), a guide for teachers in infant and junior schools offering information and teaching strategies for work on health (spiritmasters for student materials £3.95); *Think Well* (£13.50), eight units for the middle years of schooling with a teacher's guide (spiritmasters £4.95; resource sheets £8.50; combined pack, £26.95).

SCOTTISH COMMUNITY EDUCATION CENTRE (1979), *Social Education Kits*, Scottish Community Education Centre, £3 for all kits except 'Job Hunting' which is £8.
The kits cover job hunting (including a tutor's resource book); sex and the sexes; a place to live; money matters; good health; drugs, drink and tobacco; carry on learning; rights and obligations. There are exercises, cartoon leaflets, and aids for group discussion.

SWINDON AND WILTSHIRE TEACHERS, *Record of Personal Achievement*, Curriculum Study and Development Centre, Swindon.
Materials produced by a group of teachers, employers, trade unionists, etc., to develop personal qualities in school-leavers. Designed for all abilities and including work on physical fitness, communication, self-presentation, etc.

TRAINING RESEARCH AND DEVELOPMENT STATION (1973), *Lifeskills Coaching Manual*, Department of Manpower and Immigration, Saskatchewan.
Lifeskills training programmes developed for adults in Canada presented in a trainer's manual.

WAY, B. (1967), *Development Through Drama*, Longmans, £1.75.
The skills of self-expression are developed through the games and role-plays described here. They will help students to identify their creative potential.

Me: skills I need to manage and grow
How to read and write; How to achieve basic numeracy
These areas are so huge and well known to specialist teachers of English and mathematics that there seemed to be little point in surveying them for this book. There is already considerable space within the curriculum and expertise available in all schools.

How to find information and resources
ILEA (1978), *Living In A City*, ILEA, £3.75.
A kit designed to develop communications skills relevant to young people living in London: finding a place to live, getting from place to place, getting and spending, spot of bother (a motorbike accident), yo-yo (solving problems through finding out about agencies and resources).

HOPSON, C., HOPSON, B. and HAYES, J. (1973), *Speedcop: A Game For Learning About Occupations*, CRAC, £5.40.
A board game for six to eight players to help them learn a way of analysing occupations based on the mnemonic SPEEDCOP.

How to think and solve problems constructively
ADAMS, J. L. (1974), *Conceptual Blockbusting: A Guide To Better Ideas*, W. H. Freeman, $4.95.
American. A valuable discussion of perceptual, cultural, emotional, and intellectual blocks to problem-solving. A variety of techniques to tackle these blocks and to develop creativity are described.

DE BONO, E. (1976), *Thinking Action*, Direct Education Services, teachers' notes £5.50; pupils' textbook 75p.
The CORT thinking lessons with a teacher's manual to explain how to use the materials.

209

PARFIT, C. (1976), *Pro's and Con's*, Hodder & Stoughton, £3.35.
Three packs of cards: 'So I Said'; 'Girlfriends and Boyfriends'; 'Problems'. Designed to stimulate class discussion about moral issues, problem-solving skills, and relationships. Teacher's notes. Also suitable for below-average ability.

PRIESTLEY, P. *et al.*, *Social Skills and Personal Problem Solving*.

SPIUACK, G., PLATT, J. and SHURE, M. (1976), *The Problem-Solving Approach To Adjustment*, Jossey-Bass, £9.50.
American. A description of the author's approach to teaching interpersonal cognitive problem-solving skills (ICPS). Accounts of the classroom teaching methods and the research they have done which evaluates these methods very highly.

How to identify my creative potential and develop it
FARMER, P. and ATTWOOD, T. (1979), *The Top Business*, E. J. Arnold, £9.85.
A tape–slide presentation which helps students explore their musical tastes.

How to manage time effectively
HOPSON, B. and SCALLY, M., *Lifeskills Teaching Programmes No. 1*.
Teaching programme: how to manage time effectively. Eight classroom exercises to help students identify priorities, save and manage their time, and discover how they spend their time at present.

How to make the most of the present
We were unable to find materials that would help develop this skill and would be pleased to learn of any that exist.

How to discover my interests
CROWLEY, T. (1974), *PIG—Pictorial Interests Guide*, CRAC, £14.85.
54 cards designed to help the less able to discuss and discover their interests and job preferences. Accompanying filmstrip. Teacher's manual describes a variety of ways of using the material including card games.

CROWLEY, T. (1976), *Occupational Check List*, CRAC, £3.00; spiritmaster £5.06; questionnaires £7.00 per 100.
An interests questionnaire requiring no special training; designed

for students of above-average ability. It relates occupational interests to sources of job satisfaction.

How to discover my values and beliefs

CROWLEY, T. (1976), *Crowley Occupational Interests Blank*, CRAC, manual £3.00; spiritmasters £6.32; questionnaires £7.00 per 100.
For third- and fourth-year students of average and below-average ability. Requires attendance on a CRAC training course.

HOPSON, B. (1976), *Personality: A Game For Learning About People*, Careers Consultants, £4.95.
A card game for six to eight players which invites them to share their beliefs and opinions with one another.

HOWE, L. W. and HOWE, M. M. (1975), *Personalizing Education*, Hart, $7.95.
American. Over 100 strategies for values clarification plus worksheets for students.

MARTIN, J. (1979), *Last Days*, E. J. Arnold, £9.85.
Tape–slide presentation to help students explore their beliefs about old age and death. A questionnaire tests students' general knowledge about old people, explodes some common misconceptions, and provides class assignments.

McPHAIL, P., CHAPMAN, H., and UNGOED-THOMAS, J. R. (1972), *Lifeline*, Longmans.
The result of the Schools Council Moral Education Project. A teacher's book, *Moral Education in the Secondary School* (£2.25), and a handbook on the practice of democracy by secondary school students, *Our School*. Students' materials designed to help them clarify beliefs, attitudes, and values: *In Other People's Shoes*, *Sensitivity*, *Consequences*, *Points of View*, *Proving the Rule* (five short books), *What Would You Have Done?* (six booklets posing moral dilemmas to students). Project materials pack £17.60.

RAINBOW, C. (1977), *Support Group*. 'Living Well', Health Education Council Project, Cambridge University Press, £4.00.
35 work cards which reflect the needs and preoccupations of adolescents. Students are requested to say how they would react in a variety of situations.

211

SIMON, S. B. (1974), *Meeting Yourself Halfway*, Argus, $4.95.
American. By one of the founders of the 'values clarification'
approach. 31 strategies for discovering one's values through daily
living. Excellent sourcebook.

SIMON, S. B., HOWE, L. W. and KIRSHENBAUM, H. (1972), *Values
Clarification*, Hart, $5.95.
American. 79 classroom exercises to help students clarify their
value for themselves.

VALETT, R. (1974), *Self-Actualization*, Argus, $3.95.
American. A personal workbook and guide to self-determination.
Exercises covering self-understanding, purpose, love, work, self-
control, tension reduction, self-confidence.

How to set and achieve goals
HOPSON, B. and HOUGH, P., *Exercises In Personal And Career
Development*.
Teaching programme: Life planning—8 exercises to help students
examine the way they are living now, encourage them to set new
objectives and make action plans to achieve those objectives.

How to take stock of my life
HAYES, J. and HOPSON, B., *Careers Guidance*.
Tests of self-esteem and self-appraisal.

HOPSON, B. and HOUGH, P., *Exercises In Personal And Career
Development*.
Teaching programme: Life planning—8 exercises to teach the
skills of personal re-evaluation to students.

How to discover what makes me do the things I do
ADAMS, C. and LAURIKIETIS, R. (1976), *The Gender Trap: A Closer
Look At Sex Roles*, Virago, £1.25 each.
Three books which demonstrate the ways in which we are shaped
into sex roles and behaviours, using cartoons, stories, newspaper
extracts, facts and figures, questions and subjects for discussion.
Book 1: *Education and Work*
Book 2: *Sex and Marriage*
Book 3: *Messages and Images*

COUSINS, J. (1979), *Taking Liberties: An Introduction To Equal Rights*,
Virago, £8.95.
A kit of 18 workcards and a guide to teachers for suggested use of

the material. The cards give information, encourage discussion, raise awareness.

CRAMPTON SMITH, G. and HARRIS, S. (1977), *Thinkstrips*, Longmans, 85p.
A pack of 10 comics and teacher's notes for class discussion with much information: 'It's Only Fair'—about sex roles; 'It'll Never Be The Same'—about having a baby; 'It's Your Round'—teenage drinking; 'Too Great A Risk'—contraception.

GROOMBRIDGE, J. (1978), *His And Hers*, Penguin, 80p.
One of the 'Connexions Topics' series designed to give information about sex-stereotyping and to raise awareness.

GUTTENTAG, M. and BRAY, H. (1976), *Undoing Sex Stereotypes: Research and Resources for Educators*, McGraw-Hill, £3.50.
American. An account of an attempt to counter sex-role stereotyping in primary and secondary schools. Packed with ideas, classroom exercises, and techniques.

JAMES, M. and JONGEWARD, D. (1975), *The People Book: Transactional Analysis For Students*, Addison-Wesley, £3.75.
American. For sixth-form level upwards. A clear exposition of the principles of transactional analysis in workbook form. The concepts of cultural and family scripting are dealt with very well.

JONES, A., MARSH, J. and WATTS, A. G., (1974), *Male and Female*, CRAC, £1.10; teacher's book £1.00; spiritmasters £3.45.
A workbook for students to explore the changing roles of men and women and to discover their own attitudes on this issue.

LINDSAY, J. (1978), *Who Do You Think You Are?*, E. J. Arnold, £9.85.
A tape–slide presentation to combat sex-role stereotyping. Spiritmasters are available.

SARGENT, A. G. (1977), *Beyond Sex Roles*, West, £7.90.
American. 58 exercises to explore sex roles and sexual identity, many of which could be translated for the classroom. Also, excellent articles on awareness, social change and personal change.

WHITE, B. (1977), *Non-Sexist Teaching Materials and Approaches*, New Childhood Press, £1.00.
An excellent book of resources from all over the world.

How to be positive about myself
CANFIELD, J. and WELLS, H. C. (1976), *100 Ways To Enhance Self-Concept In The Classroom*, Prentice-Hall, £4.55.

American. Although many of the exercises are geared to 6–12-year-olds, they are usually translated easily for use with secondary school students. An excellent handbook for teachers *and* parents.

HOPSON, B. and SCALLY, M., *Lifeskills Teaching Programmes No. 1.*
Teaching programme: How to be positive about myself. The skill area is defined and 11 exercises are described with the objective of enhancing self-esteem. This has been used successfully also with ESN groups.

How to cope with and gain from life transitions

HOPSON, B. and SCALLY, M., *Lifeskills Teaching Programmes No. 1.*
Teaching programme: How to cope with and gain from life transitions. The skill area is described and 13 classroom exercises are presented.

How to make effective decisions

B.P. EDUCATION SERVICE AND BATH UNIVERSITY SCHOOL OF EDUCATION (1976), *North Sea Challenge*, BP Education Service, £10.00.
A simulation game to develop decision-making skills. For more able senior students.

ESSO (1975), *Students' Business Game*, CRAC, £17.25.
For sixth-formers to understand how a business is run and to develop decision-making skills.

HOPSON, B. and HOUGH, P., *Exercises in Personal and Career Development.*
Teaching programme: Learning to make decisions—9 classroom exercises to teach decision-making skills.

LYNCH, M. (1977), *It's Your Choice*, Edward Arnold, £5.00.
Role-play to develop oral and mental skills, to teach decision-making, information processing, etc. For middle and upper forms of secondary schools. Materials in the form of a pack.

WATTS, A. G. and ELSOM, D. (1974), *Deciding*, CRAC, £1.10; teacher's notes £1.00; spiritmasters £14.37.
A British translation of a highly successful American programme for teaching decision-making skills in the classroom. Students work through a variety of individual and group exercises, questionnaires, and discussion topics.

214

How to be proactive
We were unable to find materials that would help develop this skill and would be pleased to learn of any that exist.

How to manage negative emotions
HOPSON, B. and SCALLY, B., *Lifeskills Teaching Programmes No. 1*.
Teaching programme: How to manage negative emotions. Description of the skill area and seven classroom exercises to develop the skills.

KRANZLER, G. (1974), *Emotional Educational Exercises For Children*, Cascade Press, £2.50.
American. A teaching programme designed to help students recognize and combat negative feelings. Based on Albert Ellis's rational–emotive therapy.

How to cope with stress
HOPSON, B. and HOUGH, P., *Exercises In Personal And Career Development*.
Teaching programme: Progressive relaxation. The skills of this technique are described and presented in a form to be used in the classroom.

HOPSON, B. and SCALLY, M., *Lifeskills Teaching Programmes No. 1*.
Teaching programme: How to cope with and gain from life transitions. Three of the exercises in this programme are specifically geared to stress management.

Teaching programme: How to manage time effectively. Developing the skills described in this programme are in themselves techniques for preventing stress.

How to achieve and maintain physical well-being
BALDWIN, D. (1979), *Healthwise*, Harrap, £1.30.
A workbook with cartoons and case studies for class discussion designed to illustrate the skills of healthy living.

CARRUTHERS, M. and MURRAY, A. (1977), *F/40: Fitness On Forty Minutes A Week*, Futura, 70p.
A book of exercises with the rationale firmly based on research studies.

CONSUMERS' ASSOCIATION (1978), *Which? Way to Slim*, Consumers' Association, £3.95.

A comprehensive guide to nutrition, ways of maintaining and reducing weight through diet and exercise.

HEALTH EDUCATION COUNCIL (1978), *Look After Yourself*, Health Education Council, free.
Booklet with accompanying wallchart, badge, and bookmark, which describes a schedule of exercises for increasing mobility, strength, and cardiovascular ability. Also contains a more advanced schedule using weights and tips on diet.

HEALTH EDUCATION COUNCIL (1979), *Looking After Yourself*, Health Education Council, free.
Based on the booklet *Feeling Great*, published in association with the BBC television series of the same name. Presents a variety of tests for assessing stamina, suppleness, and strength, three fitness tests, and do's and don'ts of diet, exercise, and life-style.

McPHAIL, P. (1977), *And How are We Feeling Today?* 'Living Well', Health Education Council Project, Cambridge University Press, £4.00.

SCHOOLS COUNCIL PROJECT (1978), *Health Education (9–13)*, Nelson.
Health education materials in eight units for ages 9–13.

How to manage my sexuality
COUSINS, J. (1979), *Make It Happy: What Sex is all About*, Virago, £2.95.

MAYLE, P. (1974), *Where Did I Come From?* Michael Joseph, £1.95.
Well-illustrated book for students to read—for below 12 years.

SCHOOLS COUNCIL PROJECT, *Health Education (9–13)*.
Units on 'Myself' and 'One Of Many' materials on sex education.

Me and you: skills I need to relate effectively to you
How to communicate effectively
HOPSON, B. and SCALLY, M., *Lifeskills Teaching Programmes No. 1*.
Teaching programme: How to communicate effectively. The area is described and six classroom exercises are presented to teach the skills.

KRUPAR, K. R. (1973), *Communication Games*, Free Press/Collier-Macmillan, £2.50.
A teacher's manual containing a variety of games and exercises to develop interpersonal communication skills.

216

WEBB, C. (1978), *Communication Skills: An Approach To Personal Development*, Macmillan, £1.75.
A worksheet for developing communication skills. Covers the skills of self-appraisal, making contact, meeting people—and includes reading skills, using the telephone, writing letters, going for an interview, filling in forms.

How to make, keep, and end a relationship

HOPSON, B. and SCALLY, M., *Lifeskills Teaching Programmes No. 1.*
Teaching programme: How to make, keep, and end a relationship. The skills are described and 10 classroom exercises are presented to develop the skills.

SCHOOLS COUNCIL PROJECT (1978), *Health Education (9–13)*, Nelson. Units on 'One Of Many' includes sections on making relationships.

How to give and get help

PATERSON, B. (1977), *'Help'*, Peacock Books (Penguin), £1.00.
Very helpful hints and pieces of information on legal rights, getting help, etc.

How to manage conflict

We were unable to find materials that would help develop this skill and would be pleased to learn of any that exist.

How to give and receive feedback

We were unable to find materials that would help develop this skill and would be pleased to learn of any that exist.

Me and others: skills I need to relate effectively to others
How to be assertive

GALASSI, M. D. and GALASSI, J. P. (1977), *Assert Yourself*, Human Sciences Press, £6.25.
American. Although intended for adults, a valuable source book for designing assertiveness training programmes for schools. There is a small section geared to schools. Many exercises are reproduced along with homework assignments.

HOPSON, B. and SCALLY, M., *Lifeskills Teaching Programmes No. 1.*
Teaching programme: How to be assertive. The skills are described and five exercises for classroom use are presented.

217

How to influence people and systems
We were unable to find materials that would help develop this skill and would be pleased to learn of any that exist.

How to work in groups
STANFORD, G. (1977), *Developing Effective Classroom Groups*, Hart, $10.95.
American. A practical guide of activities and games to help students develop the skills of working together as an effective group. Based on a sound theoretical model and packed with tips.

WATTS, J. (1976), *Interplay: General Studies Project*, Schools Council/Longmans, £7.00.
Box of 12 units including teacher's guide with role-play situations to develop skills of working in groups and to explore issues in the areas of work, family, revolution (politics), and a hospital role-play to explore conflict, discrimination, and working with others.

How to express feelings constructively
HOPSON, B. and SCALLY, M., *Lifeskills Teaching Programmes No. 1*.
Teaching programme: How to manage negative emotions. The first exercises teach the language of feelings.

How to build strengths in others
HOPSON, B. and SCALLY, M., *Lifeskills Teaching Programmes No. 1*.
Teaching programme: How to be positive about myself. Exercises 4, 5, and 9 are specifically geared to encouraging a positive climate in the class by teaching the skills of identifying the strengths of others.

Me and specific situations

1. Skills I need for my education
How to discover the educational options open to me; how to choose a career
BELL, P. B. and GALLAGHER, B. L. (1974), *Subject Scope*, CRAC, £1.20.
A guide to the first two years of Scottish secondary education for students and their parents. It presents a course of guidance combining information, self-assessment exercises, job games and advice on subject and career choice.

HOPSON, B. and HOUGH, P., *Exercises in Personal And Career Development*.

218

Teaching programme: SPEEDCOP—choosing an educational course. Nine classroom exercises to teach a framework for assessing courses.

MARCH, P. and SMITH, M. (1976), *Your Choice At 17+*, CRAC, £1.10.
A workbook for sixth-formers to prepare them to choose what to do after A levels.

SMITH, M. and MARCH, P. (1977), *Your Choice At 15+*, CRAC, £1.10.
A workbook to help students decide whether to stay on at school, leave school to get a job, or to go to a college of further education.

SMITH, M. and MATTHEW, V. (1972), *Your Choice at 13+*, CRAC, £1.10.
A guide for students choosing O-level and CSE subjects, to help them understand the long-term effects of their decisions. Teachers' notes.

How to study

BAKER, E. (1975), *A Guide To Study*, BACIE, £1.30.
Basic hints on how to study effectively.

BAMMAN, H. A. and BRAMMER, L. M. (1969), *How To Study Successfully*, Pacific Books, £1.50.
American. For sixth-formers with a large number of self-tests to diagnose study-habit weaknesses, with excellent tips on managing time, taking lecture notes, preparing for and taking examinations, improving reading habits, spelling skills, developing vocabulary skills, using the library, writing skilfully.

BUZAN, T. (1974), *Use Your Head*, BBC Publications, £1.85.
A useful resource book although geared mostly to adult learning.

CARMAN, R. A. and ADAMS, W. R. (1972), *Study Skills: A Student's Guide For Survival*, John Wiley, £2.00.
American. Aimed at sixth-form level. An excellent workbook, amusing, many examples, written as a programmed text covering listening, note-taking, remembering, improving reading and recall ability, reading textbooks, writing and researching short papers, taking examinations.

HAMBLIN, D. H. (1978), *The Teacher and Pastoral Care*, Basil Blackwell, £4.25.
The book contains a variety of instruments to help students identify

219

their study difficulties, with suggestions for teaching skills in the classroom to remedy these.

OPEN UNIVERSITY (1979), *Preparing To Study*, Open University, free.
For adults but still useful for classroom teachers who are interested in designing a study skills teaching programme of their own.

ROWNTREE, D. (1970), *Learn How To Study*, Macdonald, 65p.
Primarily for college students but adaptable. Describes the well-known SQ3R reading method.

2. Skills I need at work

HOWDEN, R. and DOWSON, H. (1979), *The School-Leaver's Handbook*, Careers Consultants, pack of 10 £9.00.
A workbook for school-leavers covering choosing a job, self-assessment, guide to agencies and resources, information on budgeting, etc.

MARTIN, C. (1974), *Working With Other People*, Hulton, 85p.
Awareness-raising for school-leavers about relationships in work situations.

SANDAY, A. P. and BIRCH, P. A. (1976), *Understanding Industrial Society*, Hodder & Stoughton, £3.95.
Students' books and teachers' guide, giving information and using simulation for more able senior students.

How to discover the job options open to me; how to find a job; how to keep a job; how to change jobs

ADAMSON, H. (1972), *Starting Work*, Industrial Society, filmstrips £12; slides £17.
What workers need to know about how industry works; multi-media pack for use with school-leavers.

ALLSOP, K. (1974), *Earning A Living*, Ginn, £1.60.
Information on the world of work for school-leavers.

ANSTIS, R. D., *et al.* (1979), *Practical Business Education—Book 1 and Book 2*, Macdonald & Evans, £3.50 each.
An integrated approach to the development of knowledge and skills relevant to careers in the business world.

BARBER, T., LANCASHIRE, R., STEWARD, J. and WHITE, P. (1977), *Work It Out—A Pack Of Resource Materials For Careers Education*, ILEA, £12.65.

Five activities containing material for 30 students working on different activities. Follow-up group discussions possible. Teacher's notes. Covers: 'self-assessment', 'fitting people to jobs', 'analysing advertisements and obtaining information', 'getting a job', 'starting work'. An audio-cassette by young workers is also available (£2.30 extra).

BARKER, W. (1974), (1) *Business World* and (2) *Money Matters*, Nelson, £1.35 each.
Information on how business works and on some consumer issues.

BLYTHE, R. (1974), *Work Experience Projects*, CRAC, Nos. 1–5 £7.49 each; No. 6 £3.30.
For fourth- and fifth-year students; each project unit provides material for a class of 30 working in pairs. The tasks involve literacy and numeracy skills, discussion and role-playing. The projects are (1) transport clerk; (2) receptionist; (3) printer's reader; (4) sales promoter; (5) policeman/woman; (6) bank cashier.

BRENNAN, W. K. and TANSLEY, A. E. (1976), *School Leavers Series*, E. J. Arnold, handbook 80p; work tasks spiritmasters £7.00.
A workbook covering a variety of aspects of starting work including a self-analysis section. Teacher's notes with the spiritmasters.

CAREERS CONSULTANTS (1978), *Where Do We Go From Here?* Careers Consultants, £5.00.
A set of information booklets on leaving school. Teacher's notes.

CHILDWALL PROJECT (1973), *Design For Living*, E. J. Arnold, £48.15.
A social studies course with five main themes: Responsibilities of adulthood, Understanding children, The world of work, Living today, The world around us. Each theme has a kit, teacher's notes, and material for 20 students. Some of this appropriate for students of below average ability.

CHRISTIAN EDUCATION MOVEMENT (1976), *Work: Topic Folder No. 2*, Christian Education Movement, 80p.
Information for class and group discussion about the facts of working life.

CLEATON, D. (1976, 1977), *Exercises In Careers Education*, Careers Consultants, £4.95; *Further Exercises In Careers Education*, Careers Consultants, £4.95.
A variety of careers education exercises.

221

COIC (1975), *The Sponge Mix*, Careers and Occupational Information Centre, £13.25.
Three filmstrips and tape presentations designed for average and below-average ability groups to introduce them to the idea of choosing a career. Worksheets are included and transcripts of the tapes.

COIC(1976), *Thinking About Work*, Careers and Occupational Information Centre, £16.75.
23 colour overhead transparencies which cover choosing and finding a job. Teacher's guide.

COIC(1977), *Job Families*, Careers and Occupational Information Centre, £19.50.
24 overhead transparencies complementing *Thinking About Work*; also using a cartoon approach to entry to employment and occupational interest groups. Teacher's guide.

CRAMPTON SMITH, G. and HARRIS, S., *Thinkstrips*.

CRAC (1975), *Business Experience Case Studies*, CRAC, £20.00.
10 case studies and role-playing exercises illustrating basic principles of business and skills required to manage a variety of decision-making situations. For fifth- and sixth-formers.

CRAC (1975), *The Job Choice Programme*, CRAC, £19.55.
Three filmstrips and one cassette designed to help students narrow down their career choice.

CRAC (1976), *The Interview Programme*, CRAC, £12.30.
Two filmstrips and a cassette to promote the skills of being interviewed.

CROWLEY, T. (1977), *Job Quiz Book No. 1*, CRAC, 55p.
A workbook with teachers' notes to help students use occupational information more effectively. Cartoons, puzzles, and crosswords are aimed at mixed-ability groups.

CROWLEY, T. (1979), *Computajob*, CRAC/Hobsons Press, £7.32.
A set of transparent overlays which allows 150 jobs not normally requiring formal entry qualifications to be matched against a range of occupational features like 'work with children', 'work that has a link with art', etc. Questionnaires are sold separately at £7.00 per 100.

CROWLEY, T. and BRAITHWAITE, A., *The Career 'Bull's Eye' Book*, CRAC.
This contains the complete 'Bull's Eye' series of workbooks in one volume, including the teacher's notes for each section. There are also spiritmaster duplicates available for 13 of the exercises in the four individual books. The four books are:
Choosing A Job (1972), 85p. Games, cartoons, and quizzes help students to measure their abilities and preferences against a range of jobs.
Finding A Job (1972), 85p. The different ways of seeking jobs, applying for a job, and preparing for an interview.
Starting A Job (1973), 85p. Examines first-day worries, what a young worker needs to know about wages, tax, unions, further education, etc.
Keeping A Job (1974), 85p. Relationships at work, keeping fit, changing jobs, etc.

DAVIES, M. (ed.) (1975), *Work It Out*, CRAC/Hobsons Press, £12.65, cassette £2.30.
Worksheets for careers work with school-leavers.

FARNSWORTH, T. (1977), *On The Way Up: The Art And Science Of Clawing Your Way To The Top*, Prize Publications–Proteus, 95p.
Survival strategies for sixth-formers and adults. The emphasis is on fun and the skills of achieving what it is that you want.

GREATER LONDON CITIZENS' ADVICE BUREAU (1975), *Jackie and Joe*, Greater London Citizens' Advice Bureau, 3p–5p each.
A series of information sheets and comic strips for project work, class discussion. Useful for low reading ability: 'The Bust Up'—about family arguments, spouse violence and legalities; 'Out of School Out of Work'; 'Disaster at the Disco'—about bail, legal aid, court sentencing, and procedure; 'The Troubled Truant'—truancy laws; 'The Case of the Shoddy Shoes'—consumer rights; 'The Great Job Hunt'—job hunting skills; 'The Unplanned Pregnancy'—contraception and abortion; 'Evicted'—tenancy and rent laws; 'Sacked'—employment protection; 'Foiled Again'—parental duties and responsibilities, legal age limits.

HANSON, A. (1976), *Ready To Leave*, Collins, 70p.
Student record-keeping book to ensure that students become familiar with some of the skills of adult living.

HARRIS, M. (1979), *How To Get A Job*, Institute of Personnel Management, £1.50.

Job-finding information and checklists for more able school-leavers.

HEPPELL, R. (ed.) (1972), *A Practical Handbook Of Careers Education And Guidance*, Careers Consultants, £1.50.
Articles on the roles of careers teacher, careers officers, counsellor, etc., and on a variety of techniques of the careers team.

HOPSON, B. and SCALLY, M., *Lifeskills Teaching Programmes No. 1.*
Teaching programme: How to find a job. The skill area is described, much up-to-date information on the economy, special measures schemes and agencies are presented, along with seven exercises for developing the skills in the classroom.

ILEA (1978), *Working In A City*, ILEA Learning Materials Services, £3.75.

INDUSTRIAL SOCIETY (1977), *Going For A Job Interview*, Industrial Society, £7.00—filmstrip; £10.00—slides for schools.
Tape–slide presentation with teacher's notes and suggestions for discussion and role-playing.

INSTITUTE OF CAREERS OFFICERS (1978), *School To Work*, Institute of Careers Officers, £6.00.
12 cards illustrating the problems of moving from school to work.

KIRTON, M. J. (1979), *Career Information: A Job Knowledge Index*, Heinemann, £2.25.
65 indices in the form of questionnaires to test students' knowledge of jobs. Can be used for classroom discussion also.

LAW, B. (1977), *Decide For Yourself*, CRAC, classbook 90p; workbook 45p; teacher's notes £1.00.
A careers education programme for fifth- and sixth-year students to help them towards a career choice. Involves self-assessment and job assessment. The classbook is re-usable.

LEAFE, M. (1978), *Bridging The Gap Between School And Work: A School-Leaver's Handbook*, Cassell, £1.45.
A workbook to help students choose a job and to acquaint them with the facts of going to work.

LUKER, C. and YATES, A. R. (1977), *Getting A Job*, Longman Career Series, 50p.
A workbook.

MARCH, P. and SMITH, M. (1974), *Vocational Choice*, CRAC, £1.10; set of 12 spiritmasters £11.50.
For average and above-average students who are thinking of leaving school with CSE or O levels. A workbook that helps students assess their personal skills and preferences and relates school subjects to a future career.

MARCH, P. and WESTERN, T. (1973), *Lift Off From School*, CRAC, 85p.
Workbook for average and below-average students to help them prepare for career choice and starting work. Cartoons and divided into units that provide materials for 15 careers lessons. Teacher's notes.

MARCH, P. and WESTERN, T. (1974), *Touch Down To Work*, CRAC, 85p.
Workbook with units on self-assessment, job analysis, sources of information, applying for a job and preparing for an interview. Teacher's notes.

MOSS, P. (1978), *Work And Leisure*, Counterpoint Series no. 6, Harrap, £1.75.
A workbook with information designed to help students to examine the balance of work and leisure for their lifestyles.

NUFFIELD HUMANITIES PROJECT (1970), *People And Work*, Heinemann, £40.00.
This kit includes a wide range of photographs, extracts from newspapers and books, cassette tapes, and an explanatory handbook for using the material in class.

REEVES, BARRY (project director) (1978), *Just The Job—'Job Hunter's Kit'*, National Extension College, £1.36.
Materials designed to help unemployed teenagers. Produced as part of a regional approach in South-West England, but has application elsewhere.

SAINSBURY, V. (1975), *Planning Your Future*, Mills & Boon, £2.05.
Set of five booklets for individual work and class discussion: 'Leaving School', 'Your Money', 'Making The Most Of Yourself', 'Somewhere To Live', 'The Family'.

SANDYS, R. and STACE, A. (1978), *Job Finder's Book*, Kogan Page, £1.95.
Practical book for more able leavers to develop job-finding skills.

THOMAS, M. (1978), *On Our Own Two Feet*, Heinemann, £1.50.
Workbooks on 'Starting Work', 'Saving and Spending', 'Highdays and Holidays', 'Eighteen', 'Living Together'.

YATES, A. R. (1977), *Choosing A Job*, Longman Career Series, 50p.
A workbook involving self-analysis and occupational analysis.

How to cope with unemployment

CORCORAN, D. (1977), *Looking For A New Job*, Corden Publications, £1.75.
Job hunting skills and tasks to encourage their development.

TYNE AND WEAR NEW JOB HORIZONS PROJECT (1978), *Helping Job Seekers*, 50p.
10 sections on self-assessment, job hunting, self-presentation, resources. A 90-minute cassette following two young people job hunting.

3. Skills I need at home

How to choose a style of living; how to maintain a home

CURRY, J. (1974) (1) *Investigation into the Home*; (2) *Investigation Into City Life*; (3) *Investigation Into The Mobile Society*. Blackie, 85p each.
Stimulus and discussion material for upper secondary groups.

HINTON, M. (1977), *Life Chances*, Christian Education Movement, £2.90.
A board game to help students discover why people live the way they do.

JONES, A., MARSH, J. and WATTS, A. G. (1977), *Living Choices*, CRAC, 76p.
A workbook for students to explore how they wish to live and use their leisure. It explores the relative merits of living alone and sharing a flat, of different styles of family and community life.

How to live with other people

ADAMS, C., GAGG, S. and MARSDEN, R. (1971), *Viewfinders*, Macmillan, £7.95 each.
Three kits each containing 12 pamphlets with pictures, newspaper articles, etc., plus a viewchart stating the opinions illustrated. For group discussion work: 'You and Your Leisure', 'You and Your Parents', 'You and the Law'.

CHILDWALL PROJECT, *Design For Living*.

226

COMMUNITY SERVICE VOLUNTEERS (1975), *The Family*, Community Service Volunteers, £3.00.
A kit of information sheets, workbooks, and class exercises to explore family relationships.

ILEA (1978), *Living In A City*, ILEA Learning Materials Services.

MOSS, P. (1978), *Family And Friends*, Counterpoint Series no. 7, Harrap, £1.75.
Workbook.

NORTH-WEST CURRICULUM DEVELOPMENT PROJECT (1972), *School Education Kit*, Macmillan, £24.29 each. Teacher's book £1.90.
Seven themes: 'Freedom and Responsibility', 'Consumer Education', 'Conservation', 'Vocation', 'Marriage and Homemaking', 'The British', 'Towards Tomorrow'. Teacher's notes, student materials.

PARFIT, C. (1978), *The Marriage Scene*, Collins, 1978.
Resource pack of eight titles to encourage class discussion. Teacher's notes; twelve 35mm slides and a 60-minute cassette.

SOCIAL EDUCATION MATERIALS PROJECT (1979), *Families*, Curriculum Development Centre, Canberra, Educational Media Australia; Units range from $35.85 each.
A multi-media pack of materials designed to explore family roles and relationships. The approach was influenced by the Humanities Project of the Schools Council/Nuffield. The ten components are case studies, 'What is a Family?', 'Friendship and Courtship', 'Marriage and Being Together', 'Children', 'Work', 'Breakdown', 'Alternatives', 'The Family and the Media', films.

THOMAS, M., *On Our Own Two Feet*, 'Living Together'.

How to be an effective parent

ABIDIN, R. R. (1977), *Parenting Skills*, Human Sciences Press, £10.95.
American. A trainer's manual and a student workbook. Designed for running workshops for actual parents; however, there are many ideas that could be used for looking at parenting with 14–18-year-olds.

GORDON, T. (1977), *Parent Effectiveness Training*, New American Libraries, £3.95.

American. Skills development book designed for use with adults, but useful to teachers doing work on parenting with 14–18-year-olds.

KRUMBOLTZ, J. and KRUMBOLTZ, H. (1972), *Changing Children's Behaviour*, Prentice-Hall, £2.40.
American. The behavioural modification approach to child management. Very readable and humorous. Designed for adults but could be used for looking at parenting skills in the classroom, or, more intriguingly, could be used as a source book to help students manage their parents more effectively.

THOMAS, M. W. (1976), *The Family—The Facts*, Nelson, 55p.
Facts and discussion material on family matters.

4. Skills I need at leisure

How to choose between leisure options; How to maximize my leisure opportunities; How to use my leisure to increase my income

ADAMS, C., GAGG, S. and MARSDEN, R. *Viewfinders*.
You and Your Leisure.

SCHOOLS COUNCIL PROJECT, *Health Education (9–13)*, Nelson.
Unit 5, *Time To Spare*, has sections on use of leisure.

THOMAS, M., *On Our Own Two Feet: Highdays and Holidays*.

5. Skills I need in the community

CITIZENS ADVICE BUREAU (1977), *Under 18—A Guide To The Law As It Affects Young People*, Greater London Citizens Advice Bureau/National Youth Bureau, 65p.
Guide to basic legal rights.

DOBINSON, H. M. (1976), *Basic Skills You Need*, Nelson, £1.70.
Basic skills like form filling, giving directions, finding information, etc., in a workbook for individual and group work.

GREEN, B. (1976), *Facing Society*, Clearway, £1.18.
Basic information for school-leavers.

MAY, J. (1975), *Participating In Society*, Clearway, 98p.
Information on citizenship for secondary students.

NIXON, B. (1977), *Focus On The Community*: (1) *Family And Housing*; (2) *Work And Leisure*, University Tutorial Press, Book 1 £1.25; Book 2 £1.35.
Information, problems, and skills relevant to living in the community.

PHILLIPS, A. (1975), *The Living Law*, Clearway, £1.05.
Information about citizenship and how the law works; for more able school-leavers.

SCHOOLS COUNCIL GENERAL STUDIES PROJECT (1976), (1) *Politics*; (2) *Growing Up*; (3) *Interplay*; (4) *Psychology*, Longmans, £7.00.
Sixth-form materials designed to give information, raise awareness, and develop skills. Thematic units including teacher's guide.

How to be a skilled consumer
CHILDWALL PROJECT, *Design For Living*.

CONSUMERS' ASSOCIATION (1978), *Consumer Education*, Consumers' Association, £3.95.
A resources handbook for teachers to equip students with consumer skills. It includes a subject file of 64 subjects from advertising to weights and measures with student activities and teaching materials. It also has a list of organizations that produce potentially useful teaching aids, and details appropriate Acts of Parliament and Codes of Practice.

GUNDREY, E. (1976), (1) *You And Your Money*; (2) *You And Your Shopping*, Evans Bros, 98p.
Information and consumer skills for secondary students.

MOORE, N. and WILLIAMS, A. (1976), *Mathematics For Life*, Oxford University Press, £2.50.
A course in social mathematics for the slow learner from 10 to 16 years. Teacher's notes: 'Family Affairs', 'Money Matters', 'Going To Work', 'Saving and Spending', 'Around the House', 'Spare Time Activity', 'Down the High Street'.

NORTH-WEST CURRICULUM DEVELOPMENT PROJECT, *Social Education Kit*.

THOMAS, M., *On Our Own Two Feet: Saving and Spending*.

TOLFREE, W. R. (1977), *Money: The Facts Of Life*, Woodhead Faulkner/Lloyds Bank, 60p.
Information about budgeting and money management.

How to develop and use my political awareness
BRITISH YOUTH COUNCIL (1978), *Working For Change*, British Youth Council, 80p.
A political education pack with a list of games and films, and material on community politics simulation, how to get involved in local politics, etc.

COMMUNITY SERVICE VOLUNTEERS (1976), *Planning Your Environment Kit*, Community Service Volunteers, £2.90.
For class discussion and group work dealing with raising political awareness, rights as a citizen, and setting up social action groups.

CRAMPTON SMITH, G. and HARRIS, S., *Thinkstrips*.

LYNCH, M. (1977), *It's Your Choice: Six Role-Playing Exercises*, Edward Arnold, £5.00.
Eight cards per role-playing exercise with questions for class discussion. Topics are relevant to the community, e.g. motorway being planned, oil threat, etc.

MOSS, P. (1978), *People and Places*, Counterpoint Series no. 5, Harrap, £1.75.
Workbook to examine political issues and rights.

How to use community resources

ADAMS, C., GAGG, S. and MARSDEN, R., *Viewfinders: You And The Law*.

ILEA., *Living In A City*.

GREATER LONDON CITIZENS' ADVICE BUREAU, *Jackie And Joe*.

NATIONAL COUNCIL FOR CIVIL LIBERTIES (1978), *Civil Liberty: The NCCL Guide To Your Rights*, Penguin, £1.75.
A handbook of legal rights and organizations that give help and advice.

List of publishers' addresses

Addison-Wesley Publishing Co., West End House, 11 Hills Place, London W1R 2LR

Argus Communications (UK), Plumpton House, Plumpton Road, Hoddesdon, Herts

E. J. Arnold, Butterley Street, Leeds LS10 1AX

Association for Liberal Education, Thurrock Technical College, Woodview, Grays, Essex

BACIE, 16 Park Crescent, London W1N 4AP

BBC Publications, 35 Marylebone High Street, London W1M 4AA

BP Education Service, Britannic House, Moor Lane, London EC2Y 9BU

Basil Blackwell, 5 Alfred Street, Oxford OX1 3AD

Benefic Press, 10300 W. Roosevelt Road, Westchester, Illinois 60153, USA

Blackie & Sons Ltd, Furnivall House, 14–18 High Holborn, London WC1

British Youth Council, 57 Chalton Street, London NW1 1HU

Cambridge University Press, Bentley House, 200 Euston Road, London NW1

Careers Consultants, 12–14 Hill Rise, Richmond Hill, Richmond, Surrey TW10 6UA

Careers and Occupational Information Centre, Rufford Road, Cross Ends, Southport PR9 8LA

Cascade Press, 3455 Chambers Street, Eugene, Oregon 97405, USA

Cassell and Company, 35 Red Lion Square, London WC1R 4SQ

Christian Education Movement, 2 Chester House, Pages Lane, London N1O 1PR

Clearway Publishing Co. Ltd, 19 Nechells House, Dartmouth Street, Birmingham B7 4AA

W. Collins & Co. Ltd, 14 St James's Place, London SW1

Community Service Volunteers, 237 Pentonville Road, London N1 9NG

Consumers' Association, 14 Buckingham Street, London WC2N 6DS

Corden Publications, 20 Somers Road, Rugby, Warwickshire

CRAC/Hobsons Press, Bateman Street, Cambridge CB2 1LZ

Curriculum Study and Development Centre, Samford Street, Swindon, Wiltshire

Direct Education Services Ltd, 1 Alfred Street, Blandford Forum, Dorset DT11 7JJ

Educational Media Australia, 237 Clarendon Street, South Melbourne, Victoria, Australia 3205 (in Europe: 25 Boileau Road, London W5 3AL)

Edward Arnold, 41 Bedford Square, London WC1B 3DQ

Evans Bros, Montague House, Russell Square, London WC1B 5BX

Free Press of New York, Collier-MacMillan Publishing Co Inc, 866 Third Avenue, New York, NY 10022, USA

W. H. Freeman & Co., 58 Kings Road, Reading RG1 3AA

Futura Publications Ltd, 110 Warner Road, Camberwell, London SE5

Ginn & Co Ltd, Elismore House, Buckingham Street, Aylesbury, Bucks HP20 2UQ

Greater London Citizens' Advice Bureau Service Ltd, 31 Wellington Street, London WC2

Harrap, 182 High Holborn, London WC1

Hart Publishing Company Inc., 15 W. 4th Street, New York, NY 10021, USA

Health Education Council, 78 New Oxford Street, London WC1A 1AH

Heinemann Educational Books Ltd, 22 Bedford Square, London WC1B 3HH

Hodder & Stoughton, St Paul's House, Warwick Lane, London EC4P

Hulton Educational Publications Ltd, Raans Road, Amersham, Bucks HP6 6JJ

Human Sciences Press, 72 Fifth Avenue, New York, NY 10011, USA

Hutchinson & Co Ltd, 3 Fitzroy Square, London W1

ILEA Learning Materials Service, Publishing Centre, Highbury Station Road, London N1 1SB

Industrial Society, Robert Hyde House, 48 Bryanston Square, London W1H 7LN

Institute of Careers Officers, 2nd Floor, Old Board Chambers, 37A High Street, Stourbridge, Hereford and Worcester DY8 1TA

Institute of Personnel Management, Central House, Upper Woburn Place, London WC1H 0HX

Jossey-Bass, 44 Hatton Garden, London EC1N 3ER

Kogan Page Ltd, 120 Pentonville Road, London N1 9JH

Lifeskills Associates, Ashling, Back Church Lane, Adel, Leeds LS16 8DN

Longman Group, Longman House, Burnt Mill, Harlow, Essex CM20 2JE

Macdonald Educational Ltd, Holywell House, Worship Street, London EC2A 2EN

Macdonald & Evans Ltd, 8 John Street, London WC1

Macmillan, 4 Little Essex Street, London WC2R 3LF

McGraw-Hill Book Co., Shoppenhangers Road, Maidenhead, Berks

Media Resources Centre, ILEA, Highbury Station Road, Islington, London N1 1SB

Michael Joseph Publishing Co. Ltd, 44 Bedford Square, London WC1B 3DU

Mills & Boon, 17–19 Foley Street, London W1A 1DR

National Extension College, 131 Hills Road, Cambridge

National Youth Service, 17–23 Albion Street, Leicester LE1 6GD

Nelson (Thomas) & Sons Ltd, Lincoln Way, Windmill Road, Sunbury-on-Thames, Middlesex TW16 7HP

New American Libraries, 1301 Avenue of the Americas, New York, NY 10019, USA

New Childhood Press, 152 Upper Street, London N1

Open University Press, Open University Educational Enterprises Ltd, 12 Cofferidge Close, Stony Stratford, Milton Keynes MK11 1BY

Oxford University Press, Ely House, 37 Dover Street, London W1X 4AH

Pacific Books, PO Box 558, Palo Alto, California 94302, USA

Peacock Books (Agents), Lyon, Grant & Green Ltd, 20–24 Uxbridge Street, Kensington, London W8 7TA

Penguin Books, Harmondsworth, Middlesex UB7 0DA

Prentice-Hall International Inc., Durrants Hill Road, Hemel Hempstead, Herts

Prize Publications–Proteus Press, 9225 Baltimore Boulevard, College Park, Maryland 20740, USA

Publication Satellite, Centre for Training Research and Development, PO Box 1565, Prince Albert, Saskatchewan S6U 5TZ, Canada

Science Research Associates Ltd, Newtown Road, Henley-on-Thames, Oxon RG9 1EW

Scottish Community Education Centre, 4 Queensferry Street, Edinburgh EH2 4PA

Tavistock Publishing Co. Ltd, 11 New Fetter Lane, London EC4

Training Research and Development Station, Department of Manpower and Immigration, Saskatchewan, Canada

Tyne and Wear New Job Horizons Project, Monitor House, Coast Road, Wallsend, Tyne and Wear

University Associates Publications, 158 Chesterfield Road North, Mansfield, Notts NG19 7JD

University Tutorial Press Ltd, Great Sutton Street, London EC1

Virago Ltd, 5 Wardour Street, London W1V 3HE

West Publishing Co., 50 W. Kellogg Boulevard, PO Box 3526, St Paul, Minnesota 55102, USA

Wiley (John) & Sons Ltd, Baffins Lane, Chichester, Sussex PO19 1UD

Woburn Press Ltd, Gainsborough House, 11 Gainsborough Road, London E11 1RS

Woodhead Faulkner, 7 Rose Crescent, Cambridge

7. 'Yes, but . . .'

In this chapter we would like to anticipate some of the objections that might be made to the educational approach we are urging in this book, and to respond to those objections. As we have talked to people about what we feel should be current priorities in schools and colleges we have obviously encountered contrary views, some scepticism, some despair, and fortunately much energy and enthusiasm. Those who have had some difficulties with the proposals have usually been gracious enough to preface their arguments with the words, 'Yes, but . . .' Hence the title of the chapter. In it we will restate objections we have encountered and our subsequent thoughts on the issues raised.

'Yes, but your version of the post-industrial society may not actually occur'

Some of the features we have outlined of life in our post-industrial future may not emerge exactly as predicted. Foretelling the future is obviously risky at any stage, though ignoring very clear clues as to what could be ahead is, for us, equally dangerous. We do think educators have to give present indications very serious consideration. The future is one of the things we are preparing students for, and not to contemplate what may be the elements in that future seems to us to be travelling blind, failing to use the maps and navigation instruments that could indicate some of the dangers ahead. We think there is ample evidence to support the trends we outline. A difficulty in completing the writing of the opening chapters was that new evidence is emerging daily. This evidence supports the view that the future will be significantly, even dramatically, different from today; that the speed of change will be increasingly rapid; that we will have to face economic, social, and personal challenges not faced before. If educators contest or deny particular details in the trends or predictions, or even the whole of them, we think it is then required of them to become specific about what kind of future they are educating their students towards (and the evidence they have for it).

In any case, whatever economic and social scenario one feels is most likely to occur, our point would be that there can be no more valuable investment made presently than the development of individuals who are skilled and competent to deal with whatever the future brings.

Whichever of the optimists, pessimists, or ecology critics as described in Chapter 1 are correct, one incontrovertible feature is common to all, namely that people today face a future that will demand great personal flexibility and an ability to cope with rapid change—be it alternative technology and self-sufficiency or the microelectronic revolution.

'Yes, but won't an emphasis on personal development simply produce a generation of self-centred individuals ?

We have already stated strongly our belief, and some evidence to support it (Chapter 3), that there is enormous personal and social significance in individuals' levels of self-esteem and perceptions of their 'locus of control'. People who feel positive about themselves, who feel they are responsible for themselves and the lives they lead, are more likely:

1. to learn more;
2. to relate better to others;
3. to be less aggressive towards and less demanding of others;
4. to be more committed to social action, and much more besides;
5. to help others in a variety of social situations.

Our view, put simply, would be that it is very difficult, perhaps impossible, for any person to give anything that she herself has not first received. Unless we are regarded and treated as valuable and significant ourselves, it is unlikely that we will be able to appreciate the value and importance of others. Unless we experience the benefits of others' sensitivity towards us, we will be unlikely to be sensitive to others. Unless we are loved, and learn to love ourselves (recognizing our worth and having self-respect), then we will surely be less capable of loving others.

We would like to achieve the kind of society where most people operate at the level of relationships which Harris (1969) identifies as 'I'm OK—You're OK'. People who are given positive recognition themselves will be better able to give that to others.

'Yes, but our education was good for us, we've turned out OK!'

Whenever one suggests a new approach to anything, many see it as an implicit criticism of what has gone before. We are not saying this. We can see progress being made, in education as in other areas of life, which is simply building on the good that has gone before. The rote learning, rigid discipline and huge classes of Victorian era had a purpose and a place suited to that time. Developments

236

occurred in that methodology as we learned more and society changed. It is interesting to speculate on how primitive much of what we do now will seem to be to generations a hundred years on. Change, hopefully progress, is inevitable, and for education today to change some of its emphasis is not to say that what has gone before has failed, but that new knowledge and awareness invites a new response. Just as Victorian schooling did not 'fit' for subsequent generations, some of our current schooling may not fit for the future.

'Yes, but employers won't give jobs to students who have done weird subjects'

Education is clearly not simply about producing acceptable employees, though many students, parents, teachers, and employers might regard that as a priority objective. Education needs to produce more skilled and competent people who will have the versatility, initiative, and creativity to make the most of their lives, but who will also have the skills and qualities to contribute to many organizations. More aware, skilled individuals are less likely to be interested in routine, repetitive work, but increasingly those jobs will be automated, and indications are that employers' requirements will be for a much more skilled workforce (Manpower Services Commission, 1977).

That trend is already noticeable in the higher qualifications now demanded for many jobs than was the case 10 or 15 years ago. Many careers teachers feel many employers are unrealistic in requiring numbers of O- and A-level passes for entry to jobs that could be done, more than adequately, by people who may not achieve that amount of academic success. Here surely is an opportunity for dialogue between educators and employers. What many employers are really searching for are competent, reliable, industrious individuals (Industrial Training Research Unit, 1979). They measure those personal qualities, at the moment, by assuming that candidates who are successful academically are also likely to have the necessary personal attributes they are seeking. This is not always the case, and some employers will stress that they are more interested in whether candidates have the 'right attitude', are willing to learn, are reliable, punctual, can work with others, etc.

Evaluation of the Youth Opportunities Programmes (Smith and Lasko, 1978) show that 48 per cent of young people on Work Experience Projects were offered full-time jobs at the end of their six-month programmes. Once employees were given the opportunity to assess personal qualities directly, formal qualifications become less significant for a wide range of jobs.

Teachers embarking on the development of lifeskills for their students are in a position, we think, to persuade employers that this approach is in their interest as well as that of the students. This will obviously require making contact with prospective employers to explain the rationale and objectives of lifeskills teaching, to explain that it is not a substitute for literacy and numeracy but an addition to those lifeskills, and to indicate how more personally skilled workers are likely to benefit working climates by being more competent and involved. Teachers using this approach in particular localities might organize seminars with employers groups, or enlist the assistance of local careers services in arranging such a dialogue. This contact could begin to question the relevance of some of the academic qualifications on which employers place such weight. Often the subject content of some examination syllabuses is never directly usable in work situations, and it is really proof of individual application and achievement that employers want. If schools can persuade employers that there are other ways of recognizing this, then that will be an important development. Lifeskills are not a substitute for academic attainment; they could even enhance it. They are a way of saying that academic achievement is only part of what people have to offer.

'Yes, but parents would not want schools to do work like this'

We do see schooling not simply as a contact between teachers and students, but much more as a partnership between teachers, students, parents, and the community. Any development in any area of that partnership will have implications for the rest. It is unrealistic therefore for the school to think it can operate in isolation. Involving parents in what the school is doing, letting them experience some of the programmes, and considering with them the implications of the work for the students and themselves will be just as important as any work with students in the classroom. Parents usually want what is best for their children. If they are treated with respect and invited to dialogue; if teachers can with sincerity and conviction present a rationale for, and explanation of, the lifeskills approach; if they can show that it is seriously thought out, and is about developing levels of competence that are relevant to school, home, work, and the community; if they can say that it is not replacing other valuable work that the school is doing but enhancing it, then parents are likely to see its purpose and give the approach their support. It is an interesting question for teachers to ask themselves, from time to time, whether they would be happy for their own children to receive the education they are giving to the children of others. If they can justify their own work to that extent, they will probably have not too much difficulty persuading other parents of its worth.

'Yes, but won't it cause disruption in schools ?

Lifeskills cannot be developed in a vacuum. There will obviously be ramifications for school systems of using this approach with students, and developing an awareness in the system of what these might be will be important groundwork. For 'lifeskills staff' not to communicate with others about their purpose and methods would be to invite problems. Preparing other staff for what students with increased awareness and skills might say or challenge will be vital. Lifeskills development is not a passport to licence or unreality. Skill development should be paralleled by growing responsibility. Too many school situations currently are basically win–lose ones. Teachers feel they are 'winning'/'on top', when students are 'losing'/'put in their place'. Students 'assert themselves'/'are disruptive' by giving the teacher a 'tough time'. The dynamics are those of confrontation, where winning occurs only when the 'other side' is losing. Defensiveness and insecurity are sometimes a way of life.

We feel that progress can be made from these positions by seeking areas of mutuality. This would involve challenging the stereotypes we carry around of 'teachers' and 'students', laying aside the 'facades' that our defensiveness causes us to build, and co-operating in ways that demonstrate we are all 'people', with similar hopes, fears, problems, anxieties, skills, beliefs, etc. The more teachers and students behave openly and genuinely towards each other, the less likely, we believe, will there be a need to resort to win–lose outcomes.

During the trials stage of some of our own Lifeskills Teaching Programmes (Hopson and Scally, 1980), teachers have had to respond to students who comment on the skill levels of other staff in areas such as communicating effectively or making relationships with the student groups. The raising of such issues is, we think, an important opportunity to discuss with student groups some of the ground rules and values implicit in the lifeskills approach, e.g. that

239

the approach rests upon the worth of the individual and the realization that each person has some skills and is capable of being more effective in other areas. To concentrate on the weaknesses of others, rather than appreciate the strengths they have and assist them in developing others; to recognize others' current limitations and blame them for those rather than admit our own and work to remove them; to fail to see that lack of skills in one person actually demands more skills and responsibility from another is to miss out on much of the 'message' in the lifeskills approach. Individual development is not to be at the expense of others or for the exploitation of others—irresponsibility probably means a lack of awareness, sensitivity, and skills.

Skill development will require, and benefit from, much discussion of the values and responsibility on which the approach is founded. As we develop new skills in students there is likely to occur some experimentation in behaviour as part of the process. If this can be seen as a way of learning new norms and boundaries rather than simply unleashing irresponsibility, then situations can be used to illustrate the ground rules that will indicate where boundaries will be drawn (as they will always need to be—recognizing realities is an important lifeskill!). For example, some teachers using our materials as part of our trials group have found it useful to state to their student groups something like the following:

> 'I have introduced a lifeskills programme because I believe in the value of each person and the importance of developing all our potential. Each of you is important, as is every person in the school, including other teachers. Because I respect you I will treat as confidential whatever we discuss among ourselves in this room. Because I respect others also, I do not want to discuss people behind their backs. We can discuss difficult situations and what *you* might do to make them better. Simply complaining about what is wrong is not very skilled—taking the responsibility yourselves for improving situations is. Let's talk about how you might use your awareness and skills to make things better.'

A heavy emphasis therefore in any lifeskills teaching programme should be placed on the discussion of and development of responsible attitudes. Students treated responsibly are much more likely to behave responsibly.

Lifeskills teaching should offer students an opportunity to be involved in work that is interesting, because it is about themselves. It should also, by giving them good attention and a chance to air their views and share opinions and ideas, remove some of the causes of disruptive behaviour.

'Yes, but aren't there likely to be political consequences of encouraging everybody to be more aware, more in control of themselves and of different situations ?

There are some who would claim that the current education system is politically neutral. We would not accept this, believing that political neutrality is incredibly difficult to achieve. Non-reference to political matters in schools and colleges is for us a decision to support the status quo, which in fact is a political decision. That does not mean it is a 'wrong' decision, but it does mean that it is wrong to regard it as apolitical. Schools and colleges are involved in politics, though not necessarily party politics, in the values they promote, in the social models they present to their students, in the emphasis they place on respect for law and authority, in the interpretations the teachers give of the subjects they teach, consciously or otherwise.

Since it is virtually impossible to be apolitical in education, we would see some virtue in a more overt approach to political education. Even at Cabinet level recently the British government has urged the introduction of courses to develop the political awareness of students as a guard against the increasing influence of extremist political groups. Ian Lister at York University has been developing programmes that will help schools and colleges to undertake political education alongside the other subjects they teach. We would support these developments, seeing the skill of having and using one's political awareness as an important component of our lifeskills model.

What we are *not* saying above is that we want heavy party political indoctrination of students—we do not. We *do* think that democracy thrives best when individuals are aware and involved; when they communicate effectively with each other; when they can influence each other; when they have access to decisions that affect them and want to be and are encouraged to be involved in those decisions; when power, authority, and law are openly discussed and are mutable; when power is distributed and not wielded by few over many for too long; when matters affecting those in the community are dealt with openly by members of that community; when justice in all matters is widely discussed, highly valued, and is seen and felt to be done; when grievances are listened to and redress is available; where individuals are able to state their views

241

freely, subject only to the checks and balances imposed by the human and civil rights of others.

We think the best preparation for participation in a democracy is to experience living in one, and schools and colleges are in a unique position to allow that to happen. Schools that encourage individual development, which allow participation and dialogue, which give responsibility and share decision-making, which avoid autocracy and rigid authoritarianism, are doing far more than paying lip-service to preparing students for citizenship in a democracy. The more effectively functioning people there are in our society, the healthier we will be as a democracy. Apathy and indifference provide a dangerous political vacuum; empowering people will help avoid the creation of one. Lifeskills teaching is, we feel, a real investment in democracy, and would have benefits for individuals and society.

'Yes, but you can't really teach subjects like this'
The ultimate betrayal, for the approach to education through personal development, would be for it to become just another academic, routine, heavily structured, examinable item on a timetable. Lifeskills teaching will thrive best:

● where there is a recognition that there are such things as personal and interpersonal skills which can be developed through identification and practice, in something like the way we acquire the skill of driving a car. The learning process involves wanting to learn and seeing the advantages of doing so; getting help and support for one's own efforts; identifying and practising the different skill components; practising and gaining experience; 'ironing-out' any difficulties encountered; assimilating and feeling 'natural' with the new behaviour. Unless awareness and a desire to learn are present there is not likely to be any learning;

● where teachers are prepared to learn with the students and provide important models in doing so. Such teachers are likely to have energy and enthusiasm; the ability to work with individuals and small groups and to build the trust required to work in areas of personal growth; and the classroom management skills and flexibility required to present this work as not simply another lesson. Lifeskills teaching will require highly competent teachers;

● where it is appreciated that 'lifeskills' is not the subject—the students are. The approach focuses on the individual and her own development. Teaching materials are a means of allowing that to happen, but are secondary in importance to the people themselves.

242

Therefore, a teacher who treats the materials as sacrosanct, who is interested primarily in the completion of exercises or tasks, who is not sensitive to the importance of pursuing issues that are raised, who has a need to 'get work down on paper' or into exercise books, and who does not stress the importance of learning from peers will probably present lifeskills teaching as just another subject and will reduce much of its potential. Even then, at its lowest, it could be more interesting than some curriculum material that is around! Given effective teachers, with enthusiasm and skills, a climate that encourages and supports, some stimulating materials, and students who have been motivated to learn, we would reckon one can teach and learn most things. It does leave a question for us of whether our teacher-training scheme does provide sufficient numbers of the kind of teachers with the kind of skills that we are describing.

'Yes, it will be good for the more able students, but what about the others ?

In the trials stages our own teaching programmes have been tested with groups varying from those in ESN schools to adult groups in FE settings. What was required for that to happen was skilful adaptation of the materials by teachers who knew the groups very well. In other words, all materials are written for particular target groups, but the ideas they incorporate can usually be shaped to become applicable to most groups. It has been interesting to hear teachers involved with very bright sixth-form groups and those involved with so-called 'slow learners' say that there is something for everybody in a lifeskills approach. Obviously, the more intelligent and articulate the student, the greater possibility there might be for grasping concepts and expressing views. At the same time there is sometimes, in the more intelligent, greater reluctance to express emotions than is experienced by those less able to shelter behind a facility with words. In short, everybody is capable of being more skilled and effective in some areas than he is at present, and it can be just as rewarding to see those at a lower skill level make progress as to see the sophisticated become more so. In priority terms, it would be important for us to see special effort being made with the less skilled. Without personal and social skills, one is unable to make even minimal inroads into the community and make a place for oneself. If one cannot do that by one's skills, the temptation is likely to be to do it by anti-social means, and there are high personal and community costs that result from that approach. In purely practical terms in schools and colleges,

243

teachers are much more likely to be given time to do such work with the 'less able' students, because their timetables tend to be less filled with exam requirements or staff demanding more time with them. It is important however that lifeskills teaching is not limited to non-examination groups. A high number of O or A levels does not guarantee that the owner is personally and interpersonally competent.

'Yes, but aren't lifeskills very much a middle-class concept ?

The lifeskills one needs to survive and grow are obviously related to one's social environment. Children living in situations of deprivation will probably acquire naturally the skills necessary to exist in their situation, and those skills will suffice as long as they remain in that situation. Were they to move out of that or want some alternatives, they would have to acquire new skills. We would like lifeskills not to be seen in social class terms, but very much as a means of developing in each of us the ability to be and do whatever is within our potential and is important to us. Our social context is something that is given to us as a beginning. Given awareness and skills, we can begin to question whether that is as we want it to be or whether we would want to make it more to our liking. Without skills one has little or no choice, with them one has more chance of creating and shaping the environment one wants. Built into the lifeskills concept is the belief that one ultimately creates one's own environment. The more skills one has, the more options one has. Lifeskills teaching holds out the possibility of making more individuals' lifestyles a matter of choice rather than accident. It is saying that lives lived unawarely and unskilfully involve wasted potential, in whatever socio-economic grouping they occur.

'Yes, but you can't treat students like adults—they are not capable of deciding things for themselves'

Western cultures delay the granting of adulthood longer than is common in most cultures. Recently, in reducing the voting age to 18, there has been an attempt to halt that process. There remains however, a very extended period between childhood and adulthood, which can seem a kind of limbo to those who are too young for some things and too old for others. Recently research has identified for us the importance of age stereotyping in our society. There are clear social messages about what each of us should be doing at particular ages (ref. Hopson and Scally, 1979). The more fixed we are in our views about what is 'normal' at a particular age, the less freedom we are giving to individuals to develop at their own pace and to exercise their own judgement on what is appropriate for them at any particular time. One effect of having strong ideas about what fits for certain age groups is probably that we offer responsibility to our young people later than we could— we delay their maturing by prolonging their child role. Teaching lifeskills will involve an invitation to students to become more adult, more responsible, more self-directing; and if this process is a gradual one, we see no reason why more cannot be expected earlier of students by way of mature response. It is fascinating to see in some schools an emphasis placed on decision-making exercises in the classroom, while at the same time students are offered very little chance of making real decisions about what to wear, what to eat, what to study, or about rules and procedures affecting their daily lives. We separate learning from life. It is probably true that as teachers we get what we expect—if we expect students to participate sensibly, to be able to accept responsibility, to make realistic decisions, and if we give them a chance to do those things, it is unlikely we will be disappointed in the long term. Responsibility and reliability are best learned and tested experientially in trusting climates from an early age.

'Yes, but doesn't this approach destroy all the old values ?

Without being specific about which 'old values' the teaching of lifeskills might challenge, it is difficult to assess what it might replace. The value system that underpins this approach is likely, we think, to reinforce what most people would value in traditional approaches to education. Lifeskills teaching stresses the significance and the importance of the individual; it emphasizes sensitivity to and respect for oneself and others; it believes that organizations, and society, function most effectively when they encourage individual development and welcome participation and involvement from all; it challenges the right, and the desirability, of any person or group to dominate or dictate to another individual or group; it emphasizes balance and partnership in relationships; it works for the development of all human potential and regards under-development as wasteful and tragic; it invites each of us to be more able to shape the kind of life we see is important for us, saying that the more control and direction each of us has over ourselves, the more we are functioning as truly human.

We think those values are probably not too different from what most people would feel comfortable with. We do not see that what we are now presenting does any more than restate some of the old values that people have promoted in the past.

'Yes, but isn't this just another gimmicky educational idea ?

We hope not. We think teaching lifeskills does have a great deal to offer everybody but it will be effective only if it excites teachers, who are skilled enough to work in this way, and if they in turn can interest students in undertaking their own development. Good ideas and materials cannot be a substitute for good teachers and enthusiastic learners, and the lifeskills approach, like all other curriculum developments, stands or falls on that. Given that those exist, we think there is great potential in the development, and hopefully it could become a common core element in many educational settings. Its permanence will depend on the experience it gives people. Teachers involved in testing some of our programmes have found the work rewarding—some have even commented that this is the 'best teaching' they do. Some students have regarded their 'lifeskills time' as the most stimulating part of their timetable. If lifeskills teaching can be that involving, then there is hope that it will be seen as not gimmicky at all but concerned with fundamental education and real personal development.

'Yes, but isn't this simply another technique for forcing young people to adapt and conform to the demands of the economic system ?

In a recent paper, Bernard Davies raises a crucial issue of the underlying intentions behind so much of what today is called 'life and social skills training', which he differentiates from the more liberal intentions of 'social education' as it has come to be taught:

> Social and life skills training is not, of course, an entirely new form of practice. It has been used for many years in work with the mentally handicapped, with prisoners and even with those seeking help with personal and behavioural difficulties. However, in these fields of practice it has usually been possible to regard those undergoing the 'training' as victims of some personal incapacity, or as seriously deviant, or as voluntarily submitting themselves to some form of therapy. [Davies, 1979. p. 4]

The danger, Davies argues, is that the same approach, now being generalized to a much larger and undifferentiated section of the population, is a real threat to young people's rights to self-determination.

246

The Manpower Services Commission's own guide to their version of life and social skills training certainly lends some support to Davies' fear. Their *Instructional Guide to Social and Life Skills* (1973) states: 'One of the aims of the . . . training will be to *adjust* trainees to normal working conditions'; a satisfactory private life 'can contribute to a person's *work motivation*' (our italics).

As Davies correctly points out, statements like these in themselves are not sinister. 'The trouble is the absence of any explicit commitment to certain fundamental values or to certain primary aims' (Davies, 1979).

We believe that a clear statement of specific objectives and a disclosure of the underpinning values is essential. That is what this book has been about. To develop more self-empowered people, who in turn will help to create more self-empowering systems, we believe that young people must be given the tools to do the job. Those tools for us constitute the awareness, the goals and values, the lifeskills, and the information without which we are indeed subject to the knowing and unaware manipulations of powerful groups and powerful structures. Our approach to illness is a preventative one. You do not need to kill the organism when an inoculation can provide the necessary protection. Lifeskills teaching has the potential to provide that protection, if carried out from a clear philosophical base, directed towards self-empowerment and social interdependence rather than from a desire to produce certain behaviours for the 'good of the system'.

References

ABBOTT, W. (1977), 'Work in the year 2001', *The Futurist*, **11**, 1, 25–31.

ADVISORY COUNCIL FOR ADULT AND CONTINUING EDUCATION (1979), *Towards Continuing Education: A Discussion Paper*, ACACE, Leicester.

ASPY, D. and ROEBUCK, F. (1977), *Kid's Don't Learn From People They Don't Like*, Human Resource Development Press, Amherst, Mass.

BAXTER, J. L. (1972), 'Long-term unemployment in Great Britain 1951–1977', *Bulletin of the Oxford University Institute of Economics and Statistics*, November.

BAZALGETTE, J. L. (1971), *Freedom, Authority and the Young Adult*, Pitmans, London.

BILL, J. M. *et al.* (1974), *Early Learning in Northern Ireland*, Northern Ireland Council for Educational Research, Belfast.

BIRCH, D. L. (1979), *The Job Generation Process*, MIT Press, Cambridge, Mass.

BOOTH, C. (1978), 'When young people start work: a government sponsored experiment', *Trends in Education*, Autumn, 34–42.

CAMPBELL, D. (1974), *If You Don't Know Where You're Going, You'll Probably End Up Somewhere Else*, Argus Communications, Hoddesdon, Herts.

CARKHUFF, R. (1976), 'The Promise of America', address to APGA, New Orleans.

CENTRAL POLICY REVIEW STAFF (1978), *Social and Employment Implications of Microelectronics*, National Economic Development Council, London.

CHAMBERS, J. (1978), *Young People in Transition*, address on the education of the 14–19 age group to NUT Conference, 8–9 June 1978, NUT, London.

COLEMAN, J. S., *et al.* (1966), *Equality of Educational Opportunity*, report from Office of Education, US Government Printing Office, Washington, DC.

COOMBS, P. H. *et al.* (1973), *New Pathways to Learning*, International Council for Educational Development, New York.

COUNCIL FOR SOCIAL DEVELOPMENT (DELHI) (1976), *The Mabubnagar Experiment: Non-Formal Education for Rural Women*, CSD, Delhi.

COX, C. B. and BOYSON, R. (1977), *Black Paper 1977*, Maurice Temple Smith, London.

248

CURLE, A. (1973), *Education for Liberation*, John Wiley, New York.

DAVIES, B. (1979), *From Social Education and Lifeskills Training: In Whose Interests?* Occasional Paper no. 19, National Youth Bureau, Leicester.

DE BONO, E. (1970), *Lateral Thinking: A Textbook of Creativity*, Ward Lock, London.

DE CHARMS, R. (1972), 'Personal causation training in the schools', *Journal of Applied Social Psychology*, **2**, 95–113.

DEPARTMENT OF EDUCATION AND SCIENCE (1977), *Curriculum 11–16*, HMSO, London.

DEPARTMENT OF EDUCATION AND SCIENCE (1976), *Unified Vocational Preparation: A Pilot Approach*, DES Circular no. 6/76, HMSO, London.

DEPARTMENT OF EDUCATION AND SCIENCE (1978), 'Making Inset work: in-service education and training for teachers: a basis for discussion', DES, London.

DERLEGA, V. J. and CHAIKIN, A. (1975), *Sharing Intimacy*, Prentice-Hall, Englewood Cliffs, New Jersey.

DORE, R. (1976), *The Diploma Disease*, Allen & Unwin, London.

DWECK, C. S. (1975), 'The role of expectations and attributions in the alleviation of learned helplessness', *Journal of Personality and Social Psychology.* **31**, 674–85.

ELLIS, A. (1973), *Humanistic Psychotherapy: The Rational–Emotive Approach*, Julian Press, New York.

ESLAND, G. M. (1971), 'Teaching and learning as the organisation of knowledge', in *Knowledge and Control*, M. F. D. Young (ed.), Collier-MacMillan, London.

FITTS, W. (1972), *The Self Concept and Psychopathology*, Counselor Recordings and Tests, Nashville, Tennessee.

FLYNN, M., FLYNN, P. and MELLOR, N. (1972), 'Social malaise research in Liverpool', *Social Trends.*

FOGELMAN, K. (ed.) (1976), *Britain's Sixteen Year Olds*, National Children's Bureau, London.

FORDHAM, P., POULTON, G. and RANDLE, L. (1979), *Learning Networks in Adult Education*, Routledge & Kegan Paul, London.

FREIRE, P. (1972a), *Cultural Action for Freedom*, Penguin, Harmondsworth.

FREIRE, P. (1972b), *Pedagogy of the Oppressed*, Penguin, Harmondsworth.

FREIRE, P. (1976), *Education: The Practice of Freedom*, Writers and Readers Publishing Cooperative, London.

FRENCH, J. R. P. and RAVEN, B. (1959), 'The bases of social power', in

Studies in Social Power, D. Cartwright (ed.), University of Michigan Press, Ann Arbor, Michigan.

GILLESPIE, F. (1974), 'Stress costs more than strikes', *Financial Times*, 26 April 1974.

GOLDFIELD, M. R. and MERBAUM, M. (eds) (1973), *Behaviour Change Through Self-Control*, Holt, Rinehart and Winston, New York.

GOODMAN, P. (1970), *Growing Up Absurd*, Sphere, New York.

GOYDER, C. (1977), *Sabbaticals For All*, NCLC, London.

HARRIS, T. (1969), *I'm O.K.—You're O.K.*, Harper & Row, New York.

HITT, W. D. (1972), 'Two models of man', in *The Regeneration of the School*, De Cecco (ed.), Holt-Saunders, London.

HOLMES, T. H. and MASUDA, M. (1973), 'Life change and illness susceptibility', *Separation and Depression*, American Association for the Advancement of Science, New York.

HOPSON, B. and HOUGH, P. (1973), *Exercises in Personal and Career Development*, Careers Research and Advisory Centre, Cambridge.

HOPSON, B. and SCALLY, M. (1979), *The Adult as a Developing Person: Implications for the Counsellor*, CCDU, Leeds University.

HOPSON, B. and SCALLY, M. (1980), *Lifeskills Teaching Programmes No. 1*, Lifeskills Associates, Leeds.

HUDSON, L. (1967), *Contrary Imaginations*, Penguin, Harmondsworth.

HUMPHREYS, J. (1978), *A Directory of Voluntary Counselling and Allied Services*, 3rd edn, British Association for Counselling, London.

ILLICH, J. *et al.* (1977), *The Disabling Professions*, Marion Boyars, London.

INDUSTRIAL TRAINING RESEARCH UNIT (1979), *The A–Z Study: Difference Between Improvers and Non-Improvers Among Young Unskilled Workers*, IRTU Publication SY4, Cambridge.

INSTITUTE OF EDUCATION (DAR ES SALAAM) (1974), *Mtu-ni-afya: An Evaluation of the 1973 Mass Health Education Campaign*, Institute of Education, Dar es Salaam.

IRELAN, L. (ed.) (1967), *Low Income Life Styles*, Department of Health, Education and Welfare, Washington, DC.

JENKINS, C. and SHERMAN, B. (1979), *The Collapse of Work*, Methuen, London.

JOHNSON, L. D. and RACHMAN, J. G. (1976), 'Educational institutions and adolescent development', in *Understanding Adolescence*, J. Adams (ed.), Allyn & Baker, Boston.

JOURARD, S. M. (1974), *The Healthy Personality*, Collier-Macmillan, London.

KING, K. (ed.) (1976), *Education and Community in Africa*, Centre of African Studies, University of Edinburgh.

KLEINKE, C. (1978), *Self-Perception: The Psychology of Personal Awareness*, W. H. Freeman, San Francisco.

LEIBOW, E. (1967), *Tally's Corner*, Little Brown, Boston.

LONDON, P. (1969), *Behaviour Control*, Harper & Row, New York.

LOTT, A. J. and LOTT, B. E. (1968), 'A learning theory approach to interpersonal attitudes', in *Psychological Foundations of Attitudes*, A. G. Greenwald, T. C. Brock and T. M. Osram (eds), Academic Press, New York.

LOUGHARY, J. W. and RIPLEY, T. M. (1978), *Career and Life Planning Guide*, Follett, Chicago.

LUTZ, B., MERIAUX, B., MUKHERJEE, S. T. and REHN, G. (1976), 'Outlook for Employment in the European Community to 1980', Commission of the European Communities, Brussels (mimeo).

MANPOWER SERVICES COMMISSION (1976), *Towards A Comprehensive Manpower Policy*, MSC, London.

MANPOWER SERVICES COMMISSION (1973), *Instructional Guide to Social and Life Skills Training*, MSC, London.

MANPOWER SERVICES COMMISSION (1977), 'Industrial Survey' (unpublished).

MARTIN, R. and FRYER, R. H. (1974), *Redundancy and Paternalistic Capitalism*, Allen & Unwin, London.

MASLOW, A. (1968), *Towards A Psychology Of Being*, Van Nostrand, New York.

MAY, R. (1970), *Love and Will*, Souvenir Press, London.

MEICHENBAUM, D. (1977), *Cognitive Behaviour Modification*, Plenum, New York.

MIDWINTER, E. (1972), *Projections: An Educational Priority Area at Work*, Ward Lock, London.

MILLER, N. E. (1971), *Selected Papers*, Aldine, Chicago.

MUKHERJEE, S. (1976), *Unemployment Costs. . . .*, PEP, London.

MUKHERJEE, S. (1978), 'Unemployment: a note on some social and economic costs', paper delivered at NUT Conference 'Young People in Transition', June 1978.

PHARES, J. E. (1976), *Locus of Control in Personality*, General Learning Press, New Jersey.

PLUNKETT, H. D. (1978), 'Modernisation reappraised: the Kentucky mountains revisited and confrontational politics reassessed', *Comparative Education Review*, **22**, 1.

RATHS, L., MERRILL, H. and SIMON, S. B. (1966), *Values and Teaching*, Charles E. Merrill, Columbus, Ohio.

251

RAVEN, J. (1977), *Education, Values and Society*, Lewis, London.

REICH, C. A. (1971), *The Greening of America*, Random House, New York.

REIMER, E. (1971), *School is Dead*, Penguin, Harmondsworth.

REPUBLIC OF BOTSWANA (1977), *Lefatshe la Rona—Our Land*, Botswana.

RICHARDSON, C. J. (1977), *Contemporary Social Mobility*, Pinter, London.

ROGERS, C. (1978), *Carl Rogers on Personal Power*, Constable, London.

ROSENBERG, M. (1965), *Society and the Adolescent Self-Image*, Princeton University Press.

ROTTER, J. B. (1966), 'Generalised expectancies for internal versus external control of reinforcement', *Psychological Monographs*, **80**, 1 (entire issue).

ROWAN, J. (1976), *Ordinary Ecstasy: Humanistic Psychology in Action*, Routledge & Kegan Paul, London.

RUBIN, J. (1973), interview in *Psychology Today*, September 1973.

RUTTER, M., MAUGHAN, B., MORTIMORE, P. and OUSTON, J. (1979), *Fifteen Thousand Hours*, Open Books, London.

SCHOOLS COUNCIL (1968), *Young School Leavers Enquiry No. 1*, HMSO, London.

SCHULTZ, R. (1976), 'The effects of control and predictability on the physical and psychological well-being of the institutionalised aged', *Journal of Personality and Social Psychology*, **33**, 563–73.

SCHRAUGHER, J. and ROSENBERG, S. (1970), 'Self-esteem and the effects of success and failure feedback on performance', *Journal of Personality*, **33**, 404–14.

SELIGMAN, M. E. (1975), *Helplessness*, W. H. Freeman, Reading.

SINFIELD, A. (1968), *The Long-Term Unemployed*, OECD, Paris.

SMITH, S. and LASKO, R. (1978), 'After the work experience programme', *Department of Employment Gazette*, **86**, 8, August.

SPECIAL TASK FORCE TO THE SECRETARY OF HEALTH, EDUCATION AND WELFARE (1973), *Work in America*, MIT Press, Cambridge, Mass.

STEIN, R. L. (1963), 'Work history, attitudes and income of the unemployed', *Monthly Labour Review*, **86**, 12.

STEINER, C. (1974), *Scripts People Live*, Grove Press, New York.

STONIER, T. (1978a), 'Materials production requirements in post-industrial society', working paper commissioned by Central Policy Review Staff (Cabinet Office).

STONIER, T. (1978b), 'Education in a post-industrial society', *Exchange* 3, CCDU, Leeds University.

STROM, R. (1975), 'Education for a leisure society', *The Futurist*, **9**, 2, 93–7.

SUPER, D. E. and BOWLSBEY, J. A. (1979), *Guided Career Exploration*, Psychological Corporation, New York.

THORESON, C. E. and MAHONEY, M. J. (1974), *Behavioural Self-Control*, Holt, Rinehart & Winston, New York.

TOFFLER, A. (1970, *Future Shock*, Bodley Head, London.

TUCKMAN, B. W. (1965), 'Developmental sequences in small groups', *Psychological Bulletin*, **63**, 384–99.

VORAPIPATANA, K. (1975), 'Reports—World Education', no. 8, World Education, New York.

WALZ, G. (1974), 'A bill for futuristics: life/career planning and the human services', *Impact*, **3**, 1, 24–8.

WATTENBERG, W. W. and CLIFFORD, C. (1972), *Relationship of Self-Concept to Beginning Achievement in Reading*, US Office of Education, Cooperative Research Project no. 377, Wayne State University, Detroit.

WATTS, A. G. (1978), 'Using computers in careers guidance', *Journal of Occupational Psychology*, **51**, 1, 29–40.

WIDMER, T. F. and GRYFTOPOULOS, E. P. (1977), 'Energy conservation and a healthy economy', *Technology Review*, June, 31–40.